ADDICTED KIDS:
OUR LOST GENERATION

AN INTEGRATIVE APPROACH TO UNDERSTANDING AND TREATING ADDICTION IN TEENS

RONALD P SANTASIERO MD
CHERIE L SANTASIERO PhD

ISBN: 1496112091
ISBN 13: 9781496112095
Library of Congress Control Number: 2014904232
CreateSpace Independent Publishing Platform
North Charleston, South Carolina

Dedication

We dedicate this book to our addicted patients and their families. We have learned so much from them. Addiction is a disease that crosses all socioeconomic classes, and sometimes causes irreparable harm to families and other relationships. Addiction is associated with stealing, dealing drugs, jail, prostitution, serious infection, social isolation, loss of friends, alienation from family, and sometimes prejudice from medical providers. Its victims are overwhelmed by the power the addiction has over their lives. If we can give hope to patients and families through education and our experience treating addiction, we will have succeeded in our mission.

- Drs. Ronald and Cherie Santasiero

Dedication

From Dr. Cherie Santasiero

To Ron, my best friend, lover, my soul mate. For forty-five years you have always been there for me, encouraging me. Most of all, thank you for teaching me about the difference between allopathic medicine and wellness, a.k.a. integrative care. You are totally awesome and I adore you.

To my patients; I immensely admire you for your hard work and dedication to your healing. When you fell off your path, you brushed off your knees and jumped back on and we worked together that much harder. Most of all, thank you for trusting me with your psyche and soul. I honor you.

To Alex B., for giving me resounding hope in what I do.

Thank you to family, friends, patients, Dr. Ron's and mine, who sent me prayers, healing wishes, and cards while I dealt with cancer. I truly believe that without your loving thoughts I would not have finished this book with my husband.

From Dr Ron Santasiero

To my patients, who continue to teach me something new every day.

Most of all to Cherie; you are my partner, wife, best friend, and soul mate. Your battle with cancer taught me about real bravery and resolve. You always find a way to motivate and inspire me.

Acknowledgements

We want to thank all those who had a part in helping us with this book. It has taken a long time to finish, and without the following people, you would not be reading this now. Thank you to:

Matthew Shontz, our grandson, an inspiration for hard work, loyalty and love, and who gave us another chance at "getting it right" in parenting. We are blessed to have him in our lives... and for his honest evaluation and comments for this book.

Barbara and Mark Santasiero, who actually printed out the whole manuscript, maintaining its double-spaced format, in order to give us written feedback. What a job!

Cody Hughes, artist, who learned to read our minds and put it on paper for this book.

Denise O'Shei, teacher, for her eagle eye and honest feedback.

Our neice, Christina Denee Reilly, artist and musician (of Breakerbox), for her insights with the cover and marketing.

Our Sedona Holistic Medical Centre staff, for patiently taking *many* calls back and forth between us while we worked in separate offices.

To our close friends and family who helped us with this book by asking questions about addiction in kids, which helped us to realize the obvious questions a lay person would ask about this subject.

To the Create Space team, some of the nicest professionals we have had the pleasure to work with. Thank you for your guidance *and* patience.

Table of Contents

Introduction

As you are reading this, a nine-year-old boy in your neighborhood is getting his first taste of alcohol. He discovered it in an unlocked cupboard in the kitchen at home. His ten-year-old friend told him, "Let's drink some, that's how the grownups have fun." In four years, that nine-year-old will go to a party with that same friend and grab a handful of hydrocodone pills from a bowl that is filled with multiple prescription pills and over-the-counter drugs. The drugs were collected from the other teens and pooled to make it more exciting than the other parties he had attended.

At about the same time, an eleven-year-old daughter of a middle school teacher in your community is getting her first experience with marijuana. She got her first joint from a classmate who "borrowed" it from her seventeen-year-old brother. Her mother, the teacher, will not know she has a drug problem until she is sixteen and is arrested for possession of heroin. When she is arrested, she is in a car with a nineteen-year-old boy from the inner city near her hometown. Her mom is terrified, because she cannot believe this has been going on for six years without her knowledge. She is also terrified because she has no idea what her daughter faces in dealing with this problem, from a legal and medical standpoint. In addition, she and her husband do not have the four thousand dollars needed to pay a private attorney to defend her in the town court.

During this period of time, a mechanic's twelve-year-old son experiments with ecstasy and hallucinogenic mushrooms. He dabbled in marijuana, which did not do much for him after a while, and he did not like drinking on weekends with his friends. He liked the ecstasy much more. Ultimately, he will discover his true drug of choice next year, when his girlfriend gives him a 40 mg

Oxycontin, a form of long-acting oxycodone, which she bought off the street. He heard about oxycodone after using hydrocodone, a weaker opiate he had been using on weekends. The oxycodone far surpasses the effect he got from even the strongest 10 mg hydrocodone prior. When he is seventeen, he is sentenced to one year in juvenile detention for selling heroin to an undercover agent he thought was a twenty-year-old guy from a neighboring town looking for a good time. He finds out during the investigation that he had been selling to undercover agents for almost a year without ever knowing it. He also discovers that the only way his sentence will be reduced to a year is if he gives up the names of dealers and other users. These dealers and users are his soon-to-be ex-friends. His mom and dad will ultimately separate because of disagreements about how he should be handled. His father thinks hard line, no-nonsense treatment is the best way to go. His mother believes babying him and showing him some sensitivity is the way to go. After serious fights and disagreements, they decide to separate. Ultimately they resolved their issues, only to discover that their fifteen-year-old daughter, who has been watching this scenario play out, is also using prescription opiates she is buys off the street.

As hard as it may be to believe these scenarios, there are more. A judge in a nearby small town is facing an issue with his thirteen-year-old son who is addicted to hydrocodone. He was suspicious because his son, an A student until about six months ago, now misses eight to ten days of school each month because he cannot get out of bed. He found out later his son used cocaine for about a year before starting the hydrocodone, approximately nine months ago. He also discovers that his son does not like cocaine nearly as much the hydrocodone. Sadly, he learns that this is very common in opiate addicts. The judge calls a local physician who deals with addictions to ask for help. He gets his son immediately into a treatment program with the physician, and his son improves for approximately six months. He then relapses and for the next five years struggles to stay clean. He never goes to college and gives up his hopes of becoming an attorney like his dad. At first the judge is worried about the embarrassment he will face with the towns-people, but then the main issue becomes a life-and-death struggle to save his son.

The judge finds out that the police chief's fifteen-year-old son has been using OxyContin for approximately a year and recently started using fentanyl patches, a potent synthetic opiate. He could not afford the OxyContin, and found that fentanyl patches, an extremely potent synthetic form of morphine, satisfied his craving and relieved his withdrawal symptoms. The police chief has approached the judge because he found out his own son was picked up downtown in the city ten miles north of them for buying the patches from a dealer who was under surveillance. The narcotics division of the city police had been watching him more than six months. The chief asks if the judge knows any other judges in the city who might be more lenient with his son, who is facing jail time. The police chief finds out his son has not only been wearing the patches, but also scraping off the gel and snorting, which gives him a quicker high. He also finds out his son was considering buying heroin and snorting it because it was much cheaper. The police chief is also embarrassed, but soon faces the reality that his son is fighting for his life, and the embarrassment is irrelevant in comparison.

In the meantime, a prominent doctor was in the midst of trying to get treatment for his sixteen-year-old daughter, who is an intravenous heroin addict. He had no idea she had a drug problem until he was called from the local emergency room; his daughter overdosed and was near death. Luckily, she was given a dose of Narcan, an intravenous drug that reverses the effects of opiates. His daughter will leave the hospital and get into a treatment program, but sadly, three years later, her naked body is found frozen in an alleyway next to a bar in a high crime area of the city near their home. The case makes the headlines in the regional newspaper and it is later discovered that it is unclear why she died. The autopsy shows large amounts of opiates in her blood and signs of her being strangled. Since the police are unable to find the perpetrator, it will be ruled as a death from an accidental overdose. The father hires a private detective who discovers she had been staying weekends with a known drug dealer for the past nine months. The drug dealer is known to be violent and to associate with violent gang members. The father believes she was beaten and raped before the overdose. The father tries to press the issue with the authorities, but they disregard his pleas. The doctor finds out later that the police believe she was "just another junkie who overdosed." He and his wife have to live with the fact that the truth will never be discovered.

As outrageous as these illustrations seem, they all are based on facts. The circumstances and identities have been changed, but all are based on real cases from our practice. What they point out are the tragedy and unbelievable loss experienced by families, patients, and society by the epidemic of drug addiction in this country right now.

In 2009, the National Institute of Drug Abuse reported that there were 5.3 million adolescent abusers of painkillers in the United States. In the same report, one in five teens had abused prescription controlled medication in the prior year. One in ten high school children used the painkiller hydrocodone in the prior year. In addition, one in twenty had used OxyContin, a very potent opiate painkiller, for nonmedical purposes in the prior-year. The statistics are staggering. They represent a serious problem that we all face in our society and few understand the consequences our future holds because of it.

In the October 2011 issue of *American Family Physician*, an editorial reported on the status of the abuse of over-the-counter medications among teenagers and young adults. The editorial states that the medical literature shows an emerging issue of teenage over-the-counter drug abuse. In 2006, about 3.1 million persons between twelve and twenty-five years of age (5.3 percent of that age group) reported using over-the-counter cough and cold medications to get high. In the same editorial, a Utah survey showed that 38 percent of illicit drug use among teenagers and children from 1990 to 1999 involved over-the-counter drugs. It also reported that admissions to drug treatment centers for over-the-counter medication abuse increased more than 30 percent between 1993 and 2003. Cases of dextromethorphan abuse (a cough suppressant usually designated by DM on the label) that were reported to poison control centers increased sevenfold from 1999 to 2004. Most of these involved fifteen and sixteen-year-olds.

These trends are sobering at best and staggering when you consider the cost to our society and our children's futures. We have been doing adolescent drug addiction work for over ten years and have treated over 350 adolescents from ages thirteen to nineteen. A more depressing observation is that the problem is getting worse. There are a multitude of reasons for the addiction problem in our society. After seeing the tremendous scope of the problem, the devastated parents, and the alarming cost to our young people, we were compelled to document some of their stories and educate the community in our efforts to help resolve this situation. Part of the educational process is getting people to understand that addiction is serious and that it crosses all social, financial, and educational boundaries. As you will see, opiate addiction does not discriminate and can strike anyone, anywhere. Our teenagers are most vulnerable for a number of reasons, which we will also discuss.

This book is based on true stories. We have changed the circumstances and identities to protect our patients and their families. Their names have been changed. Some of the stories you read are compilations of several patients, but nonetheless will illustrate the severity of the problem. We blend as much scientific and documented research as possible, but we did not want to write a textbook on adolescent addiction; the information presented is based on our opinions about the current situation. The reader should understand that this book is based on our experience and knowledge in the treatment of adolescent opiate addicts. As you read the statistics, studies, and case reports, bear in mind that the personal and familial costs far outweigh the medical, financial, and societal costs. We felt compelled to write a book because the epidemic and serious negative affects of adolescent addiction will be with us for future generations. If we do not educate parents, teachers, students, young children, medical personnel, law enforcement officials, legislators, and the community, the problem will spiral out of control. The addicted adolescents are soon to be a lost generation.

Chapter 1

THE ADDICTION EPIDEMIC

"The United States has 4.6 percent of the world's population, but uses 80 percent of the world's prescription opioids."
- "IMS Health Survey," ABC News (April 20, 2011)

Michael was sixteen years old when he first presented to our office. He looked about twelve years old, with young features, and weighed only 115 pounds. He started using alcohol at age ten. At around age twelve, he was using marijuana with his friends. Between ages twelve and thirteen, he experimented with cocaine and ecstasy (a hallucinogenic drug commonly used by teens and easy to acquire). He never liked cocaine or ecstasy because he felt too "hyper" and "spaced out" on them. At age thirteen, his best friend gave him hydrocodone. His friend told him he would "feel high after about twenty minutes." When Michael took the hydrocodone, he did not feel high; in fact he told me he felt "normal" for the first time in his life. This is not an unusual experience for opiate addicts, as you will see later. Prior to the hydrocodone, he always felt nervous, could not focus, and sometimes felt distant and detached. After taking hydrocodone, he could focus and felt calmer. Within three months, he was using four hydrocodone per day. He was stealing them from his grandmother who had an arthritic hip. When she started noticing pills were missing and that he was visiting more often, she hid the pills but never confronted him. Soon he was buying them from friends and low-level dealers at his middle school. He was stealing from convenient stores and the local home improvement store and selling what he stole, or he would return the items for cash until the stores refused to give him any money without a receipt. By age fourteen, he was using six to eight pills a day. His school grades were dropping, and since he was never a great student, he was now close to failing. He also skipped school, about ten days per month. Most of the time he was too tired to get up or was sick from withdrawal symptoms. The nausea was the worst, but the anxiety and joint pain were a close second. His father, a single parent, gave up trying to get him up for school. He was tired of seeing him sick all the time, but had no idea his fourteen-year-old was experiencing the unrelenting grip of opiate addiction. Michael refused to see a doctor because he feared being exposed. Since he could no longer steal enough to supply his addiction, and his grandmother was suspicious, his supply of hydrocodone was in jeopardy. Soon he discovered his only alternative was to buy larger amounts and start selling to kids at school to make enough to supply his habit. He had to sell about forty pills a day to supply his habit of eight to ten pills a day. One day his supplier, a guy who dealt from a drug house in a dangerous part of the city fifteen miles from his house, gave him a new pill. He told him it was a lot more potent than even the strongest hydrocodone (10 mg). He went home and tried the new pill. After an hour, he felt good again. He discovered his new pill was Oxycontin. Oxycontin is a highly potent opiate narcotic that can be made ten to twenty times more potent than the hydrocodone. The pill taken was only 20 mg, but pills can be bought as high as 80 mg each. The cost was about a dollar a milligram at the time, but well worth it. One 20 mg pill could keep him from going into withdrawal for up to eight hours.

Oxycontin was originally approved and marketed for terminal cancer pain. Opiate addicts quickly discovered its value and the illicit market exploded in the late 1990s and into the next decade. Frequently, Oxycontin is the drug young addicts start using after they "max out" on eight to ten or more hydrocodone a day. Michael also discovered Oxycontin was easier to deal. It also made it easier to satisfy his unrelenting craving and hunger for the opiate. Right after his fifteenth birthday, he realized he was using three 80 mg Oxycontin per day. His habit was costing him about $150 to $200 per day. His ability to get that much money a day sometimes amazed him. Since he was now rarely in school, he found it harder to deal the opiates to other students. He started hanging around the mall in town where there was never a lack of willing teens to buy Oxycontin. He often wondered where these kids got the money. Some were obviously better off financially than he was. Some even got ridiculous allowances from their parents, which they promptly spent on the Oxycontin. A few used it for "fun" on the weekends with friends, but most were hooked just like him. At times, he felt guilty for selling to the thirteen and fourteen-year-olds, but the alternative—not feeding his hunger for the drug—was much worse. He could even justify selling to them by telling himself they would buy it somewhere else if he did not sell it to them. He mostly felt sorry for the young girls. He knew it ultimately would end up worse for them than for the guys. The older girls were more than willing to sell themselves for an Oxycontin 80. They would do anything he asked. After the first few times, even he did not have the heart to supply them that way. However, he was in the minority. Most of the older dealers had no problem asking for the demeaning and sometimes unspeakable sexual favors. He knew of several girls from his school that dropped out at sixteen and were now prostituting at the drug house where his supplier set up business. At around age sixteen, Michael was given a Duragesic (fentanyl) patch by a guy he met at the drug house. At first he scraped off the gel from the patch. The patches are meant to be put on the skin and absorbed slowly. Fentanyl, as stated previously, is an extremely potent synthetic form of morphine; it is measured in micrograms. A microgram is one thousandth of a milligram. In other words, it would take one thousand micrograms to equal one milligram. Most drugs are dispensed in milligrams. Duragesic is measured in micrograms, rather than milligrams, because the synthesized drug is so potent. When Michael started scraping the gel off the patch and snorting it, he felt a little buzz. He had not felt any "buzz" since his early days of hydrocodone. Within two months he was using two to three of the most potent Duragesic patches (100 micrograms) per day. Of course, he no longer felt any buzz. That disappeared two days after his first exposure to the Duragesic. He could not afford to buy the patches, even with full-time dealing at the mall to friends and their acquaintances. He approached his dealer to see if he could get the patches cheaper if he bought more. Instead, his dealer gave him a small packet of powder and told him to snort some of it. Michael was not sure what it was, but he had his suspicions. Without ten seconds of reconsidering, he opened the packet and snorted the powder. Within five seconds, he had the most unbelievable rush and sensation he had ever felt. It was a hundred times better than his first hydrocodone. It was like nothing else he had ever experienced. He was immediately hooked. The dealer told him the price and he bought twenty pack-ets. The twenty packets were cheaper than the Oxycontin and the feeling was much greater. After going home, he snorted two more packets over the next eight hours. The sensation was unbelievable, although it never matched that first snort at the drug house. The powder, as he suspected, was heroin.

Michael, now seventeen, and pretty much never going to school, was preoccupied with using the heroin and periodically going to the mall to sell what he could. He did not waste his time stealing from friends, relatives, and local stores anymore. His new life was using and selling heroin. His father had no clue what was happening to Michael. He knew he was no longer going to school by the letters and phone calls from the school. Michael's dad was at a total loss as to what to do. Being a single parent, he had all he could do to work fifty hours per week to barely pay the bills. When he was not working, he was busy keeping the house up and preparing meals. Many days Michael would sleep through meals, and his hygiene was becoming a serious issue. When his father confronted him about his hygiene, at first Michael was defensive. After thinking about it, he realized he had not had a bath or shower for over two weeks. He had not changed his clothes in more than a week. Since he slept in them, there was no need for pajamas; he could not even remember the last time he had clean sheets on his bed. He had not seen his mother in over three months. She had her own problems with alcohol, the reason his father was now his sole parent. Michael realized he was in a downward spiral, but did not have a clue what to do about it. He only knew selling and using drugs. He had essentially dropped out of school at sixteen, and ninth grade was the last grade he actually finished. Working for minimum wage was ludicrous. He certainly did not have the time and could never support his habit working a real job. Even if he worked a full forty hours, it would barely be enough to supply his habit for a few days. His emotional and physical downward spiral was accelerating exponentially.

Two months after snorting heroin, Michael was using ten bags (a bundle) a day. To make matters worse, he no longer got a buzz; he now used just to stop the horrible feelings of withdrawal. If he went more than five hours without the heroin, the nausea and joint pain were unbelievable. Forget the high, now he was fighting for survival. When he was seventeen and a half, Michael made the decision to start injecting the heroin. It would give him a bit of a high and his tolerance for the drug was becoming a serious issue with only snorting. Getting needles was not a problem. They had hundreds of them lying around the drug house. He bought four bundles (40 bags) of heroin on his next trip to the drug house. The dealer did not have any new needles, but he gave him what looked like a relatively "clean" syringe. He told Michael to clean the needle with alcohol and it would be okay. No chance of a serious problem. The fifteen-mile trip home felt like four hours. He was getting withdrawal symptoms and feeling like crap. He had not snorted in over six hours. Upon arriving home, he walked in leaving the door wide open in spite of the 25-degree weather. He had not noticed the cold, because he was sweating like it was 125 degrees. The withdrawal was excruciating and his anxiety was at a level of twenty out of ten. He felt like he was coming out of his skin. He mixed the bag of heroin just like the dealer told him, filled the syringe the dealer assured was clean, and used his jacket as a tourniquet. He could not find a vein so he just injected into what he thought was a vein. The burning in his arm felt like he touched a red-hot coal. He also had a bruise the size of a walnut at the injection site. The good news was his withdrawal was starting to improve. He knew he could not do this injecting thing without some help. He knew a lot of IV (intravenous) drug users from seeing them at the mall. He decided to travel to the mall. He hopped into his twelve-year-old rusty Chevy and headed to the mall. On his way, he was thought about all the money he spent on drugs and how he could have a much nicer car if he could just stop using. The car his dad bought him when he turned sixteen was junk even then. And now the dream of owning a decent vehicle was as distant as waking up and not craving heroin.

When Michael arrived at the mall, he saw one of the guys who used IV drugs. After explaining his dilemma, the guy offered to give him a lesson on proper IV drug technique. They went back to his car and Michael was given a crash course on proper use of a makeshift tourniquet and needle technique. He was also shown the quickest way to prepare the powder to use in the syringe. His newfound teacher was a bit reluctant to use the syringe and needle Michael brought from the dealer. He warned Michael that he could get something unbelievably bad by using "dirty needles." Michael heard the words but did not really care. He also did not believe that would happen to him. After all, he was a healthy teenager. At least he was before the drugs. That kind of crap only happened to homeless addicts who lived in a box under a bridge. After the crash course, Michael was ready to "do it right." He applied the tourniquet, found a good vein and was ready to do it. When the needle went in he saw the dark bluish red liquid fill the hub of the needle, just like his "teacher" had said he would. As soon as he saw that, he injected the fluid from the syringe. Within seconds, he felt a sensation that could only be described as "out of this world." It was like a hundred orgasms all at once. He barely remained conscious for the first thirty seconds. Soon he came back to reality and could focus. His instructor was long gone as the mall police would be around soon looking for addicts getting high in cars. Michael got his bearings and drove home.

Michael thought his problems were over. That night the withdrawal symptoms started again, only this time it was different from before. The withdrawal came on quicker and the symptoms felt worse sooner. He was anxious to use his new skills and couldn't wait for that "out of this world" feeling. After he found that same vein and injected the heroin he waited for that incredible feeling to happen again. Thirty seconds later he felt no withdrawal; there was also no orgasmic sensation. Disappointed, he went to sleep, anticipating better times with the next dose. Being new at this, maybe he just needed a little more practice. He woke up four hours later sweating, feeling sure he would throw up, even though he had eaten nothing in thirty-six hours. To make matters worse, this was the absolute most horrible anxiety he had ever experienced. He felt like he could not catch his breath, like his lungs would not fill with air, even if he took a deep breath. "Keep moving, keep moving," he told himself. Michael had to breathe some fresh air in spite of it being 19 degrees outside. The sensation lasted twenty minutes, but this was something he had never experienced before and did want to feel ever again. He was tempted to wake his father for some comfort and reassurance that he was not going to die. That, he thought, would be a big mistake. His dad had no idea he had a drug problem. He thought Michael was "just a typical lazy, unmotivated teenager." Better he think that than know the real truth, Michael thought. Then Michael decided to try his newfound skills again. Maybe he did something wrong the last time. After repeating what he learned and injecting that same reliable vein, he waited. Thirty seconds, one minute, two minutes, no out of this world sensation. The withdrawal stopped, but the disappointment he felt about the lack of buzz had him feeling as low as he could ever remember feeling.

The days and weeks passed with Michael injecting his now scarred and increasingly red arms, causing him to have severe pain when he injected himself. The track marks on his arms forced him to wear long sleeves at all times. At least it was winter. He had no idea what he would do in the midsummer heat, but that was a life-time away. He was injecting ten bags of heroin a day when he could get it. His drug dealer would not give him any drugs unless he showed cash first. He was so drugged up most days, so he could not get to the mall to sell his drugs to support his habit. His dealer gave him the job of delivering and selling drugs in the most dangerous part of the city when he had no money. He generally sold to people in the immediate area around the drug house. Occasionally he would sell in areas away from the drug house. It had been four months since his first experience with injecting heroin. Sometimes Michael would be so stoned he did not go home and would sleep at the drug house with thirty or forty other "users." He would try to keep the same syringe and needle as much as possible. This did not always happen, and sometimes he would borrow a syringe and needle from one of the other users. He was so preoccupied with getting his drugs; the thought of disease never crossed his mind. His dad stopped asking where he was when he was out all night and did not have a clue what was going on; he had a suspicion but was afraid of what the truth might be. He was struggling to keep his job and keep the house going for Michael and himself.

Michael's boyish looks were an advantage in dealing drugs in the neighborhood surrounding the drug house. Nobody would suspect he might be an undercover agent, and they were more than willing to buy from him. This gave Michael confidence to deal outside the neighborhood when he saw a disheveled looking guy in his twenties, two blocks from the drug house. He had seen the guy before buying from other dealers, so he approached him and offered to sell him two bags of heroin. After all, Michael needed another customer. The guy agreed, paid him twenty dollars and walked away, apparently happy to soon be getting high.

Several months later, while standing on the front porch of the drug house making small talk with his main dealer, three police cars slammed to a halt with sirens blazing and twelve police officers in full battle gear, flying out of the cars with guns drawn. Michael was told to drop on the ground with his hands above his head. An officer came up behind him and kicked his legs apart so he was spread eagle on the ground and handcuffed him. He was abruptly lifted by the handcuffs and slammed into the police car. The rest of the police stormed into the drug house and dragged out thirty-three other "users," including his dealer.

Michael was taken to the police station and put in a room to be questioned. His fear was unbelievable. He had no idea what to expect, but knew it would not be good. Not only did he fear what would to happen to him if he had to stay in jail, but mostly how bad his withdrawal would be. How would get through the withdrawal if he did not get a fix? Probably the worst fear was what would his father say. Up to now, his father had no clue and was insulated from the dark side of the drug world. Now he would be exposed to it through his only son. After sitting in the room alone for forty-five minutes, the door opened. Two detectives walked in, one dressed in a suit, the other in baggy jeans and a tee shirt. The guy in the suit looked like someone you would not want to mess with. The other guy looked vaguely familiar. After he spoke, Michael's heart almost stopped. It almost stopped not because he was starting to feel the early effects of what would be his worse withdrawal ever, but because he recognized the guy in the jeans and tee shirt. Michael had sold him two bags of heroin several weeks earlier. He knew he was done. It was only a matter of time now. After his interrogation, it was clear they knew Michael was a low-level dealer and a teen in deep trouble with an addiction that had taken over his life.

What they wanted was for him to agree to testify against his drug dealer in exchange for *some* leniency. They offered to let him call a lawyer if he wanted. Michael thought, why bother? I don't know any lawyers, and even if I did, where would I get the money to pay one? The police officers told him he could think about it overnight in jail. They would notify his father who could pick him up in the morning after his arraignment in court, another new experience for Michael. They sent him to his cell to "think about things," and give him time to "come to his senses," as they put it. Michael had a feeling that the officers had a much better understanding of what he had in store in the next twenty-four hours than he did.

The night in jail was the worst hell he could imagine. Worse than anything he had experienced in his seventeen short years on this planet. He did not know chills could feel that horrible. It felt like he was outside in 50-degree below-zero weather with a 60 mph wind against his naked wet body. The freezing and shaking was only tempered by the unbelievable nausea and vomiting he experienced. He vomited until only a dark green sour material came up in his throat, out his mouth and nose. The burning in his esophagus was like a hundred hot pokers stabbing him there. The joint pain felt like he had broken both knees and hips and was forced to run a mile on them. The anxiety from what he now knows was a prolonged panic attack made him pray for death. Death would be better than the sensation of suffocation he felt. It was as if a cement truck was parked on his chest while he was fully awake trying to get a deep breath. He also couldn't stop yawning (a common symptom of withdrawal). The yawning made the air hunger from the panic attack a hundred times worse. Two hours of horrible chills was bad enough, but the six hours of profuse sweating was even worse. It felt like he was trapped in an oven being cooked alive. He took all his clothes off and did not notice any difference. He noticed all the puke on the floor where he was lying, because he could not get to the toilet in time. He screamed for help from the guards, but they either did not hear him or pretended they couldn't. After eight hours of hell, they finally sent for the jail's physician assistant. The PA at least seemed like he cared but told Michael he could not prescribe anything, and it would get better each hour. He would just have to wait it out.

What seemed like eternity finally ended the next morning. Michael woke up at about eight o'clock in the morning, naked, and surrounded by vomit, urine, and perspiration-soaked clothes. They brought him breakfast, but he had no appetite. He knew the worst was about to come, and this was just the beginning. At about nine o'clock, the guards opened his cell and told him he was going to court for arraignment. He was not sure what exactly that was, but he would soon find out. He was still feeling like crap; he had a hard time walking and felt like he had gotten beaten up, and now the craving was becoming worse than the withdrawal. He started to feel like he had not eaten in a month, and no food was in sight. He thought about the breakfast he couldn't eat earlier. When he got to the courtroom, accompanied by a burly guard, he was to experience his worst nightmare. Sitting in the second row was his father, looking like he had not slept, with his head down, look-ing at the floor. Suddenly his father looked at Michael. The sense of disappointment Michael felt was so much worse than any with-drawal or craving he had ever felt before. His father would soon know the "real" Michael, he thought. His father worked so hard for so many years, and how did he repay his dad? By becoming a drug addict, a dealer, a worthless excuse of a human being.

The arraignment was a blur. All Michael could think about was what his father would say, and think, and what he could possibly say to his father to make it better. Michael's father had retained and paid for a lawyer, who had told the judge that Michael would enter a plea of not guilty to the charge of selling drugs to an undercover police officer. Michael did not quite understand this, since he did sell the drugs and was in fact guilty. The judge asked Michael what he wanted to do. He asked if Michael wanted to go to jail until his trial or go to rehab. Apparently in this court, they had something called drug court. In drug court, first-time offend-ers are offered the option of rehab and staying clean for one year, or jail time. If they stay clean for a year, the charges are reduced or dismissed. Michael had to make a decision. He thought that if he went to rehab, he would not have to feel the now worsening craving and hell of withdrawal. Maybe they could even "fix" him so he did not do drugs anymore. On the other hand, if he went to jail he would continue the hell of withdrawal and craving, but he wouldn't have to face his father every day. He was definitely lean-ing toward jail and the hell of withdrawal and craving rather than the comfort of rehab. However, facing the disappointment of see-ing his father everyday, now knowing that his son had become an addict, seemed worse. While he was deciding, his lawyer said that since he was under eighteen and still under his father's custody, his father wanted his only son to do drug court and rehab. "Case adjourned," the judge agreed. Michael would be taken to rehab per his father's request and would appear in court in two weeks.

He walked out of court with his father and a guard and was on his way to a local hospital for rehab. His father did not say a word. He did not have to; he showed what he felt on his face and in his eyes. He was devastated. His only son was a heroin addict at seventeen and on his way to rehab. A criminal, worthless, damaged, a disgrace to his family. This is what Michael believed his dad was feeling. In reality, his father felt none of those things.

Michael's dad was in a state of disbelief that this could be happening. How had his little boy gotten into so much trouble with a drug that was only used by junkies who lived on the street when he was growing up? Was it really possible that his son was injecting a lethal illegal drug into his own veins? How could he possibly know how to do such a thing? Was it possible all those days he was not coming home he was selling drugs? Did his little boy sell drugs to a police officer? How could this be going on without him knowing? With the wonders of modern medicine, they must be able to fix his boy. They must have a pill, a treatment, and a therapist who would fix his little boy. Michael started rehab and stayed in drug court for about six months. He did not finish drug court or rehab. Not because he was not doing well, but because his disease took an unexpected turn.

We met Michael after his rehab counselor called to see if we would accept him in our Suboxone treatment program. I will explain this in detail in subsequent chapters. In simplistic terms, Suboxone is a drug that blocks the effects of opiates and dramatically relieves withdrawal and craving. By law, to be in a Suboxone treatment program patients must be active in counseling, visit the prescribing doctor at *least* once a month, and stay clean, verified by regular urine drug screens. We took Michael into our program. When we first met Michael, we were struck by his youthful appearance. He was seventeen but looked twelve. He was shy and appeared somewhat frail. He told us his history, about the alcohol at a young age, the progression through hydrocodone Oxycontin, Duragesic, and heroin. The history could be a script for 90 percent of the young addicts we see.

His story does not end with rehab and there is no happy ending. When we first started Michael on Suboxone, he seemed to do well. At his first follow-up visit a week after starting, like most opiate addicts, he was feeling better. About a month after we first saw him, he came in sweating and nauseated. He reported not feeling well, but not like withdrawal, of which he was very familiar. We adjusted his dose, thinking he may need more medication. If patients are under dosed with Suboxone, they feel like they are in withdrawal, or have the flu. We had him come back a week later and he was no better. He also complained of some abdominal pain. By now he had an elevated temperature and tenderness in the area over his appendix. Thinking he had appendicitis, unrelated to his addiction, we sent him to the emergency room. He was admitted. Diagnostic studies were performed to see if he had appendicitis. The surgeon was unsure, so he operated on Michael and found an appendix that really did not look bad. Michael rallied for about a week after his surgery, went home, and then worsened. He was readmitted to the hospital and got sicker and sicker. After several days, in the hospital he grew bacteria in his blood culture and soon after developed symptoms of heart failure. The heart failure was found to be secondary to an infection on his aortic heart valve. The valve was infected by bacteria he was exposed to when he used dirty needles to inject heroin six months before. He had a condition known as bacterial endocarditis.

His heart failure progressively worsened as the valve became more infected. It reached a point where the valve could not close properly and blood was leaking backward into his heart. A decision was made to do open heart surgery to replace his infected valve. He had the surgery and the valve was successfully replaced. Unfortunately, this was not the end of problems for Michael.

In the period immediately post op, he developed a very slow heart rate. This sometimes happens after an infection in the heart, from damage to the electrical system of the heart. The surgeons and cardiologist decided to put a permanent pacemaker into Michael's chest to protect him from the slow heart rhythm. This is a typical treatment; however, the patients are usually much older. After the pacemaker, another complication occurred. A small clot formed in his heart from the infection and the artificial valve. The clot traveled to his brain and caused a stroke. Michael became paralyzed on one side.

He left the hospital in a wheelchair under the care of his father. A seventeen-year-old young man who six months before was worried about staying out of jail and trying to recover from addiction, was now paralyzed on one side, wheelchair bound, and had a pacemaker and an artificial heart valve. THIS IS THE DEPRESSING FACE OF ADDICTION.

Addiction is not about someone taking too many drugs and hurting himself. It is about a disease that is poorly understood and inadequately treated. It is a disease that rips apart families, causes divorces, does irreparable harm to relationships, and destroys lives. It is a disease that manifests with patients lying, deceiving, and hurting those around them. It destroys families financially, emotionally, and spiritually. Victims of addiction are not weak people who lack willpower. *The drugs involved in addictions are more powerful than the willpower of even the strongest among us.* Accepting that the drugs are more powerful than our willpower is part of the recovery process. It is a disease where relapse and backsliding are the norms, not the exceptions. Drugs *do not* cause addiction. Defective brain chemistry causes addiction. Drugs are what make addictions hard to treat. You can be addicted to many things: gambling, sex, food, sugar, sports, TV, your job, or even constructive things like reading or gardening. Drug addiction has more negative aspects because of the cost, illegality, and emotional and physical destruction associated with it.

In subsequent chapters, we will discuss some facts about drugs and addictions. Treatment and prevention will be dealt with in detail. Much of what we write will be our opinion, based on our experience treating over 350 young opiate addicts. In the next chapter, we will look at some of the reasons we have this epidemic of addiction.

Chapter 2

THE MAGNITUDE OF THE PROBLEM

"In 2010 the cost of substance abuse (alcohol, tobacco, and drugs) in the United States, including health, crime-related costs, and loss of productivity exceeded $600 BILLION."
- The National Institute on Drug Abuse,
updated December 2012

The cost of addiction, financially, socially, emotionally, and spiritually, to the United States is staggering. The sad news is that it continues to worsen in spite of enormous sums of money and effort spent by our government. The United States has spent over one *trillion* dollars on the war on drugs in the last forty years. To give you an idea of the magnitude of a trillion dollars, imagine spending one million dollars a day from the day Jesus Christ was born until the present. You still would not have spent a trillion dollars, but only about ¾ of a trillion. In 2008, we spent seventy-four billion dollars on criminal and court procedures for drug offenders, but only $3.4 billion for treatment. Spending twenty-two times more on drug-related crime than on treatment explains why we are losing the war. The amount spent on prevention and education is a tiny fraction of the treatment expenditure.

Addictions are the number one cause of death in the United States, if you include all causes of disease related to addiction. Think about the numbers. Over 400,000 deaths per year from tobacco use and over 100,000 deaths per year from alcohol and drug-related cirrhosis of the liver. From 1999 to 2005, deaths from *prescription* opioids, *not* illegal drugs, rose from 4,042 to 14,459. Far more people die from prescription opioid addiction than AIDS. Abuse of prescription opioids has risen rapidly in the United States. From 1997 to 2002, the number of Oxycontin prescriptions written went from about 200,000 per year to almost two million, a tenfold increase. That number continues to increase. Prescription opioid emergency room visits went from 41,687 in 1994 to 90,232 in 2001, a 117 percent rise. From 2004 to 2009, over two million emergency room visits were recorded for opioid abuse. In 2009, people hospitalized for cocaine overdose totaled 442,896. Hospitalized heroin overdoses numbered 213,118. In 2004, the number of people needing treatment for substance abuse was about 22.4 million, but only about 3.8 million received treatment. In 2009, opioid overdoses numbered a staggering 513,896. The prescription opioids were by far the worst problem. Fifteen years ago, drug rehabilitation center populations were mostly due to alcohol addiction. Today, the vast majority of patients in rehabilitation centers are there due to opioid addiction. Many of these centers report 90 to 95 percent of patients are there to treat opioid addictions. In addition to the emergency room utilization, 50 percent of psychiatric hospitalizations are related to drug abuse and addiction. It has been estimated that 25 percent of medical/surgical hospital admissions are related to drug abuse and addiction.

The cost of addiction in terms of psychosocial issues is immeasurable. How do you measure the cost of suicides, intentional or accidental? The toll it takes on families cannot be measured.

The scars last forever. Teen suicide or death from addiction also affects schools and the fabric of entire communities. Friends and schoolmates of teen suicide victims, or teens accidentally overdosing, have a difficult time assimilating these events. A high percentage of homicides also can be traced back to drugs or addiction. How many are the result of drug deals gone bad or due to people out of control? How many occur because a drug-crazed person reacts to a situation in a violent way? How many fires are the result of carelessness caused by an addict who falls into a stupor while smoking a cigarette? The number of fires related to methamphetamine labs is increasing at an alarming rate. In a recent documentary, a Tennessee hospital's burn unit was filled with people who suffered major third-degree burns after their meth labs exploded. The hospital was taking care of these people, at a tremendous loss, since most had no insurance. These individuals were also hospitalized for months, preventing other patients' access to the specialized care. Auto accidents, spousal abuse, child abuse, and sexual abuse have a high correlation to drug abuse.

In the workplace, drug abuse is a serious problem. In 2010, a study done by the National Institute of Drug Abuse found 8 percent of full-time workers and 10.2 percent of part-time workers abused illegal drugs. The highest incidences were in the food service sector, construction, and durable goods. In our area, western New York State, a high incidence is also seen in collection agency workers. Restaurants have a particularly difficult time with workers and drug use. Wait staff, cooks, and support staff are the main users. This is probably due to the young age of many of these workers. In 2009, the National Institute of Drug Abuse also found that nonprofessional truck drivers between twenty-one and twenty-five years old tested positive for illegal drugs 35.4 percent of the time. They also found that illegal drugs were found in drivers involved in 54 percent of all traffic accidents. The majority of the time, the drivers were poly-drug (multiple drug) users.

Much of the blame can be traced to prescribers: doctors, dentists, podiatrists, nurse practitioners, and physician assistants. There were enough prescription painkillers prescribed in the United States in 2010 to medicate every American adult around the clock for one month. In New York State, the number of prescription narcotic painkillers increased from 16.6 million in 2007 to 22.4 million in 2010. The number of prescriptions for hydrocodone increased by 16.7 percent from 2007 to 2010. The number of oxycodone prescriptions (a much stronger drug) increased by 82 percent from 2007 to 2010.

The problem with teenagers is no better. A study published in the *Archives of Pediatric Medicine* in 2011 looked at a population of seventh to twelfth graders in two school districts. They surveyed four classes of controlled substances, pain medications, stimulants, sleeping pills and anti-anxiety drugs. The survey was completed by 61.7 percent of students. Over 18 percent of the students said they were prescribed at least one of those medications, and of these 22 percent reported misusing a prescribed controlled medication within the past year. Close to 10 percent of students said they used their prescribed medications to intentionally get high or increase the effects of alcohol or other drugs. Overall, students abused pain drugs more than any other class of drugs, but painkillers were the least popular for getting high intentionally. In the study, 9.2 percent of students admitted misusing pain pills to get high or to augment other drugs. About 17 percent misused sleeping pills, 15.8 percent misused antianxiety pills and 11 percent misused stimulants to get high. Dr. McCabe, the lead researcher, found that those who misused prescription medication were more likely to divert the drug (give it to friends or sell it) and abuse other substances. They were 7.4 times more likely to have used another illicit drug in the past year, and 4.4 times more likely to have engaged in binge drinking in the past two weeks.

Our own experience dates back to 2004. I originally started treating addictions and using the drug Suboxone in my practice in 2004. A close friend, Dr. Tom Small, MD, CAc, board certified addiction medicine specialist and medical school classmate, initially told me about Suboxone for treating opiate addiction. I had been interested in ways to help people get off opiate analgesics for years. My practice is a holistic medical practice, which specializes in acupuncture, primary care, and pain management. I also had been looking at nutritional therapies and supplements for patients trying to get off opiate analgesics. Many of the patients that came to our medical center wanted help getting off the drugs. My wife, Dr. Cherie Santasiero, PhD, uses spiritual counseling, including hypnosis, Neuro-Linguistic Programing (NLP), and reframing, to help these patients. She has since added EFT (emotional freedom technic). These processes will be discussed in a later chapter. Some patients did very well, but many couldn't get off the prescription drugs because of the awful withdrawal and craving. After looking into Suboxone, I decided to attend the training. To be able to prescribe Suboxone for opiate addiction requires special training and a waiver from the DEA (Drug Enforcement Agency) and the state in which you practice. This is the only drug that requires this extra training and the legal waiver for physicians to prescribe it. This will also be discussed in detail later. After completing the training, the doctor's name is listed on a Suboxone website. Patients looking for doctors to prescribe the medication will often go to the website to locate physicians who can prescribe the drug. An interesting and not fully explained stipulation connected to the waiver to prescribe the drug states that *a physician can only have thirty patients on Suboxone in his/her practice the first year. After two years that number increases to one hundred patients* but never goes higher. As stated previously, the rationale for the numbers and limitations is not clear and has been the subject of much debate by physicians who prescribe Suboxone. The penalty for having more than one's quota of patients is loss of the waiver, which prevents a physician from prescribing the drug from that point on. Patients in the practice then have to find another prescribing physician. Also, according to a DEA official who audited my practice in July of 2011, if a physician exceeds the quota, he/she is subject to a fine of $10,000. The extra training required, the DEA's unannounced visits and audits, and the possibility of the $10,000 fine, make the physician community reluctant to cultivate a Suboxone population of patients. In addition, dealing with addicted patients, especially teens, presents a constant struggle for any practice, including ours. They can be difficult patients, and as you will see, lying and manipulation are common symptoms of addiction. Most of these patients are actually decent people, but they have a difficult disease. They often see lying and manipulation as necessary for survival and have become quite skilled at it.

Within two days of my name appearing on the national Suboxone website, (www.suboxone.com), we began receiving calls for help from patients. To my surprise, a large number of the requests were coming from high school students with an addiction to heroin. Within three months, my practice was filled. I had reached the thirty-patient quota. This was the point at which we decided we wanted to focus on young opiate addicts. The main reasons were: There was (and is) a serious problem with young addicts, the numbers were alarming, and it appeared this population had the best chance of staying clean in the long-term. Many of the initial older addicts were too entrenched in the addiction lifestyle, and I believe they have significant physiologic problems with their brains. After using heroin for years, it is my opinion that the older addicts have biologically and structurally changed the neuro-receptors in their brains. They could stay clean with the proper treatment, but it was a constant struggle. Some even admitted they always felt a craving and could not function in a "normal" society because of this constant craving. They also had long-engrained significant anchors, or connections, to the opiate that were difficult to change in their situations. They felt more comfortable living the addicted lifestyle than living under the normal societal rules. The younger addicted patients had not done extensive damage to their brains and had much more at stake than the older group. Although we focused on younger patients, we still received calls from people of all ages who were looking to get treatment. It would not be unusual to get five to six calls a day from teens or their parents looking for help and for a doctor to prescribe Suboxone. We have been doing Suboxone treatment for almost ten years, and not a day goes by without a call from a young person seeking help. The tragic stories we have heard, and still hear, from parents and teens, comprise one of the main reasons for writing this book. The problem is not going away. It is getting worse. In our area, only a very small percentage of opiate-addicted patients have access to a doctor able to prescribe Suboxone. It is probably in the 20 to 25 percent range. As you will see, the answers to the problem come from education and prevention. We cannot stop the supply of opiates coming into our country illegally, and we have yet to find ways to decrease the number of opiate prescription written by providers. *We must decrease use by decreasing demand.* If there is no demand, there will be no market for illegal drugs. In the subsequent chapters, we will try to educate providers, teens, parents, and interested readers, and give concrete ways to deal with the treatment and prevention of this epidemic.

Chapter 3

WHAT IS ADDICTION?

"A nondependent user controls his/her use.
A dependent person is controlled by his/her use"
- Dr. Charles Gant, *End Your Addiction Now*

Many people think that if someone uses a drug, legal or illegal, and has difficulty stopping the drug, either for psychological or physical reasons, he is addicted to that drug or substance. For instance, if someone loves chocolate and always wants it, they are addicted to chocolate. Actually, that is not true. Craving is part of addiction, but not the whole story.

Some definitions and explanations will help clarify the misconceptions. Some basic definitions are as follows:

NARCOTIC AND OPIATES

A *narcotic* is defined as "a substance that produces insensibility, narcosis or stupor." Narcotic analgesics (pain relievers) derived from opium or produced synthetically alter the perception of pain and induce euphoria, mood changes, mental clouding, and deep sleep. They depress respiration and the cough reflex, constrict the pupils and cause smooth muscle spasm, decreased peristalsis (the involuntary movement of substances through the bowel), and can cause vomiting and nausea. Repeated use of narcotics may result in physical and psychological dependence. Opiates (defined below) are narcotic, but not all narcotics are opiates. For example alcohol is a narcotic because it is sedative and a depressant. Cocaine and amphetamines are not depressant or sedative, but are sometimes called narcotics, because of their euphoria and mood-altering characteristics. Many people use *narcotic* and *opiate* interchangeably, but that is not correct from the actual definition of *narcotic*. As you will see, an *opiate*, by the strictest definition is a substance derived from opium or its derivatives.

OPIATE

An *opiate* is "any of various sedative narcotics containing opium, or one or more of its natural or synthetic derivatives."

OPIOID

An opioid is "a drug, hormone, or other substance having a sedative or narcotic effect, similar to those containing opium or its derivatives. Something that dulls the senses induces relaxation or stupor. Because opiates and opioids slow the bowel and decrease the cough reflex, they are commonly used to treat diarrhea and severe coughing. Unfortunately, one of the severe side effects of opiates is suppression of breathing. This occurs in the brain and is the main cause of death from opiate overdose. As you will see later, the difference between the amount of an opiate that induces euphoria and the amount that causes breathing suppression and death is very slim and unpredictable.

TOLERANCE

Tolerance is a part of addiction. *Tolerance* is defined as: "a state of adaptation in which constant exposure to a substance results in diminution of one or more of the effects of the substance over time." In other words, it takes more of the substance to create the same effect. Not all addictive drugs cause tolerance. Not all people experience tolerance if they take or use an opioid narcotic. We have many pain patients who use opioids for pain relief. Many can use the same dose month after month and get reasonable relief without increasing the dose. They may get relief using three or four opioid analgesics a day and never need more. Virtually all opiate-*addicted* people experience tolerance. Some experience it very quickly, some not as quickly. It is not unusual to have an addict tell me he or she started with three or four hydrocodone per day, and within six months needed ten to twenty per day to get the same effect. Interestingly, the tolerance is mostly to the euphoria (feeling high or intoxicated) effect. The analgesic, or pain-relieving effect, is not nearly as susceptible to the phenomenon of tolerance. Most people who use opiates for pain relief are not looking for the euphoria, which is why they do not need more of the drug to get the desired effect. I have seen addicts using as many as seventy hydrocodone per day. The dose of acetaminophen (Tylenol) in this many pills is staggering and generally dangerous. Generally, the liver toxicity dose of acetaminophen is around 4,000 mg per day. At sixty pills per day, an addict would be ingesting over 20,000 mg per day. Surprisingly, we rarely see liver failure in these patients. It may be something in the genetic makeup of opioid addicts, or related to the liver accommodating these massive doses of acetaminophen as a survival mechanism. Regardless, it is playing Russian roulette with your liver. Liver failure from acetaminophen overdose is very difficult to treat and often fatal. Usually when addicts get up to twenty hydrocodone per day, they start using more potent opiates like oxycodone or OxyContin. Also, because of tolerance, many addicts use the large doses of opiates to prevent withdrawal symptoms and do not feel the euphoria. They take the drugs trying to feel normal, not high.

DEPENDENCE (PSYCHOLOGICAL)

Psychological dependence is "a *subjective* sense of need for a specific psychoactive substance or behavior, either for its positive effects or to avoid negative effects associated with its abstinence." This is different from *physical* dependence, which is more related to a withdrawal syndrome generally manifesting severe unpleasant symptoms. Opiates, as well as other narcotic substances, cause *psychological* dependence. Other substances that cause psychological dependence include alcohol, cocaine, amphetamines, marijuana, ecstasy, tranquilizers, LSD, and other drugs of abuse. Although many people would describe the effects of hallucinogenic drugs like ecstasy and LSD as disturbing, psychologically dependent people actually desire these feelings as an escape or as recreational activity. Many people have such negative existences, that even disturbing feelings are better than what they normally feel. Most drugs of abuse cause a psychological dependence syndrome.

DEPENDENCE (PHYSICAL)

Physical dependence is "a physiologic state of adaptation to a substance characterized by the emergence of a withdrawal syndrome during abstinence. The withdrawal may be relieved in total or partially by the readministration of the substance." Dependence is *not addiction*, yet it is often confused with addiction. Many people who use opiate analgesics for pain relief develop dependence. If they stop the analgesic, they get withdrawal, but they are not addicted. Dependence, in contrast to tolerance, is much more common in people who use opiates for pain relief. Stopping the analgesic can result in severe symptoms of withdrawal in these people. Giving the same or similar drug to the person experiencing the symptoms relieves the withdrawal. Withdrawal in addicted people can be life threatening because of their generally poor state of health, and the large doses of opiates they use. Physical dependence is very common with alcohol and opiates. It is not as common with other drugs of abuse. People can die from withdrawal from opiates and alcohol. That is not likely to happen with other drugs of abuse. People may get very sick, but generally they will survive. Opiate and alcohol withdrawal often need to be treated in a medical environment to prevent serious complications.

ABUSE

According to the DSM-IV (the diagnostic guideline authority utilized by most clinicians), *abuse* is characterized by:

1. "A maladaptive pattern of substance use leading to clinically significant impairment or distress, as manifested by *one or more* of the following, occurring in a twelve month period:

   a. Recurrent substance use resulting in a failure to fulfill major role obligations at work, school, or home (e.g., repeated absences or poor work performances related to substance use; substance related absences, suspensions or expulsions from school; neglect of children or household)

   b. Recurrent substance use in situations in which it is physically hazardous (e.g., driving an automobile or operating a machine, while impaired by substance use)

c. Recurrent substance-related legal problems (e.g., arrests for substance related disorderly conduct)

d. Continued substance use despite having persistent or recurrent social or interpersonal problems caused or exacerbated by the effects of the substance (e.g., arguments with spouse or parent about consequences of intoxication, physical fights)."

Even people who meet the criteria for abuse may not be addicted. The addicted person goes beyond abuse.

ADDICTION

Addiction is "a neurobiological disease with genetic, psychological, and environmental factors influencing its development and manifestations. It is characterized by behaviors that include one or more of the following:

1. Impaired control over its use

2. Compulsive use

3. Continued use despite harm

4. Craving."

The craving is extreme, and causes the addicted person to focus most of their energy into obtaining drugs. If a person exhibits one or more of these behaviors, he/she has crossed the line from dependence to addiction, or the line between abuse and addiction. An addicted person cannot control the use of the drug. If he/she has a hundred hydrocodone, he/she could never make it last a long time. They would use ten or fifteen a day, maybe more, if they possess them. Addicts cannot ration the dosing. They do not worry that they will get withdrawal if they run out. They cross that bridge when they come up to it. Logic does not come into play.

Addicts also have a compulsion to use the drug. It is a behavior that literally compels them to continue using. Much like someone with a compulsion to wash his/her hands fifty times a day regardless of whether they are dirty or not. This is a behavior similar to the behavior of obsessive-compulsive disorders. It is beyond the voluntary control of the individual.

Addicts continue to use in spite of harm to themselves. They have disconnected the sense of right and wrong in their brains. Even if they stand to lose careers, family, health, and freedom, they cannot stop. This is not a behavior they can control unless they get help. It is hard for parents to fathom a child continuing to use an addictive drug after he/she has been told what will happen. This is particularly common in teens, because their sense of right and wrong is not fully developed when they become addicted. However, even adults with a developed sense of right and wrong will continue to use despite known harm. It is as if a primitive part of their brain dictates their behavior, without input from the frontal lobes, which generally control voluntary activities and behaviors.

They also *crave* the drug. *Craving* is defined as an intense desire or yearning for something, a hunger, if you will. This is similar to hungering for food when we haven't eaten. Imagine not eating for three or four days, and then someone puts your absolute favorite food in front of you. What you experience is *craving*. Imagine that craving magnified a hundred times. That is what addiction to opiates does to one's brain and behavior.

Once a person exhibits one or more of the addictive behaviors, he/she is considered addicted. It is important to understand that it is extremely difficult to control these behaviors, and it is not something addicts can do without help. The debate continues about addiction being behavioral or biological. Our position is that addiction occurs because of biology, because of a brain chemistry deficiency. However, the decision to get treatment, if it is available, and continue in treatment *is* behavioral and under a person's control. We have good treatments for some addictions. For others, we do not have good treatments. Prevention and avoidance comprise the answer for those addictions.

In our experience, most teens become addicted quickly if they have the predisposing brain chemistry issues. They pass through the abuse stage quickly or bypass it entirely.

PSEUDOADDICTION

The term *pseudoaddiction* has emerged in the pain management literature to describe inaccurate interpretation of certain behaviors in patients who have severe pain that is undertreated. These patients exhibit some behaviors seen in addicted patients. They appear to be preoccupied with obtaining opioids, but their preoccupation reflects a need for pain control rather than an addictive drive. Pseudoaddictive behavior can be distinguished from addiction by the fact that once adequate pain relief is achieved, the patient who is seeking pain relief demonstrates improved function in daily living activities. For example, such patients may have severe pain and do not get relief with three pain pills per day. They may constantly ask their provider for more pain medication. However, if they are given four pain pills per day, they get better pain relief and do not seek more medication. In addition, they use prescription drugs as prescribed, and do not use drugs in a manner that persistently causes sedation or euphoria. It is important to note that such behaviors may occur occasionally, even in successful opioid therapy of pain. If the patient displays a more frequent pattern of sedation or impaired mentation, further assessment for addictive behaviors should occur. A small percentage, 2 to 4 percent of patients, become addicted following pain treatment with opioid narcotic pain relievers. This is a fact providers and patients need to know. Some of our addicted patients became addicted after being treated for severe pain with opiates.

PSYCHOTROPIC DRUGS

We have been using psychotropic drugs (chemicals that act on the brain) for thousands of years. Initially these chemicals were used for survival or for ceremonies. They were also used as elements of cuisine or as medicines. They were found in their natural forms as plants, herbs, or extracts of plants. Our ancestors smoked, chewed, or swallowed these substances. However, they had very rudimentary ways to process them. They could not concentrate the chemicals that much, and they did not have ways to make synthetic potent derivatives or analogues of them.

The main reason we have more severe addictions and more widespread use of these chemicals is because of technology. We can make more concentrated chemicals, supercharge chemicals, and get an exaggerated effect. We have designer drugs and pharmaceutical analogues today that are sometimes thousands of times more potent than the parent chemical found in nature. Pharmaceutical companies have a vested interest in creating these potent versions of narcotics because they can then be patented; a natural substance cannot be patented. Most painkillers today are derivatives of morphine, but hundreds or thousands of times more potent than morphine, which allows the pharmaceutical companies to patent them and sell them at great profit. They can also make drugs that have a similar chemical structure to naturally occurring compounds and market them exclusively for a profit. Pharmaceutical companies can also patent a delivery system, such as a patch applied to the skin, or an extended release oral delivery system, for a naturally occurring chemical. The extended release forms of morphine have morphine in them, which cannot be patented, but the delivery system can be patented. Drug companies can also make a pro-drug, a drug that is the precursor of an active opioid, which is metabolized into the active opioid in your body, and patent the pro-drug. The other way they can vary this theme is by making a metabolite of a drug, which can then be patented. For example, Opana is a patented and often abused drug. It is actually a metabolite of hydrocodone (Vicodin, Lortab, Norco, etc.,). By taking Opana, you are essentially skipping the first step in using the hydrocodone, thus making it more potent for the user. This theme of making extended release drugs into different delivery systems, precursor drugs, and metabolites of drugs, allows the pharmaceutical giants to deliver a steady and unending supply of drugs to our population.

As these drugs are prescribed, sold, and utilized in larger and larger numbers, the cost to make them drops and the profits increase. Once a drug is off patent, it can be made generically by any company willing to get into that market. You would think the cost would go down dramatically, but typically when a drug goes generic, if it is a narcotic, the generic version is only marginally cheaper. Many times, the company that held the patent still keeps a large share of the market, because cost difference is not that great for someone paying cash for the pills and then selling them on the street. Many patients have prescriptions written by doctors, filled at pharmacies, paid for by insurance companies, and then sold at great profit on the street. An OxyContin 80 mg tablet may have been filled at a pharmacy with no co-pay by the patient, as many patients are on Medicaid or other insurance programs, and sold on the street for $1 per milligram. So a patient may get a prescription from a doctor for ninety 80 mg OxyContin, fill it for no cash out of his/her pocket, then sell them on the street for as much as $7200 per month. It does not take long to see why so many patients try to scam doctors into prescribing these drugs. Since many of these patients have little or no income, this is not an unusual scenario. Some patients with legitimate pain will use some of the prescription for themselves and sell the rest. It is difficult to control this revolving door of narcotic abuse. We will discuss this in a later chapter.

In addition to pharmaceutical enhancement of narcotics, we are now creating genetically engineered plants to produce more potent forms of previously abused psychoactive drugs. The THC content of marijuana plants is much higher today than it was twenty years ago. The same could be said for the plants from which we derive cocaine and opium.

The Internet has also played a major role in the explosion of addiction. Anyone knowledgeable with a computer can do a search to learn how to process pseudoephedrine (an over-the-counter decongestant) into potent methamphetamine. To obtain drugs illegally and to buy drug paraphernalia, drug addicts and abusers also use the Internet. It is also used to find ways to get around drug testing, but this is becoming much more difficult with new drug testing technology. You can even buy "clean" urine on the Internet to bring with you for your drug test. This is also becoming more difficult because it is possible to tell the temperature of a urine sample when it is given, and whether the urine has been adulterated in any way.

Some of the characteristics of opiates are interesting and make them attractive as drugs of abuse. At low levels, opiates are very good pain relievers (analgesics). If you have severe pain, low levels of the drugs will relieve a good portion of the pain, especially acute pain. This is their forte. Opiates are meant to be used after surgery, trauma, or whenever severe pain occurs. They stimulate a cellular receptor (the *mu* receptor) that is responsible for pain relief. However, in the brain, this same receptor is also responsible for a sense of well-being. It is the same receptor that is stimulated by endorphins, which are naturally occurring chemicals made in our brain that make us feel good (Acupuncture helps to release endorphins). In higher doses, the opiates stimulate the *mu* receptor to a point that goes beyond feeling good and we feel euphoric (high). Falling in love, seeing your first newborn child, experiencing your grandchildren—all these things release endorphins in our systems. In controlled doses at physiologic levels, we feel extremely content and happy. At the higher levels experienced with opiates, we go beyond this normal level. We feel very high, out of touch, even disoriented. Many people do not like the experience. It may give them a sense of loss of control and disorientation. To others, it may be a very positive experience, especially if they have some of the risk factors for addiction. If, for instance, they have experienced severe abuse, in any form, the experience of detachment, disorientation, and feeling high may be a welcome change. For most of us, this is not the case.

If you take opiates at doses beyond the sense of feeling high or euphoric, the effect is suppression of breathing. This is a direct effect of the opiate on the area in your brain where breathing is initiated and regulated. Early signs would be shortness of breath or difficulty initiating breathing. However, most drug abusers use such high doses of these drugs or rapid onset opiates (like heroin), they pass *through that stage of breathing suppression right to breathing cessation.* Once this happens, an individual will die within minutes unless he/she is given an antidote for the opiate, which is extremely unlikely if one is doing drugs with friends. Medical professionals, or emergency paramedics, in a supervised setting, usually a hospital, have to give these antidotes. Some police departments are now instructing police officers on using the antidote and supplying them with the antidote for opiate overdoses. Most opiate deaths occur because the user takes the drug, gets high, and keeps taking more to get higher, not realizing they are bumping up against the ceiling of the high effect and going into the breathing suppression/cessation range. Another problem occurs if users are buying street drugs like heroin. They have little idea of the actual dose they are getting. The drug is cut (diluted) so many times from grower to wholesaler to street dealer that it is impossible to determine potency from one day to another. Some dealers will actually make doses more potent to periodically get addicts to buy from them instead of another dealer, or sometimes just to see what happens to users. A sick and criminal behavior, but that is typical of the morality of many drug dealers. A common practice we have seen is a dealer selling a young addict a more potent heroin as an initiation to the drug. They do this to get them "hooked" so they become a desperate and needy buyer, and later, a seller. This is most disturbing when we hear about this practice with young females. We have seen sixteen and seventeen-year-old females get their first dose of heroin from a dealer who sees them not only as a new buyer, but as a potential sex slave or prostitute who will have no choice in future behavior. They get them so addicted and dependent, they will do *anything* for the drug. This has happened to more teen females than you can imagine. This is one of the worst scenarios, because recovery is difficult when a young teen is trying to rebuild self-esteem after this type of experience occurs. Many drug dealers have no conscience and few morals. Many are not even drug users; they are the lowest kind of predator, only interested in making money using vulnerable people. Control and superiority are what they live for.

Opiates are potent stimulators of the *mu* receptor (described in detail later) in cells and in the brain. They eventually block the effects of inherently produced endorphins. When this occurs your body eventually stops making these endorphins, so you become dependent, then addicted to the opiate. Recovery is complicated by this phenomenon and is difficult without addressing this shutdown of inherent chemicals. To make matters more complicated, people who are vulnerable to becoming addicted usually have a deficiency of endorphins or other neurotransmitters (chemicals made by our brains to enhance pleasure and well-being) that the opiate replaces. There is no doubt that some people are genetically more vulnerable or predisposed to opiate addiction because of this neurotransmitter deficiency. We will discuss this in detail later.

WITHDRAWAL

It is the small dose difference between the sense of euphoria and breathing suppression/cessation that makes opiates so mortally dangerous. It is the dependence and addiction potential that makes them so difficult to stop. When a dependent or addicted person tries to stop the opiate, he or she gets a severe reaction called *withdrawal*. It is this withdrawal that makes the person go back to using the drug to stop the severe symptoms. He/she cannot participate in counseling to see what is going on in his/her life, which compels him/her to seek the euphoria, or to help stop feeling the emotional, spiritual, or psychological pain that the drugs relieve. One cannot focus on these issues when one feels like one has the worst flu imaginable. It is naïve and irrational to tell an addict to "just stop the drug and you can do counseling to find out why you use." That would be like me telling a patient, "Don't eat for three weeks, then come in and we will talk about your problems." All they would be thinking about is food at that point. It is even worse with addiction. Counseling is all but impossible until you address the withdrawal and chemical deficiencies.

Some of the signs of opiate withdrawal include:

1. Distressed mood

2. Nausea and vomiting, sometimes severe

3. Muscle aches and cramping

4. Tearing

5. Yawning

6. Runny nose

7. Dilated pupils

8. Sweating

9. Chills

10. Diarrhea

11. Insomnia

12. Craving

13. Irritability

14. Severe anxiety

15. Depression

16. Dysphoria (just not feeling well)

It should be noted that opiates and alcohol are the drugs with the worst physical withdrawal. All drugs of abuse cause some psychological withdrawal, but usually not as bad as opiates and alcohol. The physical withdrawal from alcohol and opiates can be life threatening. Alcohol withdrawal can also cause seizures, hallucinations, and delusional thinking. This is not seen nearly as often with opiates. Unfortunately many drug addicts use multiple drugs so alcohol may also be an issue with opiate withdrawal, and vise versa. Withdrawal from a drug of abuse should only be done under supervision of a medical professional that has experience with treating withdrawal.

We previously looked at a simplistic definition of addiction, which included craving, a compulsion to use a drug, continued use in spite of knowing it is bad for you, and loss of control of dosing the drug. To make a clinical diagnosis of addiction, a person must demonstrate three or more of the following in the last twelve months:

1. Tolerance

2. Withdrawal symptoms

3. Use of the drug to avoid or reverse withdrawal symptoms

4. Compulsion to use the drug, especially when trying to stop

5. Narrowed repertoire of behaviors associated with drug use; their day revolves around using or getting drugs

6. Drug related behaviors become more important than other previously important activities or behaviors, they stop going to school, work, seeing family and friends

7. Early relapse after withdrawal

If a loved one demonstrates only one or two of these behaviors, but not at least three of the behaviors, they may not be clinically addicted, but they are well on their way to becoming addicted, and should seek medical attention.

Commonly used opiates and common brand names include:

1. Morphine (MS Contin)

2. Demerol

3. Dilaudid

4. Oxycodone (Percocet, Percodan)

5. OxyContin (sustained-release oxycodone, can have as many as 16 Percocet equivalent tablets in each pill)

6. Hydrocodone (Vicodin, Lortab, Norco)

7. Fentanyl (Duragesic), a synthetic morphine

8. Methadone

9. Codeine

10. Zohydro ER; FDA approved in February of 2014, a new and potentially dangerous form of extended release hydrocodone. This will be discussed later.

In 2011, Darvocet, commonly used in older people, was taken off the market, but may still be in people's medicine cabinets. You will commonly hear people in authority saying OxyContin is a drug "only prescribed for cancer patients." This is not true. OxyContin was originally approved by the FDA for severe cancer pain; however, it is a common drug prescribed by physicians for chronic pain. The main reasons are:

1. If someone has tolerance to a short-acting oxycodone (Percocet, etc.,) and the need eight or nine of them a day, it is common practice to go to a long-acting preparation like OxyContin. It is sustained release and has a higher dose per pill because of this.

2. Generally most physicians will go to oxycodone preparations if hydrocodone fails to relieve pain. Hydrocodone was the number one prescribed drug in America for years, until recently. Tylenol with codeine is not a potent pain reliever so it is not used as a first line analgesic as much as it was in the past. Hydrocodone is generally the first opiate analgesic prescribed. Darvon or Darvocet was used as first line treatment in the past, but it is no longer available.

3. Insurers pressure physicians to use sustained-release medications when a patient is on six or more short-acting medications per day. OxyContin is a *relatively* low-level sustained-release medication, even though it is one of the most abused drugs on the street. After OxyContin, you would have to use a sustained-release morphine derivative, generally more potent.

4. Physicians get a lot pressure from patients who read about drugs on the Internet or from "friends and neighbors" of that patient, making recommendations for OxyContin or other potent narcotics. Many times the "friends and neighbors" are just looking for a new source of drug, so they try to convince a person to get a script so they can steal it and use it, or sell it. It is very difficult to convince patients of the danger of OxyContin when the alterna-

tive is a more potent sustained-release medication like sustained-release morphine, fentanyl, or other potent opiate.

5. Occasionally a pharmacist will tell a patient to ask for OxyContin when they are taking a number of short-acting opiates per day. This puts pressure on physicians to write a prescription for it. Many patients view the pharmacist as an expert in medication, so it is difficult for physicians to dismiss their advice as unwise. Pharmacists are very knowledgeable about medications. However, they do not know the medical history of the patient as well as the physician. Also, many have rudimentary knowledge of addiction.

6. Opana was an alternative to OxyContin in the past, but it is quickly becoming more abused and more street-valuable than OxyContin. It is also more expensive for insurers. Consequently, it will end up as a tier two or three drug requiring a higher copayment for patients.

7. Although OxyContin is a drug diverted to the streets a large percentage of the time, it is still widely used for moderate to severe pain treatment because of the above reasons. It is difficult as a physician to argue with four or five people a day who insist upon it. It is not an excuse, but it is not something we care to do daily. Medical practice is very stressful today, and this is just one of the stressors practitioners have to deal with. Sometimes practitioners choose to pick other battles. In my practice, I rarely put people on OxyContin; however, if they are on it when they start as new patients, I try to look at alternatives. This is often unsuccessful. The lesson for the reader is to do everything in your power to not use long-acting narcotics for your pain and your family's pain treatment. It

is a dangerous and sometimes deadly practice. Once you and your provider make the decision to go to long-acting opiates, it will be a lifelong issue. It is very difficult to stop these drugs.

Opiate analgesics are valuable when used properly for acute pain. If the pain is mild to moderate, look for alternatives to opiates. Herbal remedies, acupuncture, massage, chiropractic, hypnosis, meditation, acetaminophen (Tylenol), non-steroidal anti-inflammatories (ibuprofen, aspirin, Aleve, Advil, or prescription non-steroidal anti-inflammatories). Many Americans think pain medication should "eradicate or eliminate" pain. In reality, pain medications should modify or attenuate pain, not completely relieve it. We have to get expectations in line with reality.

Chronic pain should be treated with opiate analgesics with great caution. They are not the best choice for treatment of chronic pain. Chronic pain is a syndrome different from acute pain, from surgery, or from injury. Treating chronic pain with opiate analgesics is likely to produce dependence on the medication, making it difficult to stop. Tolerance is also common in chronic pain treatment with opiate analgesics. In reality, many patients treated with opiates for chronic pain find the pain medication is really just preventing the pain of withdrawal and not really affecting the underlying chronic pain. In the next chapter, we will look at why some people get addicted and others do not.

Chapter 4

WHY DO PEOPLE GET ADDICTED?

"Our brain seeks a drug or chemical to achieve
homeostasis (balance)
- Dr. Charles Gant, *End Your Addiction Now*

What really causes the symptoms of addiction? Is it a psychiatric problem? Is it lack of social support? Do people who are addicted lack a spiritual path? Are they lacking morals? Is it the boss, the kids, lack of friends, money, or spousal issues? Are people who are addicted victims of previous emotional trauma? Do they have biochemical, nutritional, or other chemical imbalances in their brain? All of these have been postulated as causes. Some have merit, and some are just outdated thinking. Much of the interpretation of the neurochemical basis of addiction in this book comes from the work of Dr. Charles Gant.

Let's look at some myths about addiction and substance abuse.

Myth #1—Compulsive use of a substance is a sign of lack of willpower. Addicts have underlying spiritual problems or moral problems. They are basically defective socially and morally and should be treated that way. If you incarcerate or sequester addicts they will learn right from wrong and they will not be addicted.

Myth # 2—Drugs, alcohol, and casinos are the causes of substance abuse and addiction. If we could eliminate them, we would eliminate addictions and abuse.

Myth # 3—Once you have stopped drugs or alcohol, you have to engage in a constant struggle not to relapse. You will never be "cured" and should accept that "once an addict always an addict" is yours to bear.

Myth #4—People have a choice about whether they become addicts or not. If they had strong enough willpower in the beginning, they would not get addicted.

Myth #5—Addiction is really not a disease. It is a mental and psychological problem and cannot be treated like other "medical" diseases.

The treatment of addiction has changed dramatically in the last ten years. Looking at the previous myths one at a time, we can start to understand how it has changed.

Myth # 1 Reality

I have never met an addict who liked being addicted; neither do they enjoy the lifestyle of addiction. People with moral or social defects do not feel that way. They generally like their immorality and are sociopaths. That is not to say that some addicts are not sociopaths. Some also perform immoral acts; antisocial behavior and immoral activities are symptoms of addiction, not the underlying cause. They are viewed as part of survival for the addicted person. Teens we have treated hate that they have to steal from family and friends to get drugs. Young females hate selling themselves sexually to pay for their addiction. They do it because they cannot stop the drugs. Lying becomes a symptom of the disease, not the reason they are addicts.

Myth # 2 Reality

Drugs and alcohol do not cause addictions. If we could eliminate illegal drugs, stop prescribing opiates, and ban selling alcohol, many addicts would become addicted to other substances or acts. They may become addicted to gambling or sex or chocolate or shopping, but they would substitute something else for the drugs. The reason for addiction is that people who become addicted have an inherent brain chemistry issue and the addictive drug helps alleviate the brain chemistry symptoms. I hear people argue that if we only brought attention to someone's addiction and could prevent addicts from obtaining the drug, they would stop the addictive behavior. That is false. It is my opinion that, once patients start an effective treatment for addiction, they become responsible to stay in treatment. Becoming addicted may not be a choice; however, seeking and staying in treatment is a personal choice and responsibility. Relapse becomes something over which addicts have much more control. If they continue to use the drugs, the odds of getting clean are stacked against them, for reasons we will explain later.

Myth # 3 Reality

Once you have stopped your addictive drug, it does not have to be a constant struggle to stay clean. Understanding that the brain is lacking a biochemical substance (neurotransmitter) is important for the addict. An addicted individual is partially replacing the *effect* of the neurotransmitter depletion with the addictive drug. If an addicted individual helps the brain rebuild the lacking neurotransmitter through diet, lifestyle, and supplements, he or she can effectively overcome a major barrier to recovery. Are addicted individuals cured if they do this? No. It will, however, make sobriety much easier. It will always be something addicted individuals have to monitor, and they will have to do a great deal of counseling to look at other issues, but it is effective treatment. *They do not lack moral or social character, they lack brain chemicals.* As Dr. Cherie Santasiero says when addressing her young patients, "The reason you started drugs is psychological; becoming addicted is biological." Recovery is best achieved by treating the biochemical and the psychological issues.

Myth #4 Reality

Addicts do not lack willpower. They are dealing with something much stronger than the willpower of the vast majority of our population: Addictive drugs. As we explain to our addicted teens, these drugs are much stronger than you, and you must have a great deal of respect for that. It is a case, for most, of coming up against something beyond our ability to control. Biochemical forces are much stronger than we imagine. Dr. Gant, a holistic physician with an interest in treating addictions and author of books on addiction, has demonstrated this with a simple experiment: try to hold your breath for ten minutes. Of course, that is impossible for most of us. Why? Because the buildup of a substance in our brain, carbon dioxide, forces us to take a breath after several minutes. It is not about willpower or strength. It is biochemistry, beyond our voluntary control. Addictions are the same, except it is about neurotransmitters, not carbon dioxide. Let's say your brain lacks a neurotransmitter GABA (gamma-amino butyric acid). This is a substance that helps keep us calm. Drugs like Valium, Xanax, Ativan, and Klonopin mimic GABA in our brains. They are not exactly GABA, but close chemically. Now let's say you take an opiate at a party. The opiate behaves like the GABA you are lacking, although it isn't a perfect match. Your brain says, "This is close to what I have been waiting for." Once the brain starts experiencing the neurotransmitter substitute (the addictive drug), it says, "I really want that again, to achieve balance" and the craving begins.

Most of our addicted teens lack GABA. They tell us when they started taking the opiate they felt "normal," not high. That is because the opiate helped calm the receptor in the brain where GABA is needed. The opiate kind of fools the brain. Think of it as the chemical brake in our brain. Many of the addicted teens have a history of anxiety or hyperactivity. They may even have been on the Valium, Ativan or Xanax (benzodiazepine), and/or Ritalin (a stimulant) before becoming addicted. The opiate satisfies the GABA receptor and at first they feel normal. They go on to feel high after they start increasing the dose of the opiate. Most opiate addicts have tried cocaine or other stimulants and they do not like them, because they get overstimulated by these drugs. When they try the opiate, they are calmer and feel closer to normal. In medical terms, they are approaching homeostasis (balance), which is what the brain wants to do. One of our patients described the experience before he took the opiate as having a "race car engine with bicycle brakes." When he used the opiate, it helped apply the chemical brakes to his anxiety and nervousness. Most nonaddicted people would not react that way. This is unique to GABA-deficient opiate-addicted people. So how can we blame someone who has a brain chemistry deficiency for becoming addicted? As stated before, once an individual finds he or she has a neurotransmitter deficiency, it becomes his or her responsibility to get into and continue treatment. Becoming addicted is not the fault of these individuals; staying addicted once treatment is started becomes an issue of motivation, education, and willpower. This explains why they get addicted to opiates. As Dr. Gant says, "You do not choose the drug, the drug chooses you." In other words, our inherent biochemical deficiencies dictate what drugs we are susceptible to becoming dependent or addicted to. If we lack GABA, we are more likely to get addicted to an opiate rather than a stimulating drug like cocaine. The cocaine will make brains with this type of composition feel more "out of balance."

Myth # 5 Reality

Opiate addiction has many characteristics in common with chronic diseases. Compare addiction to diabetes: both type I (insulin dependent diabetes) and type 2 (noninsulin dependent diabetes) are controlled with diet and oral medications. Both diseases are chronic and tend to relapse. Both have a genetic vulnerability. Both have origins and symptoms that occur because of physiologic brain and body changes. Both respond to chronic disease management strategies better than short-term relief. If you treat an insulin dependent diabetic with an elevated blood sugar by giving more insulin, you may lower the blood sugar, but not address the underlying causes: diet and lifestyle issues. If you increase a type 2 diabetic's oral medication, again you may temporarily lower the blood sugar, but not address the long-term diet and lifestyle issues. If you take away the addicted patient's drugs and get them over withdrawal, you do not solve the addiction problem. You must educate, counsel, monitor, and motivate them, as you would the diabetic. Type 1 diabetes would be analogous to the IV heroin addict. It is a more severe form of the disease and more prone to relapse and lack of control. Individuals addicted in this way need more intensive therapy. The opiate addict that has not progressed to intravenous drug use is more like the type 2 diabetic patient. These individuals are less prone to relapse and still need treatment, but not necessarily as intensive. The IV drug abuser is also more likely to need inpatient treatment for his or her disease when he or she is at his or her worst, as will the type 1 diabetic. Whether treating a patient for diabetes, hypertension, heart disease, or addiction, the similarities are more numerous than the differences. We need to recognize the similarities in order to help remove the stigma of addicted patients and their families, because this stigma interferes with addiction treatment.

Our model of addiction treatment is based on the model promoted by the drug treatment program at Passages in Malibu, California. Passages uses a holistic model that gives a comprehensive and hopeful view of why people become addicted. We have created our own version of treatment based on the Passages model for treating teen addicted patients. Other models of addiction treatment are widely used. Some work for some people, and all have some good points. We will discuss some of these in our chapter on treatment. What is good about the Passages model is that it gives patients a reason to believe their addiction can be controlled long term. The Passages model is also a concise model that incorporates the concept of chemical imbalances as well as psychospiritual issues as causes of addiction. Most of all, it gives a patient hope that the saying "once an addict always an addict" does not have to be accepted as the norm. The Sedona model (our model) of addiction treatment is based on the Passages model; through our years of experience in treating addiction, we have modified it for the teenage population.

The model is based on these premises:

1. The vast majority, probably 98 percent of teen opiate addicts, has a brain chemistry imbalance. Most of these individuals lack GABA, as described above. Unless this imbalance is addressed with substitution therapy, nutrition, stress reduction, supplements, and integrative therapies, the other parts of the treatment are destined to fail.
2. Many teens have a history of abuse in their past. This may not be our interpretation of overt abuse. It may be neglect, perceived abuse, actual abuse, or *perceived* emotional deprivation.

3. Many teens have issues of abuse in their present situation. The issues are the same as with past abuse.

4. These addicted teens have a view of themselves that does not match the reality they perceive would be adequate for their well-being. It may be low self-esteem, spiritual depletion, lack of a viable path to success, or inability to live up to the expectations of their parents. To make matters worse, the addiction robs them of what little self-esteem they may have had. Many have disrupted family situations. It is common to see families polarized or torn apart by the addicted teen. Parents will choose sides between tough love and trying to be supportive. The supportive parent may feel sorry for the teen and enable the addiction. It is a fine line between enabling and supporting in these situations. Many times the teen has dropped out of school, cannot get a job and has legal issues that are hanging over his or her head. The family may be in constant turmoil over legal fees, jail time, medical expenses, and "babysitting" the addicted child. Siblings get neglected and are resentful toward the addicted teen. The teen has to change friends at work or school. As part of the recovery process, the teen is unable to hang out with friends that use drugs. Addicts will sometime crave by just being with a friend with whom they did drugs in the past. It is dangerous to put them into that situation during treatment. Sadly, if they go to school, the friends that are users can no longer be a part of their social group. On the other hand, the kids that do not use want nothing to do with the addicted teen, since their drug use is well known in the school. They become loners, which damages self-esteem even further. Many of our teens are good students or leaders in their schools. We have had valedictorians, cheerleaders, and star athletes. When these individuals

become addicted, it all falls apart. Families, friends, and schoolmates shun them. As one teen told me when we discussed his situation, "When I was in high school, I was a star athlete; now I am a piece of crap." He was struggling for survival emotionally, while trying to recover from his chemical imbalance.

If the addicted teen is working, many have dropped out of school; they usually can only get jobs in restaurants or for minimum wage. In our area of the country, they can also get jobs with collection agencies. Both of these kinds of jobs have high rates of drug use among the employees. These individuals are stuck working that type of job, but they are constantly bombarded with the drug use. It becomes a vicious cycle. The biggest challenge in treated teen addicts is the rebuilding of their psyche and self-esteem.

The significance of the chemical imbalance is underscored by the statistics for recovery in outcome studies. If a person tries to quit opiates "cold turkey" with no outside help, they have a **3 in 1000** chance of staying clean (drug free) for one year. In other words, 997 out of 1000 patients will relapse during that year if they receive no professional help. Patients in intensive inpatient counseling, who participate in a thirty or sixty-day treatment at a cost of $30,000 to $100,000 at the best facilities in the country, have a **15 to 17 out of 100** chance of staying clean for one year. That means eighty-three to eighty-five out of a hundred will relapse in that year after treatment. This explains why so many celebrities do poorly after inpatient rehab. They are a reflection of the accepted success rates for this type of treatment.

So what is the answer? If you look at patients treated with Suboxone, a prescription medication that calms the brain neuro-receptors crying out for the lacking neurotransmitter, the success rate of patients who stay clean is about *80 to 85 out of 100*, *if they also do counseling.* This is a type of substitution therapy. This is almost

the complete reverse of the best inpatient treatment center's statistics. This will be discussed at length in the treatment chapters.
Substitution therapy is essential to initiate before you get therapy
for abuse, emotional, psychological, or self-esteem issues. In addition to the substitution therapy, initiation of lifestyle changes and
supplements is critical to rebuild the brain chemistry.

If we look at another aspect of addiction, we see why young
people get addicted. Statistically, if a hundred people use an opiate for the first time, ten will not like it. They will get nausea and
feel sick. They will tell us, "I don't see what addicts see in these
drugs; they make me sick." Approximately eighty of the hundred
first-time users will say: "It relieved my pain, but I could take it
or leave it." About ten of the hundred first-time users will very
much enjoy the effect of the opiate. They will say, "I really like
the effects; it makes me feel really good." Of the ten out of one
hundred who really like the drug, four out of the ten will like it
so much; they become dependent and ultimately addicted. They
will typically say, "I have never felt like this in my life!" Or, "This is
the first time I have felt 'normal' in my entire life." *Unfortunately,
we cannot predict who these four out of one hundred people are who will
get "hooked" with the first use of the opiate.* This is the frightening
part of opiate addiction. Whether a person uses the drug for an
acute pain issue or recreationally the first time, the statistics are
similar. The addiction potential is only slightly less likely if the
first use is for acute pain relief. The vast majority of teen addicts
we see first use the opiate recreationally. They start by using at a
party, with friends, or out of boredom. The nature of teens is to
be daring and experimental as they begin to experience a desire
for independence in their early teens.

The statistics stated above relate to hydrocodone, (Lortab,
Vicodin, Norco), as the first opiate drug of abuse. It is the one used
by 95 percent of teens as the first opiate; it is a relatively low-level
opiate. Hydrocodone is prescribed for minor to moderate acute

pain and refills can be given on the prescription. This law changed in New York State as Of February 2013. As of that date, no refills are allowed on hydrocodone. Most other opiates are only prescribed as a thirty-day prescription with no refills. As the potency of the opiate increases, the statistics get worse. If a teen's first exposure to opiates is with a more potent opiate, the addiction potential increases dramatically with first use. It may be as high as thirty out of one hundred who get addicted with first use if the opiate is heroin. As bizarre as it sounds, we have seen heroin as the first opiate used by teens.

Amanda, a very shy eighteen-year-old, presented for opiate addiction treatment and related the following story: When she was sixteen and at a party, she met an older nineteen-year-old guy. He convinced her to try a "powder" that would make her "feel really good." Although initially reluctant, she did not have the assertiveness to say no. As you will see later, most teens do not have as sense of right and wrong *hard wired* into their brains at this age. She snorted the powder and felt "a rush like nothing I have ever experienced before." The powder was heroin. Amanda spent the next six months focusing all her efforts on getting more heroin. Her grades dropped like a rock and she stopped going to school. Her parents were extremely concerned because she had always been a good student with nice friends. Subsequent to her first use, over the next nine months she worked her way up to injecting the heroin. Her new "boyfriend," the young man she met at the party, convinced her to start dealing the drug in order to keep her supplied. Over the next eighteen months, she spent most of her time getting high and dealing heroin. During this time she also had a pregnancy, ending in an abortion. About two months prior to seeking help at our center, she and her boyfriend were pulled over by local police. As they were being pulled over, her boyfriend tossed a sandwich bag filled with powder (which was cocaine) onto her lap. When the police approached the car, she tried hiding the package in her pocket. After they searched her, they found cocaine in the package and arrested her and her boyfriend. The police soon found out the truth. The boyfriend was wanted on other drug charges. Amanda, though, was put on probation and mandated to go for treatment. When we first saw her, she was more upset about the betrayal by her boyfriend than about her addiction. She was now using eight to ten bags of heroin at a cost of up to $100 a day, to support her addiction. She quickly found that addiction has no friends, only "drug buddies." A dealer, for sexual favors and to deal his drugs, used Amanda's addiction against her. She did not comprehend that he felt this way about her, when she cared so much about him. Subsequent to this episode, she has had four pregnancies, with two living children. She completed tenth grade and cannot get a job because she struggles with addiction and getting her life in order. Her parents were initially supportive, but after three years of addiction with relapses, they gave up on her. Amanda's parents are fighting for the survival of their marriage and to salvage their two younger children. This is not an unusual situation. It is actually a common scenario to see families ripped apart by addiction.

Can we predict who will be the four in one hundred people who are susceptible to first-time addiction to an opiate? The answer is, we can see certain tendencies and possible predictors. It is becoming more and more clear that addiction, at least a tendency to addiction, may have a genetic origin. If one or more grandparents, parents, or siblings have a drug or alcohol problem, it raises the possibility of a child being susceptible, or of being one of the ten in one hundred people who will really like an opiate if they are introduced to it. Another predictor is a child who is extremely anxious and has used benzodiazepines such as Valium, Ativan, or Xanax, or a stimulant such as Ritalin, for the anxiety; these kids are more susceptible. Ritalin and Adderall are stimulants. However, they are used in young children and teens to treat hyperactivity and anxiety. The reason is stimulants have a paradoxical effect in young brains. This occurs because if you expose a young hyperactive brain to a stimulant, it triggers the brain to make calming neurotransmitters to "balance" the excess stimulants. This effect is more predominantly seen in younger brains. We tend to lose this ability as our brains age and become less sensitive to fluctuations in neurotransmitter levels. Remember the GABA receptor is partially satisfied by the benzodiazepines and the opiate. Individuals will use the opiate to feel "normal" at first, then to get high.

Many of the susceptible people have brain starvation for neurotransmitters that calm them down. Their brains may lack a vitamin, mineral, or amino acid that is needed to make these calming neurotransmitters so they become deficient. They may not have proper diets or may eat toxic foods that prevent them from making the neurotransmitter and they become deficient. On the other side of the equation, they may make adequate amounts of the neurotransmitter, but deplete it quickly because of stress, poor diet, or physical stress. Regardless of whether it is an inability to make the neurotransmitter or whether it is depleted too quickly, these individuals are susceptible to opiate dependence and addiction if the deficiency is not corrected. The correction of the deficiency is a major part of the treatment, as you will see. Counseling is also critical, because it can help slow down the depletion of the neurotransmitter from emotional, psychological, or spiritual stress. Many times the depletion is from both too little manufacture and too much utilization of the lacking neurotransmitter.

Other predictors of addiction potential include teens that are thrill seekers, lacking in goals, always complaining of being bored, and overly rebellious. The opiate serves to stimulate another neurotransmitter, dopamine, which is the pleasure neurotransmitter. The use of the opiate can cause tremendous surges of dopamine in the brain, which cause the brain to feel pleasure. A normal teen might experience the release of dopamine by getting a great report card, winning a sporting event, or falling in love for the first time. The release of the dopamine is a more sustained lower level release, but still pleasurable. As a way to compare the magnitude of the release of dopamine, Dr. Nora Volkow of the Nation Institute of Health (NIH) has done work in this area. Her work demonstrates that an orgasm releases about 200 units of dopamine very quickly, but fades over a period of minutes to hours. The surge of dopamine from the first IV injection of heroin releases about 1200 units of dopamine., which is about six times the amount of an orgasm release! The dopamine stimulates a part of the brain called the nucleus accumbens. This area of the brain is where the final pleasure is experienced. Unfortunately, the level of dopamine release from the first IV heroin experience is never achieved again. It would very quickly cause brain depletion, and the brain prevents that kind of release in subsequent IV doses of heroin, as a mechanism to preserve neurotransmitters. This causes the addicted person to "chase the high" by increasing the dose of heroin to experience that first feeling. This is what causes tolerance to the opiate. After several weeks of using the IV drug, the addicted person uses just to prevent the withdrawal, not to feel high. Feeling high quickly becomes a rare event and can only be achieved by using after a period of abstinence, or using a more potent dose of heroin. This is extremely dangerous because the dose of opiate causing the extreme high, breathing suppression, and subsequent death, is very close. Many addicts die trying to get a high; they only experience breathing cessation and death. It is the thrill-seeking nature of teens, and the potent stimulation of the dopamine receptors from opiates, that make the teen more vulnerable to addiction. Dopamine receptors are also more sensitive in young people than in older people. This is a normal aging phenomenon.

If a teen is lacking GABA (the brakes in the brain) and gets a tremendous release of dopamine (the pleasure neurotransmitter), the engine, from an opiate, the setup for addiction increases dramatically. The engine, dopamine, will run faster and longer, because of the lack of GABA, the brakes. Additionally, when people experience the pleasure from normal events like love, the birth of a child, doing well at work, being close to nature or being with family, these events are associated with sights, sound, smells, and series of events. When the dopamine release from these normal experiences stimulates the brain at the nucleus accumbens, it normally goes through structures that cause the brain to filter, remember, and associate these sights, smells, sounds, and events. They are called *anchors* and will be discussed later. When opiates stimulate dopamine and cause massive initial surges, the nucleus accumbens gets stimulated, bypassing many of these brain structures. This is because the dopamine release occurs so quickly from the opiate; this prevents the normal filtering mechanisms to control the dopamine stimulation of the pleasure center. To complicate and exacerbate this, the teen brain has poor filtering and control mechanisms to begin with. These individuals also lack inherent chemical attenuating neurotransmitters (GABA) in most cases. The anchors become where they get high, who they get high with, and what caused them to want to get high; these are the "people, places, and things" they are told to avoid in therapy. It is like riding a roller coaster, but skipping all the twists, turns, and minor hills and just experiencing that first major drop instead of the whole ride. This is exciting at first, but quickly becomes less than thrilling. Once an addict bypasses these normal pleasure circuits, and in essence short-circuits the brain's normal pleasure circuitry, it takes a lot of reprogramming to correct the short circuit. Before long, normal pleasurable events, such as getting good grades, pleasing parents and teachers, and winning at sports, become mundane and unimportant. This is a serious issue in recovery.

RISK FACTORS

Other risk factors, specifically for teenagers, have been studied. These risk factors include:

Family and Genetic Issues

1. Family history. If alcoholism is seen in parents or siblings, the rate of alcoholism is four times greater in teens. This is probably similar in opiate addiction. Even if the genetic tendency may be less, the potency of the opiate drug is greater.
2. Prenatal complications. Premature delivery, head injury during delivery or shortly after delivery. Also, exposure to toxins such as heavy metals (lead, mercury, arsenic, cadmium), tobacco, alcohol, cocaine or opiates pre- or post-delivery. These can predispose a teen to aggressive behavior and addiction.
3. ADHD, ADD, or persistent conduct disorders can lead to addiction.
4. The earlier a child initiates drugs or alcohol, the more likely he or she will use frequently and become addicted in adolescence. We typically see addicted teens that started to use alcohol at the age of nine or ten years old.
5. Parents' use of drugs, or permissive attitude by parents of a child's use of drugs, increases the risk of addiction. I cannot tell you how often we hear, "my child is going to experience his or her first joint with me," or, "I don't mind if my child smokes marijuana; everybody smoked it when I was growing up," or, "I can smoke marijuana, but that does not mean my children should. They can do what they want when they're on their own. I shouldn't have to stop smoking in front of my children, it's my house." A

child learns by seeing how a parent behaves more than what he or she says. We treated two siblings of parents who smoked marijuana regularly in front of them. The children were very bright. One was a valedictorian. The parents made no attempt to hide their smoking and drug use. When the children left home after high school, both dropped out of college in their first year and struggled with addiction and life after quitting school.

6. Allowing children to serve drinks or light cigarettes. Also letting children use candy cigarettes. Although this may seem cute, it desensitizes children about the use of these substances. They get a reward, an anchor, by appearing "cute" in front of parents, removing any stigma or reservations about using these substances. This may not directly apply to opiates, but a teen's brain many times cannot distinguish one behavior from another at this level. To a teen, using opiates might be no different from parents using cigarettes or alcohol.

7. Parents who punish excessively or inconsistently can predispose a teen to escape by using drugs.

8. Children whose parents divorced while they were adolescents can cause addiction as a way to escape or cope with the negative feelings of the divorcing parents.

9. Low maternal attachment or paternal permissiveness can be a serious risk factor for teen addiction. This is especially true if the mother is an addict or if the parents are divorced and the custodial parent is the mother and the father is permissive as a way to win favor from the child. I am sure the opposite is likely, but we have less experience with custodial fathers. Sometimes the low attachment to the mother can be a deterrent if the mother is not in the picture because of opiate addiction. These teens may "not want to be like their mother, in this situation."

Peer Factors

Friends who drink, smoke, or use drugs are strong predictors of future drug use. Many of our teen addicts used with friends the first time, sometimes as a dare, many times to be "part of the group." This is a very strong predictor. This, combined with potent drugs (opiates), is a deadly combination. Keep a close eye on your teens' friends. If parents are not major role models for the teens, friends will be surrogate role models.

Community Factors

Addiction to alcohol is more prevalent in communities where it is readily available and relatively cheap. This is more pronounced with opiates. In many areas, heroin is cheaper than marijuana, so teens start using heroin to get high. It is cheaper and causes a better initial high. This is a serious health and community problem. Availability and cost are issues dealt with by police, legislators, schools, parents, and general education. It is a huge part of prevention.

Protective factors

1. A resilient temperament is protective for teens. If they are very sensitive, rigid, compulsive, or not assertive, they are susceptible to addiction. Teach teens and young children about self-esteem and assertiveness. Help to build their self-esteem and teach them how to stand up for themselves.
2. A positive social orientation is protective. If they are encouraged to make healthy friendships, respect adults, respect authority, and education, they are less likely to get addicted. Teens are naturally inquisitive

and will be exposed to drugs and drug use. If they have respect for the power of these drugs and have good self-esteem, they are less likely to use drugs excessively. If they get positive encouragement and rewards from good grades and pleasing parents, teachers, and friends, they will not look to drugs for self-gratification.

3. High intelligence and skills are also protective. Cultivate a child's skills, whether it is art, sports, music, writing, or another skill. If a child feels self-worth, he or she will not look to drugs for gratification. If a child gets good grades, reward the behavior to anchor them to future achievement.

4. Strong beliefs or behavioral standards make children less likely to use drugs. If they feel a sense of opposition to illegal drug use they are less likely to use them for self-gratification.

Although most of the above risk and protective factors have been studied for alcohol and lower level gateway drugs, the principles apply, in most cases, even more with opiates. *Prevention is much more effective than treatment.* As you will see in subsequent chapters, teen opiate addiction is not easy to treat. The outcomes, even with good treatment, are emotionally, physically, financially, and spiritually expensive. A teen addict is never the same, and can rip a family apart before he or she recovers, if recovery is achieved. We will look at specific issues with teen addiction in the next chapter.

Chapter 5

BEHAVIORS AND SIGNS OF ADDICTION

"I was only holding that joint for my friend so he wouldn't get into trouble."
- Fifteen year-old teen caught with marijuana by his mother.

Signs and behaviors related to addiction can be broken up into several categories. These include symptoms of withdrawal, personal appearance, personal behaviors at home, behaviors at school, and behaviors in the workplace.

As stated in previous chapters, withdrawal can be manifested by a number of symptoms, which overlap with other diseases and are demonstrated to varying degrees depending on the seriousness of the withdrawal.

Withdrawal symptoms include:

• Distressed mood

• Nausea and vomiting

• Muscle aches or cramping

• Tearing

• Dilated pupils

• Sweating

• Chills

• Diarrhea

• Yawning

• Insomnia

• Craving

• Irritability

• Severe anxiety

As you can see, many of these symptoms could be manifested by an acute viral infection, food poisoning, situational anxiety, stress, lack of sleep, hormonal issues, use of nonaddicting drugs, or a number of other illnesses. It is important to put the symptoms in the context. For instance, demonstration of any one of these would not necessarily make you suspect that your loved one is going through withdrawal. However, if multiple symptoms occur at the same time, and the person has other behavioral symptoms, your suspicion for withdrawal should be elevated. A lot of parents make an issue of the child's pupils being "constricted," or dilated when they are looking into their eyes. It is important to note that dilated pupils are a sign of opiate withdrawal, not opiate use. In addition, constricted pupils don't necessarily mean that person is "using" an addictive substance. In our experience most people in withdrawal will experience GI issues such as nausea, vomiting, or diarrhea. They also usually will experience some element of muscle aches or joint pain. In addition, many experience anxiety. This is due to the fact that most teenagers we see lack GABA, a calming neurotransmitter, and the opiate serves to modulate or control this deficiency. The benzodiazepines, drugs such as Valium, Xanax, and Ativan, are synthetic forms of GABA and stimulate the GABA receptor in the brain. Therefore, since anxiety is many times caused by lack of GABA in your brain, it is relieved by taking these drugs. Although opiates are not chemically as close as the benzodiazepines are to GABA, they do stimulate the receptor to some degree. Therefore when you withdraw the opiate, the anxiety gets unmasked and is magnified because of the overstimulation by the opiate, and the rapid withdrawal of the drug. Opiate addicts will go beyond the use of opiates to make them feel relatively normal. They usually get to the point where they go beyond the sense of normalcy to euphoria and even sedation or coma. Although they may experience craving, it is difficult for you to observe this sensation as it may manifest as some of the other symptoms or behaviors such as the irritability, anxiety, restlessness, or hyperactive behavior.

The muscle aches and cramping can also be a fairly severe symptom and can cause a great deal of distress to the patient. For some patients, this is the worst symptom and the pain can be excruciating. For other patients, the muscle cramps aren't very bad, and not the main reason they seek treatment for the withdrawal.

Yawning is a curious behavior. It is involuntary and demonstrated frequently. It is unclear why yawning occurs in withdrawal but it is likely mediated through the brain and central nervous system. It is also commonly seen an opiate withdrawal, although not as distressing as some of the above symptoms. Patients describe it more as a annoying behavior rather than a serious issue.

Changes in personal appearance can be a significant indicator of an addiction problem in teenagers. These behaviors include:

- Messy appearance, although many teenagers are normally somewhat messy this would be a behavior seen in someone who is not ordinarily a disheveled person

- Poor hygiene

- Burn or soot marks on the fingertips, which may be an indication that they are smoking heroin or other addictive substances

- Marked change in clothing

- Red flushed cheeks

- Heavy use of over-the-counter medications for red eyes, nasal irritation, or bad breath, which occur usually in the withdrawal phase of the addictive substance

- Eyes appear puffy all the time

- Dilated pupils, although as stated previously, these are not a reliable indicator of drug use.

- Track marks on arms or constantly wearing long sleeves even when the weather is warm.

These signs again have to be taken in context. For example, are these normal behaviors for someone in adolescence, or is this totally out of character for this person? It's important to note that when these symptoms appear, and if it is a deviation of the norm for that person, it is much more of a warning sign. Also if the individual appears to be using over-the-counter medications for puffy eyes or red eyes and refuses to be checked out by a health professional, it is also a warning sign that you may discover a behavior that he or she doesn't want you to know about, most likely addiction. Since many adolescents go through a period of personal discovery and growth, it is a good idea to gauge whether these new behaviors are a variation of this particular stage in life. If unsure, it is wise to get a urine drug test or have them evaluated by a health professional that is knowledgeable with addictions. Also teenagers have a general distrust for authority at this stage in life and may demonstrate resistance to being evaluated by a health professional. In that case, it would be wise to get a urine drug test from pharmacy and test them at home. It's important to note that these drug tests are screening tests and can have cross-reactions with legal drugs or even common foods. If the test shows any positive substances, it would be imperative for the teenager to be then checked out by a health professional who can send the test for verification at a more sophisticated lab.

Signs of addiction demonstrated by personal behavior include:

- Going out every night, much more of a red flag if that is not their normal behavior

- Increased use of caffeine or coffee

- Cash flow problems

- Secretive phone calls, emails, texting

- "Munchies" or sudden voracious appetite

- Avoiding eye contact

- Locked bedroom doors

- Increased use of air fresheners, candles, incense

- Loss of valuables and money

- Disappearance of prescription drugs, alcohol, cigarettes

- Appearance of unusual containers or wrappers left on surfaces

- Unusual smell in car, or bedroom

- Bottles, pipes, or drug paraphernalia left in glove compartment of car or found in room

- Hidden stashes of alcohol

- Loss of interest in hobbies and sports

- Significant change in relationships, family, and friends

- All new friends

- Periods of sleeplessness or high energy

- Slurred or rapid speech

- Unusually tired

- Always sleeping

- Mood changes or emotional irritability

- Periods of prolonged silence or being uncommunicative

Again, it is important to note that some of these behaviors occur with normal adolescents. However, it is the dramatic change or rapid change that is the worrisome feature of some of these behaviors. With the advent of the Internet, much more interest is seen by teenagers signing into drug-related Internet sites for drug information and ways to obtain drugs. It is important for parents to monitor their teenagers' use of the Internet to avoid this behavior. It is also reasonable for parents to question where their child's money is going when they are using it up much quicker than in the past. This is a time in their life when they learn responsibility and consequences for undesirable behavior. Rewarding these negative behaviors without teaching consequences can be extremely dangerous later in life even if they have successfully overcome addiction problems. It is also important to monitor where they are going, and whom they are associating with. Although they are trying to be "adults," teens' behavior is much more precocious now than it was twenty years ago. They also can get into more serious problems than they could twenty years ago. Illegal drugs are much more potent, much more available, and much more addicting than they were twenty years ago. This is also a time when teens are developing their sense of right and wrong. Since the use of opiates and other addicting drugs can disrupt the normal brain chemistry and "hardwiring," it is important to be diligent with reinforcing good behaviors and not rewarding undesirable behaviors. It is also important to note that their sense of right and wrong is not developed at this age and they are not thinking the way adults think.

Behavioral signs of addiction at school include:

• Decrease in grades

• Making endless excuses for getting into trouble or poor grades

• Truancy or loss of interest in school

• Failure to fulfill responsibilities at school or work

• Loud obnoxious behavior

• Sullen withdrawn or depressed while in school

• Intoxication at school or work

• Hostile, angry, uncooperative

• Slurred or rapid speech

• Inability to focus

• Sleeping in class

• Loss of interest in activities at school that they normally are interested in such as sports, chorus, plays, cheerleading, clubs

These behaviors are sometimes noticed first by teachers, principals, or coaches. Making sure you have an open and cordial relationship with school officials is extremely important. Since teachers, principals, and coaches see these problems much more than you might, they may be more able to recognize these behaviors as aberrant. It is also important to create an environment where they do not feel reluctance to report these behaviors in anticipation of a negative reaction from parents. The vast majority of school officials are interested in the well being of their pupils, and in many cases, they can be closer to the pupils than even the parents. This is especially true in situations where the parents are not in the home when the child gets home due to work or other obligations. In many cases, the teachers spend more time with the teenagers than the parents. As a parent, if you are unable to spend quality time during the week, you must try to do this as much as possible on the weekend. Since many teens like to socialize when not in school, this can be somewhat challenging. We have noted in our practice that sometimes a single event is perceived as "my parents don't love me" by the adolescent. They may take comments or conversations much more literally than the adults around them. Many times parents will say things like "are you stupid?" These comments are not meant to be a judgment or evaluation of the teenager, only used by some parents to make a point. This type of comment was much more common when their parents were growing up; however, many teenagers will start believing they are "stupid" if they hear it enough from their parents. Since self-esteem and sense of lack of love are two of the common denominators in predisposing one to addiction, it is important to be careful about saying these types of things. This will be dealt with in more detail in later chapters.

Workplace addiction is getting worse because of a number of factors. Emotional and physical stress is increasing on the job. Boredom can be a factor. Prescription drugs are much easier to obtain and may affect work behavior. Workers may have a family history of alcohol or drug problems. Workplaces are not testing employees for drugs as often as they should. Lack of consequences for coworkers who use or abuse drugs is perceived as a sign of permissiveness on the part of employers. Financial problems are more prevalent today than they were a few years ago. Workers may have strained relationships with coworkers or supervisors and may look to drugs for solution. In addition, teenagers may have issues with relationships, school, parents, or self-esteem and may feel more comfortable using drugs in the workplace than even at home. It is been our experience that certain occupations and places of work have higher incidences of drug use. These include restaurants, collection agencies, truck driving, and fast food out-lets. It is difficult for someone trying to avoid drugs to not use when coworkers are openly and commonly using drugs. This is a challenge in treating patients who end up working at some of the above places. They may be trying to quit drugs and constantly see them being used around them. This makes it very difficult to abstain. Signs of addiction in the workplace, which can include teenagers in many cases include:

- Frequent tardiness

- Unexplained or unauthorized absences

- Extended breaks

- Avoidance of supervisory contact especially after breaks or lunch

- Accidents on or off the job

- Careless or sloppy work

- Excessive use of sick time

- Poor personal hygiene

- Many excuses for missed deadlines or incomplete assignments

- Unusual weight loss or gain

- Unmet production quotas

- Strained relationships with coworkers

- Attitude changes (mood swings, anxiety, belligerence, short temper, argumentative behaviors)

- Erratic or unusual behavior, such as talkativeness, paranoia, sleepiness, tremors, sleeping on the job

- Noticeable financial problems, borrowing money from coworkers or asking for paycheck advances

- Always having to leave for lunch

- Needing to frequently leave to go home because something was forgotten

More and more employers are doing pre-employment drug testing to prevent drug use in the workplace. They also are increasing the use of random drug testing for employees, especially in jobs that would be adversely affected by drug use. In addition, many employers have employee assistance programs to treat employees that have addiction problems. Employers should develop a policy that defines their position on drug use. It is important to make these policies confidential, to clearly point out what is expected of the employee, and to try to be as fair as possible. More and more employees are starting to realize that drug addiction is a disease and not a voluntary behavior. That does not condone the use of any type of drug while working, but encourages a position of awareness, expectation, and empathy when an employee is found to have a drug problem.

Most parents know their children better than anyone. If you observe any behavior that would make you suspicious that addiction may be an issue, do not ignore it. Addiction is more biology and genetics then most people appreciate. We have seen addicted teenagers come from all cross-sections of society, all socio-economic levels, many cultures, and many good families. You can watch your diet, exercise, and keep your weight at a good level, and still develop type II diabetes. It is the same with addiction. You can be doing everything right as a parent and your child may still be at risk for addiction. Additionally, if you are unable, for whatever reason, to be present with your teenagers after school, you may have to rely on the observations of school personnel. Many times, teachers are able to observe suspicious behaviors before parents are able to recognize them. It is also possible that your health-care provider may have suspicions of addictive problems, and it is a mistake to ignore these opinions. It is better to be overly cautious than to miss an addiction problem, which could devastate your child and your family. Prevention, early intervention, and effective treatment are critical with teenage addiction. The most important message is *none of us* are immune to the devastation addiction can cause in a family. As parents, we can do everything right and still have an addicted child. It decreases the odds of addiction, but it is not 100 percent preventative. Biology and genetics are not to be underestimated. We can certainly minimize the chance of a child getting addicted but cannot totally prevent it.

Chapter 6

TEEN ADDICTION

"I want my son to smoke his first joint with me. I want him to have that experience with me so I can show him that it is something he can control later on."
- Father of a sixteen-year-old who later became a teen heroin addict

The above statement is something that we have heard on more than one occasion. As outrageous as this sounds, it is not uncommon for parents to want to have their teenage child's first experience with drugs or alcohol to be with them. The parents believe this is the best way to introduce them to drugs or alcohol, and their child will be less likely to abuse them. This is faulty and very dangerous thinking and behavior. Our brains are not fully developed until we get to our late twenties or early thirties. The area of the brain that controls compulsion and behavior in many teenagers has only begun to develop in their late teens. Although they look like adults and sometimes even act like adults, their neurologic system is far from being adult. More than one in five adolescents have abused their prescription-controlled medication in the past year, according to an epidemiologic study conducted among middle and high school students in Michigan in 2011. This includes painkillers, drugs for ADD and ADHD, antidepressants, tranquilizers, and other drugs that are used to modify behavior. In addition, because of the previously mentioned problem with neurotransmitter production, if they introduce an illicit, addictive, or psychotropic drug or chemical into their system, it can have serious consequences. They have an unfortunate and potentially dangerous combination of incomplete neurologic development with poor impulse control. This, coupled with introduction of a chemical, reduces the ability to control behaviors and reduces inhibitions. The neurologic immaturity and the introduction of psychoactive and addictive substances will trigger addictive behavior at a much higher rate than seen in adults.

To demonstrate the magnitude of this issue, in 2008 one third of twelve- to seventeen-year-olds used alcohol. Twenty percent used illicit drugs. On the average day in the United States in 2008, 4365 adolescents used an illicit drug for the first time. Over 7500 adolescents per day in the twelve- to seventeen-year-old age group used alcohol for the first time in 2008, and almost 2500 used a painkiller that was not prescribed for them. The number of adolescents twelve to seventeen years old admitted to publicly funded substance abuse treatment facilities in 2008 from a criminal justice system was 184 per day. In that same year, 198 twelve- to seventeen-year-olds were admitted to substance abuse treatment facilities daily, through their own volition or through school, providers, or community organizations. In other words, almost four hundred twelve- to seventeen-year-olds per day were admitted to a substance abuse treatment facility in 2008. Also in that same year on an average day, according to statistics from the National Institute of Health, 76,484 teenagers under eighteen were in substance abuse treatment centers. In addition, 9219 were admitted per day to nonhospital rehabilitation programs, and 762 were admitted daily to hospital treatment facilities. Two hundred and fifty thousand emergency visits were recorded in that same year for drug-related illness; 43 percent of them were from the misuse or abuse of prescription drugs. One in five teens has tried hydrocodone (Lortab, Vicodin, Norco type drugs), one in ten has tried OxyContin, one in ten has used stimulants (Ritalin, Adderall) for nonmedical purposes and one in eleven has used cough medicine to get high.

Teen addiction has some unique triggers and characteristics. It is a combination of behavior, belief, and biology. Teen pain-killer addiction involves nonnarcotic and narcotic painkillers. In order to get relieved from emotional and/or physical pain, teens get addicted to nonnarcotic and narcotic painkillers. Nonnarcotic painkillers are the over-the-counter medications, such as dextro-methorphan, commonly found in cough syrup, but they can also be prescription drugs. They are very easily accessible by teenagers, which may lead to drug abuse. Any drug that alters the mind's perception of pain or dulls the perception of pain can become addicting whether it is narcotic, prescription, or over-the-counter. Narcotic opiate painkillers are mainly used for chronic illnesses or they are prescribed to the people who are severely injured or while dealing with surgery. It is not unusual to see a teen with the right biology and the right emotional problems become addicted after receiving a narcotic pain reliever for an injury or post surgery. The vast majority, however, get addicted by using the drugs illicitly. Commonly abused painkillers as mentioned previously are opiates like Vicodin, Lortab, Norco, codeine, OxyContin, Demerol, mor-phine, methadone, Opana, and Dilaudid.

Teenagers may also get addicted to painkillers for various rea-sons, which may include experimentation, emotional and physical stress, family history of painkiller addiction, low self-esteem, fam-ily tension, relationship problems, or school issues. Probably the most common reason for painkiller addiction among teenagers is because of the influence of their friends. Sometimes these friends even urge them to try these harmful painkillers. They imitate other addicted peers in school or the addicts in their neighborhood. They generally start with experimentation of these hazardous painkillers but end up with addiction.

It is easy for teenagers to get painkiller medications prescribed for others. These medications are readily available for the teenagers in many households. Due to their easier availability, many of the teens are getting addicted to painkiller medications without knowing the dangerous effects of them. They may steal the prescription if their parents or elders are using the pain medications. An addict may also take painkiller prescription meds from different doctors by faking an illness to get the prescription medications, although this is getting more difficult as awareness is becoming more common among the medical community and providers.

It is impossible for health providers to measure someone's pain level. There are no tests to determine pain level. It is a subjective complaint. Additionally, genetics, experience, culture, and anchors shape our perception and reaction to pain. A child's first experience with pain will shape how they react to pain in the future. If a child falls and gets hurt, and the parents overreact or get hysterical, this will influence how the child will react to future pain. It is important to be calm and nurturing when a child first experiences pain. Also, if a child is raised with the philosophy of "a pill for everything," he or she will be prone to not respecting the power and danger of pain-relieving medication.

Teens may mistakenly believe that prescription drugs are not harmful. Many of the teenagers wrongly perceive that they are not harmful, as doctors medically prescribe them. They believe that prescription drugs are safer than illegal street drugs, such as heroin or cocaine. Many of them fail to understand that they are powerful drugs that need to be monitored and dosed properly. In many cases, the illegal drugs *are* more potent because of poor ability of the midlevel and lower-level dealers to dilute the dose.

Lack of supervision and communication between parents and teenagers may lead to painkiller drug addiction among the teenagers. Therefore, parents or elders should always keep an eye on teenagers. They should be regularly checked to monitor if they are stealing prescriptions, medications, or money. This is especially true if someone in the family has a legally prescribed prescription painkiller and is not careful in storing them. These pain medications should be kept out of the reach of teens and either locked up or kept in a very safe place. Unused medications should be discarded. Giving the medication to a medical provider who can dispose of it properly best does this. It is a very bad idea to flush these pills down the toilet or throw them in the garbage. Traces of narcotic painkillers, antidepressants, and tranquilizers are now being found in most municipal water supplies. Creating awareness and educating teenagers about the harmful effects of painkiller medication abuse will help prevent them from getting addicted to the painkiller medications. The vast majority of teens report getting their first narcotic prescriptions from a legally prescribed source, usually a friend or relative. In the majority of cases, the friend or relative does not have any idea that he or she is being used by the teen.

In 2010, the government compiled some startling statistics. They found that most prescription drugs were obtained from parents or relatives. Forty percent of high school seniors had smoked marijuana in the past twelve months. Twenty-five percent have used stimulants. The use of designer drugs, such as ecstasy and GHB (a drug very similar to GABA but much more potent) were dramatically higher. Of the twelve and older population, 8.7 percent had used an illicit or prescription drug nonmedically. And even more disturbing, the fastest-growing drug of abuse in high schools was heroin. Also, in our practice, we are seeing a spike in the use of "bath salts." These are drugs bought over-the-counter, which are labeled as "bath salts," and are specifically labeled as "not to be ingested"; however, they are specifically bought to be ingested and smoked. These are drugs that are really analog or copycat drugs that are specifically designed to mimic illegal drugs. They are usually imported from Asia and are made in chemical laboratories. Chemists will take a drug like THC, which is the active ingredient in marijuana, and change it slightly through chemical manipulation, so that is technically not THC. This allows them to import it under the label of "bath salts," knowing that it will be abused and ingested usually by a teenager. The danger with these drugs is they can be bought over-the-counter at fast food shops, tobacco shops, and many other small or unregulated businesses. When the government finds out about these, they specifically ban that particular formula of "bath salt." However, a new copycat hits the market very quickly. These drugs are both very dangerous and potent. In addition, we do not know the long-term effect of these drugs because they are synthetic analogs of already dangerous drugs. Legislation is being introduced to ban any substance that is similar to an illegal drug from being sold over-the-counter. In many cases, our patients will come in not realizing that these substances are both dangerous and illegal because they are sold over-the-counter. A number have failed drug tests thinking that they had no cross-reactivity to the drugs we were testing for; however, this is generally not true. Many times these "bath salts" will turn a drug screen positive.

The teen-addicted brain is unique. Teens are unable to see the long-term negative consequences of using addictive substances acutely. They do not think about what might happen down the road because they live in the moment and are looking for instant gratification. There is also a sense of immortality and it is not in their thought process to think about danger in many cases. This is not only true about the use of addictive substances but about behaviors in general. They tend to take more chances while driving, playing sports, and in recreation. Most parents would never consider going to a party and reaching their hands into a bowl of unknown pills and swallowing a handful of them to see what happens. However, this is a more common behavior than we would like to believe. We hear this scenario quite a bit in our practice. Teens will bring whatever pills they can gather around their homes, throw them in a large bowl and then everybody takes a handful to see what happens. These are called "pharma parties" or "pill parties." A hand full of drugs is referred to as "the trail mix of pills." Not only is this immature, it is extremely dangerous. But it happens commonly. Teens are unwilling to put off personal gratification in the interest of a bigger long-term reward. They don't think about what might happen to their college chances or their chances of becoming successful in an occupation or sports in the future. They only think about what it would be like to get high now. Instant gratification is the hallmark behavior of many teens. They typically proceed with a behavior without processing all the information. Their brains are not hard wired to do that until they have more life experiences, learn the consequences of negative behaviors, and develop a more mature neurologic system.

Some of their behaviors bypass the normal pleasure circuit in their brains. For instance, when they get high from an opiate it does not pass through the areas of the brain that process it and separate out the consequences and negative aspects of the behavior. It is been well documented that using an opiate goes right to the part of the brain called the nucleus accumbens, which is responsible for the feeling of pleasure. Once teens use the addictive substance and get this sense through the bypassed circuitry, they may not feel pleasure in the same way through the normal channels. If an adult with a fully developed neurologic system gets "high" for the first time, the sensation will actually travel through pathways that modulate it before it hits the nucleus accumbens. This attenuates the response and although they get a very positive feeling, it is not of the same intensity, as a teen would feel. Unfortunately once the circuitry is

developed that bypasses this, later in life the teenager may have serious issues about feeling pleasure or the intensity of a pleasure. This is
another reason teen addiction has serious long-term consequences.
Once the bypass circuit is created, the brain will prefer that circuitry
until normal channels develop. If individuals abstain, the brain
will not choose to bypass the normal circuitry. It will choose the
healthier, more normal pathway or circuit. Our brain wants to be
balanced, so it will choose a healthier neurologic pathway if it is not
bombarded by potent chemicals that bypass the normal pathway.
This is why it is very dangerous to use drugs after someone has been
abstinent. We always tell our patients it is like clicking the icon on
your computer. When you use the addictive substance, it opens up
that abnormal program as if it was never closed. In the case of the
brain, it actually reactivates and enhances that hardwired bypass circuit that has been dormant for a long time. Long-term abstinence,
along with learning normal pleasurable behaviors, will help to keep
the bypass circuitry dormant.

The question always comes up as to whether it is safe to use
opiates after one is addicted. The answer is, it depends. If the opiate is later used for pain, for instance if someone has surgery or a
fracture, it is relatively safe. However, dosing has to be such that it
is used only for pain relief and does not reach a level that causes
any type of euphoria or feeling high. If this is not followed, the
addictive bypass circuitry will be awakened. The person will then
have cravings and without a good support system and knowledge
of negative consequences, along with a great deal of motivation,
he or she will be prone to reestablishing the addictive behavior.
You can see that since the circuitry is not hard wired until an individual is in his or her twenties, the use of addictive substances in
the teenage brain is extremely dangerous.

The teenage brain has difficulty repatterning autonomic behaviors. Autonomic behaviors are behaviors that occur in our body without our conscious control. The autonomic nervous system is divided

into two divisions, the sympathetic and parasympathetic nervous system. The sympathetic nervous system is involved with reactions that we have hard wired in our system from our primitive ancestors. It is involved in getting us ready for a potentially dangerous or life-threatening situation. It is the system primarily responsible for the "fight or flight" reaction. When the sympathetic nervous system is activated, our heart rate increases, our breathing increases, and our pupils dilate to get us ready for the upcoming "battle." It also causes our body to release glucose and increases the circulation to our muscles in case we have to fight or run away from the danger. This is the part of the system that is most affected by addiction.

The parasympathetic nervous system is more responsible for the bodily functions that keep us alive and healthy. When it is activated, it causes food to move along our gastrointestinal tract and it slows our heart rate. It controls our breathing and blood pressure, so we get enough oxygen, and blood circulation under normal circumstances. It is the activation of the sympathetic nervous system that helps us to deal with or to avoid a stressful situation. After someone is addicted, especially in his or her teen years, the response to danger is blunted. For instance, he or she may not recognize something as being as dangerous as it should be after he or she has become addicted because the addictive substance may have blunted the brain's response to that particular type of stimulation. They must essentially relearn how to react to danger or threatening situations in the future. A good demonstration of this follows. Let's say a relatively normal teenager, who you would never think would get addicted, goes to a party where there is a bowl of pills. The teenager takes that handful of pills on a dare and swallows them. The teenager gets feelings he or she has not ever felt before. The brain processes this as tremendous pleasure since the normal circuitry that would tell them that this is not a good thing to do in the first place has been bypassed. The teenager feels tremendous strength, confidence, lack of inhibition, and pleasure. Something he or she may have never experienced before. This leads to serious behaviors in the future. Suddenly he or she is spending his or her allowance on drugs to get high. Soon the teenager runs out of enough money and starts stealing to pay for their habit. The teenager also starts to interact with unsavory people. These are people they would never relate to prior to becoming addicted. In addition, the negative behaviors accelerate. The teenager starts stealing from relatives, local stores, and friends. He or she also travels to parts of town that are dangerous and places that were previously unthinkable as destinations. The teenager looks for drug houses, drug dealers, and drug users. These behaviors would have caused extreme anxiety and extreme stimulation of their sympathetic nervous system under normal circumstances. By the time the teenager is using intravenous drugs, it takes a tremendous amount of danger and stress to trigger a normal response. After they have been abstinent, their autonomic nervous system, especially the sympathetic nervous system, does not function properly. The teenager is desensitized to risky behavior and danger. This is similar to parents allowing children to watch violent movies or TV programs. Soon the children are not as upset with violence and they need a very violent scenario to create the same reaction. This is a problem seen in most addicts. Since they have engaged in behaviors that were unthinkable before they became addicted, the autonomic nervous system has to be reprogrammed. Engaging in a more normal lifestyle that does not have as many risky behaviors does this. The problem with reprogramming this part of the nervous system in teens is they do not have enough of the normally patterned circuitry prior to the addiction. They essentially have to create these circuits after they have stimulated the sympathetic nervous system with abnormally high levels of stimulation. This leads to depression and the inability to experience normal pleasures, something called anhedonia, later in life. They must slowly learn about the "normal" pleasures in life as substitutes for the "highs" of addiction. The normal pleasures related to getting good grades, winning a sports event, meeting their first love all pale in comparison to that first high they felt with drugs. This is an area that takes years of counseling and re-patterning. It also makes teen addiction that much more serious.

The part of the brain responsible for knowing right from wrong is "disconnected" after a teen becomes addicted. The brain seeks pleasure much more than it worries about the consequences of negative addictive behaviors. The brain goes from a mode of self-preservation, to a mode of seeking pleasure. Seeking pleasure supersedes all other functions. When parents say, "Why does my child not see what he is doing to himself?" they do not realize their child does not have that ability when he is addicted. The area of the brain that processes the negative consequences is not functioning. The teen is essentially incapable of seeing the behavior as negative. I tell parents it is like speaking a foreign language. The teen does not register the information. The brain is only seeking pleasure and cannot go into a mode of survival or understand the negative future consequences of behaviors. If the teen has been addicted for a longer period of time, the brain additionally does not want to feel the negative consequences of withdrawal. The brain's only purpose becomes seeking pleasure and avoiding withdrawal—nothing else matters. Consequences, family, friends, grades, future, career, or bad health are not considerations. Overall, it is a very bad situation.

In our practice we also hear some myths about the behavior of teenagers and parents.

Myth #1:

Parents are talking to teenagers more than ever. This may be true in some cases, but the vast majority of teens that we see do not talk to their parent about addiction, drugs, and alcohol. They get most of their information from friends or the Internet. In our high-energy society, parents are spending more time out of the house. In addition, more families have both parents working, or the corollary, many families are single-parent families, leaving little time to discuss these issues. Many times parents do other things very well, but they do not communicate as much as they should. We also see parents who believe it is the school's responsibility or that their child is "smart enough" to get the information off the Internet or from books. Parents forget that the children may have access to the information but since their sense of right and wrong and their knowledge of consequences associated with negative behavior are not fully developed, they cannot assimilate this information properly. It is *not* the role of schools, teachers, friends, relatives, the Internet, medical providers, or any other source to be the main source of information about the dangers of addiction. The vast majority of teens trust their parents more than any other source, and it is up to the parents to become educated in the dangers of drugs. Other sources, including schools, teachers, and health professionals should be sources that reinforce the messages. As a parent, if you do not understand about the perils of addiction, at least try to educate yourself, so you can be a source of information. In many states, schools are legally limited as to how much information they can give to students. Also, many medical providers do not have a good background in addictions to be the main source of information. Aside from this book, there are other sources of information available on the Internet or at your local bookstore. Do not depend on others to educate your child. In addition, as parents we are the main source of teaching our children about the consequences of negative behavior, as well as the rewards of positive behavior. Since a child's brain has not "downloaded" this information while the child is in high school, if we allow negative behaviors without consequences, it will lead to fundamental lack of development of a sense of right and wrong in the child. Rewarding good behaviors is just as important as teaching the negative consequences of bad behaviors. Striking a balance between the reward and the consequences can be difficult. Parents should not focus on the negative without giving some positive rewards. Once their child's brain is fully developed physically, the sense of right and wrong that is "installed" through their teens will be permanently hard wired in their brain.

Our children not only look to us for guidance, they observe our behaviors as a source of learning right from wrong. The parent who thinks having that first drink or that first joint with his or her son or daughter is going to be a positive experience ends up universally disappointed. Even if that child has surrogate role models for learning right from wrong and has learned to be a respectable adult, the child will forever have a lack of respect for that particular behavior of his or her parents. While raising teenagers, it is not our role to become their friends. It is our role to teach them to be independent, respectable adults who will contribute to society. Obviously there are situations where the parent is not capable or chooses not to be a respectable person who demonstrates good behaviors, but most of us fall into the former rather the latter category. In situations where the parent is incapable, for whatever reason, of being a role model or teaching these behaviors, other relatives, or in some cases, teachers or other professionals, may have to be the ones to serve that role. In some families, grandparents, aunts, or uncles are the role models. When we speak of parents, we don't necessarily mean the biological parent, we are referring to the functional parent. Do not underestimate your value and importance as a role model in your child's life.

Myth #2:

Getting high on legal drugs is "safer" than getting high on illegal drugs. This could not be further from the truth. Many of the legally prescribed narcotics and opioids are more potent than the illegal drugs obtained by addicted people. One of the main reasons we have such an addiction problem is that the potency of drugs has dramatically increased due to the technology and manufacturing processes of the last twenty years. Even "homegrown" marijuana is much more potent because of the ability to obtain seeds over the Internet and because of advances in cultivation easily obtainable by most people. The Internet has dramatically changed the information obtained as well as the raw materials obtained to grow, manufacture, and experiment with the substances. Legally prescribed drugs are less likely to have toxic materials or contaminants in them. This makes them a better and more likely source of drug-addicted people looking for the substances. Thirty years ago if you got high on marijuana, it was not nearly as dangerous as it is today. The marijuana circulating on the streets is many times more potent than what was grown thirty years ago. These myths tend to perpetuate themselves, but they are dangerous to believe. Technology has also dramatically changed the illegal drugs that we see. Advances in growing, manufacturing, transporting, concentrating, marketing, and distributing drugs have improved geometrically. Again, the Internet is a major source of these issues. Information travels throughout the world in a matter of minutes rather than weeks to years as it did thirty years ago. The reality is, legal drugs lead to addiction just as rapidly and in many cases more rapidly than illegal drugs. The only difference between many of these drugs is whether they are legal or not. Potency is generally not as much of an issue as it was in the past. Sometimes the only difference between an illegal drug and illegal drug is the health ramifications of using the illegal drug. For instance, you may be able to get just as high from injecting OxyContin as you can from injecting heroin. The only difference may be that it is usually unknown what else is mixed with the heroin, and many times dealers will dilute or cut the heroin with substances that should not be injected. I've seen heroin cut with talcum powder, baby powder, baking soda, scouring cleanser, and almost any other powder imaginable. Imagine injecting scouring cleanser in your veins and the devastation it does to these veins. Injecting the drug also leads to major health issues, such as hepatitis, HIV or AIDS, or other bacterial or viral infections when needles are used by more than one person. The bottom line is that all opioid and narcotic drugs are dangerous. In addition, although alcohol is legal in most places, it can be the most devastating to your mind and body. The health effects from chronic long-term alcohol abuse are some of the most devastating imaginable. While training as a resident in family medicine, I observed some horrible results from chronic alcohol abuse. Seeing people bleed to death from a gastrointestinal bleed. Watching individuals in their thirties or forties mentally deteriorate to the point where they constantly hallucinate was very difficult. Although alcohol is legal and easily obtainable, it will lead to an early and painful death just as well as narcotics and opioids. The time frame may be a few years longer, but the outcome is generally the same with alcohol.

Myth # 3:

Only "bad "kids get addicted. As stated earlier, we see teenagers from all socio-economic backgrounds and all types of families. *No one, and no family, is immune to the devastation from addiction.* If you or a loved one is one of those people who are genetically predisposed to the biochemical deficiencies related to addiction, the odds of you becoming addicted increase dramatically. Doing all the right things as parents is the best insurance we have at preventing predisposed children from getting addicted. It is important as parents that we realize that the biochemical deficiency may be the trigger that leads to addictive behaviors, but that shouldn't prevent us from doing all the things we should be doing as parents. If someone from a good family gets addicted, it is just as important to have the social support and parenting that you gave before the individual became addicted. We've seen children from upper socio-economic backgrounds, educated families, prominent families, and families that have had good parenting become addicted. We've also seen children from the other end of the spectrum. In our experience, poor parenting with a biochemical predisposition is a time bomb waiting to explode. We have seen children of physicians, judges, lawyers, teachers, police officers, college professors, and almost any other occupation you can imagine. We have seen valedictorians, cheerleaders, star high school athletes, and about every other mix of students you can imagine, seeking treatment. As stated previously, no one is immune, and no family is immune.

Myth #4:

Only "bad" parents get addicted children. As parents we would like to believe this, but it is not true. We have seen all types of parents including overprotective parents, absent parents, permissive parents, abusive parents, addicted parents, well-meaning but ignorant parents, and what we would call "good parents" come in with their addicted children. Our definition of a *good parent* would be one that is involved with his or her child, who communicates with his or her child, who actively discusses issues, and is a good role model for his or her child. Even with those characteristics, if the child has a biochemical deficiency he or she may become addicted. The difference between the two types of parents is that the generally involved parent will be involved in the treatment of his or her child and the outcomes will be better. A support system is critical for long-term sobriety. It is also critical for the parents to be involved in the counseling that is needed and in many cases the pharmaceutical and medical treatment needed for their child. Generally, parents that are involved will recognize that their child is in trouble much sooner than parents who are not involved. Parents who are overprotective may pay a dear price for the overprotection.

A very bad combination is a teenager with biochemical predisposition, an abusive parent, and access to potent drugs. This child will become addicted very quickly and will be difficult to treat. They will have significant numbers of relapses coupled with a difficult time putting their life together. Abuse in any form is like throwing gasoline on the fire of addiction. On the other hand, parents that enable their child may have very bad outcomes. It is sometimes difficult to distinguish between helping and enabling. This is a topic that will be discussed later and is sometimes difficult for parents to grasp.

In addition to the difficulties of being a parent, we have so many variations of children even within a family that sometimes one child needs a bit more structure and guidance than another child. Also some children need more distinct boundary management and definition than other children. Raising children is the most difficult job any of us will encounter in our lives. It is also the most important job. A child that has a biochemical propensity toward addiction, hormone surges seen in teenagers, and the normal variation in human behavior can be extremely challenging. In addition, the immaturity and lack of neurologic development of teens adds to the difficulty. Our fast-paced society, with access to information of unlimited scale and dangerous and potent drugs with easy availability, leads to serious problems. We can only change so much of this individually. It always distills down to the core family being the most important variable in the equation. Much of the addiction issue with teenagers is out of our control, so we have to exert control and influence where we can.

Chapter 7

TREATMENT

"For every dollar spent in treatment, we save seven dollars in costs to society."
- The National Institute on Drug Abuse, updated December 2012

Treatment of drug addiction is very cost-effective. It saves society money in terms of decreased emergency admissions for overdoses, detoxification, and medical complications. Society also saves from decreased legal expenses. Patients are able to get their lives back and in many cases to start earning a living again. Youth and entitlement are two of the biggest obstacles to recovery because they insulate the young addict from the negative consequences of addiction and instill a false sense of self-identity and security. Because many have a sense of indestructability, they have a hard time grasping the seriousness of their behavior and the effect on loved ones. They need to take an ownership role in their recovery. Parents sometimes insulate their children from negative consequences of irresponsible behavior and actions. They might have the attitude that "I do not want my child to go through all the hardship I had to endure." In reality, those hardships are what shape our resourcefulness, responsibility, and self-reliance. We learn more from our mistakes, than from our successes. For some reason, many parents do not want their children to experience any type of failure. Our society is moving toward everyone having the same rewards. Schools choose not to have valedictorians, and children play sports where nobody wins or loses. We have educational policies that keep our students moving ahead, even if they do not pass all the courses in a particular grade. These policies do not teach a responsible value system to our youth. We see parents paying for cell phones, cars, cigarettes, and luxury items, without asking for anything in return. It is these same teens that are not equipped to follow rules when they start a job. They don't show up on time, or they show up impaired or not at all. We are raising teens with no connection to reward for doing actual work. We have the perfect storm of teens without a sense of self-responsibility, low self-esteem, and exposure to potent addicting drugs. Our biology has not changed significantly in the last fifty thousand years. It is their lack of parenting in many cases and their experience and technology that has exacerbated the addiction problem.

By treating and preventing addiction, society saves resources and costs for associated health issues such as HIV, hepatitis, and complications of drug abuse. Savings also are derived from the lower cost of the crimes associated with drug addiction when addicts are treated and stay clean. Increased treatment access equals an increased savings for society, period. Not only are patients less involved in extensive criminal activity, but also the cost for prosecuting and incarcerating people who are users of drugs saves a tremendous amount of money. In addition, patients who undergo multiple detoxifications would no longer need that, which results in a very substantial savings. The savings for society from making our environment safer and healthier are incalculable. As you can see, money invested in treatment saves and both healthcare and criminal costs.

Treatment for drug addiction has dramatically changed in the last fifteen years. Until fairly recently, addicts were thought to be people who had psychiatric illnesses or were criminals or socio-paths. Treatment was aimed at giving them psychiatric drugs to suppress their "unusual and aberrant" behavior. It was felt that incarceration or sequestering them away from the rest of society was the best way to treat them. In the last fifteen years, we realize that addicted people have a medical illness that manifests with behavioral and physical symptoms. Because of this, they should be treated the way we treat people with medical problems such as diabetes, hypertension, or heart disease. Recent advances in treatment approach addiction from a nutritional, behavioral, biochemical, energetic, and spiritual approach.

As stated previously, because of the significant biochemical deficiencies in opiate addicted people, if they try to quit "cold turkey," with no outside help, they have about a three in one thousand chance of staying clean for one year. Another way of stating this is that 997 out of 1000 opiate addicts will go back to using drugs if they do not get help with the biochemical deficiency and the behavioral issues. If they are treated at a residential treatment center where they have thirty to sixty days of intensive daily treatment, the statistics show that somewhere around 17 to 20 percent of opiate-addicted people will remain clean for one year. If they are treated with substitution therapy, which calms the chemical receptor of the neurotransmitter that is deficient, it give them about an **80 to 85 percent** chance of staying clean for one year. This assumes they are also in counseling and have a reasonable support system. To paraphrase, the days of someone staying in a room and being observed while they go through horrible withdrawal for two weeks as a way to treat addiction is both archaic and grossly inadequate. In my opinion, it is malpractice. During my residency in the mid-1970s, we would admit heroin or opiate addicts to the hospital for a two-week stay. During that time, we would slowly decrease the dose of narcotics given to them until they were off the narcotics completely. We assumed that once they were off the narcotics and through withdrawal they were "cured." What we actually observed was that the same patients would return shortly after with the same problem. Many times they would tell us that on their way home from the hospital they started using drugs again. Obviously this is a flawed approach to treating addiction.

UNDERSTANDING BRAIN CHEMISTRY

As stated previously, to understand addiction, you have to understand brain chemistry. This is because the vast majority of addiction people, over 95 percent, have a deficient brain chemical, which makes them more likely to become addicted. In our experience, most of these people lack a chemical in their brain called GABA (gamma-amino butyric acid). GABA is a chemical that calms the brain down. It is somewhat like putting the brakes on a system. Imagine running your car with no brakes. In a brain with a GABA deficiency, the person has difficulty focusing, calming down, sleeping, issues of self-control, and in general feels out of touch. When an opiate addict first uses an opiate, if they are GABA deficient, the addict almost universally tells us that he or she felt "normal," for the first time, not high. After an addict uses the drug more frequently, he or she becomes somewhat euphoric or high, and then the dependence and addiction starts. However, it is this sense of normalcy when they first use the opiate that makes an opiate addict feel like they should not stop. The brain is seeking balance or homeostasis. Although the opiate is not identical to GABA, it stimulates the receptor that GABA stimulates, enough where the user does initially feel calm. It is difficult to measure GABA levels with a blood test because the level fluctuates markedly throughout the day. However, we administer a questionnaire, developed by Dr. Eric Braverman, which gives us a good idea of what neurotransmitters are lacking in a particular patient. Although the vast majority of patients lack GABA, some also lack serotonin, another calming neurotransmitter.

Serotonin also is deficient in people who are depressed. The most frequently prescribed antidepressants, the serotonin reuptake inhibitors or SSRIs, are drugs that cause a temporary increase in our brain serotonin. Common drugs in this class of medications include Prozac, Paxil, Effexor, Cymbalta, Wellbutrin, Zoloft, and Celexa. There are also a number of newer drugs in this drug class. All of these drugs have a similar effect. This is how they work: When a brain cell fires, it causes the cell next to it to fire due to a release of chemical in the space between the nerve; this space is called a synapse. Once the second nerve fires, the serotonin in this space, or synapse, gets partially reabsorbed by the first nerve, to be reused for the next time the nerve fires. The first nerve then manufactures more serotonin, and when needed will release it into this synapse to allow the second nerve to fire again. The way the serotonin reuptake inhibitors (SSRIs) work is to prevent the first nerve from absorbing the serotonin after the second nerve fires. By keeping the serotonin in the synapse, it makes it easier for the receptors on the second nerve to fill up, finally getting enough receptors filled to allow the nerve to fire. The problem is, this only works short-term; when the brain perceives that enough serotonin is lingering in the synapse, eventually it will tell the first nerve to severely limit the serotonin, or stop the manufacture of the serotonin altogether. This process causes a rebound effect; it stops working. Subsequently, if an individual tries to withdraw the SSRI, he or she will become more depressed because not only does he or she have a deficiency to start with, but after allowing the SSRI to keep the serotonin in the synapse longer, it diminishes or even shuts down the production of serotonin inherently in the first nerve. By shutting down this production, the parts of the brain that need serotonin become deficient and the original symptoms of depression or anxiety worsen. This makes it very difficult to wean yourself off of antidepressants; therefore, you will probably report to your provider that your symptoms are worse after stopping the medication. The usual response from the medical provider is to either increase the dose or add a second SSRI. If you know someone on these medications, you know it is very difficult to stop them. This is something known by the drug companies that produce them, a problem that they do not like to make public. The reason an individual might have a deficiency in a neurotransmitter like serotonin, is that either they do not have the raw material to make it or our biochemistry is deficient in the enzymes or cofactors such as vitamins needed to make it. The second possibility is that we use up these chemicals very quickly due to stress or personal problems, which may cause us to become depressed or anxious.

Below is a schematic of the process (modified from a lecture by Dr. Charles Gant):

TRANSMISSION OF A NERVE IMPULSE VIA NEUROTRANSMITTERS

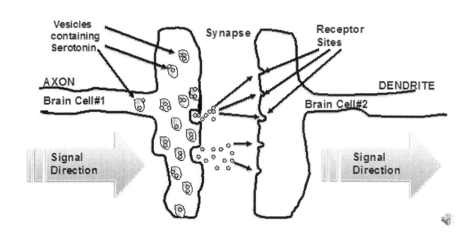

Brain Cell #1 makes neurotransmitters in the vesicles, or parts of the cell that manufacture these chemicals, which are released in the synapse between the two cells. Once the receptor sites are all filled on brain cell #2, that cell fires. The SSRIs make the molecules of the neurotransmitter stay in the synapse longer, so less of the neurotransmitter is needed to be released in order to fire brain cell #2 the next time. SSRIs work by preventing unused molecules of serotonin in the synapse from being taken up again from the first synapse, so brain cell #1 needs to make fewer molecules of serotonin to make brain cell # 2 fire. This selective inhibition of the reuptake of serotonin in the synapse is what gives the selective serotonin reuptake inhibitor (SSRI's) their name. They generally only work on serotonin, not other molecules of neurotransmitters such as GABA

In the case of addiction to opiates, it is usually not serotonin, but GABA, which is lacking. Drugs that mimic GABA include the benzodiazepines, Valium (diazepam), Xanax (alprazolam), Ativan (lorazepam), Klonopin (clonazepam), Serax (oxazepam) or sleeping pills such as Restoril (Temazepam) . Also in this category are drugs that were originally developed as antiseizure medications, such as Neurontin (gabapentin), Lyrica (pregabalin), or Topamax (topirimate). None of these drugs is identical to GABA but they are what we call partial agonists (partial or incomplete stimulators) of the GABA receptor in the brain. Although they are not identical, the brain will be satisfied and the receptor will calm down if these drugs are administered. When a brain lacks a neurotransmitter such as GABA, receptors are constantly crying out for it and will cause the person to feel anxious, nervous, or unable to focus. If the brain does not get GABA but is introduced to a similar molecule such as a benzodiazepine or similar drug, the receptor will be satisfied enough to not "cry out" for more. This is exactly what happens when a woman is going through menopause because her estrogen or progesterone levels have dropped. The hot flashes associated with estrogen deficiency during menopause are actually the hormone receptors looking for the hormone to calm them down. Since our brain is made up of nerves, receptors, and neurotransmitters, when we lack the neurotransmitter, it causes the receptors to look for whatever will satisfy it so it can cause the nerves to fire, or in some cases, calm down. GABA and serotonin are calming neurotransmitters, the brakes, so to speak, in our nervous system. If we do not make enough GABA or serotonin when we use the opiate drug, the drug will cause the system to be more in equilibrium. Our brains always seek equilibrium or a state of homeostasis, which is a balanced and healthy state. To reach this healthy state, the brain will seek whatever it needs to keep balanced brain function.

Patients sometimes ask why doctors do not recommend GABA or serotonin instead of the benzodiazepines or SSRIs. The answer is many doctors do not realize that you can actually give GABA as a supplement. In the case of serotonin, it is not available in supplement form, however, if you give the supplement 5- hydroxy-tryptophan (5-OH-tryptophan), or 5-HTP, it will actually convert to serotonin, as the 5-hydroxy-tryptophan is the chemical precursor to serotonin. Interestingly, tryptophan, which is abundant in turkey, converts to 5-HTP and subsequently to serotonin. Many of us know that if we eat a large turkey dinner at Thanksgiving, within a few hours we feel tired and would like to nap. This is because of the increased levels of serotonin derived from the tryptophan, which calms us down. If we are generally calm, the increased serotonin will make us feel sleepy. If we are generally somewhat anxious, the increased serotonin will make us feel calmer or more normal. As you can see, these chemicals have a role in keeping the brain normalized. To get back to the original point, in a holistic or naturopathic practice, you can take either GABA or 5-HTP and achieve effects similar to taking benzodiazepines or SSRIs. The problem is GABA and 5-HTP are not nearly as potent as the prescription drugs, so people will not feel an immediate and pronounced an effect. So why take GABA and/or 5-HTP instead of benzodiazepines or SSRIs? The answer is GABA and 5-HTP are natural and a better fit for the brain. Although the benzodiazepines and SSRIs are not what the brain needs, the fact is, they are very potent, which overcomes the fact that they are only partial agonists or stimulators of the receptors; they work more quickly, which makes people assume they are better or preferable. Patients feel the effects sooner, so they assume they are better. However, the quicker a drug works, and the more potent a drug, the easier it is to become dependent. Dependency is when you stop the drug and feel lousy, more anxious and/or depressed, and often worse than before starting the medication. In addition, sometimes the medications just stop working and you need to take more to get the same effect, which is known as tolerance. Some patients come to us complaining that they have been on Prozac, or another SSRI, for several years. They will say, "it worked in the beginning but not anymore, and the dose is so much higher than when I started." Dr. Eric Braverman, MD, a specialist in brain chemistry, explains that if your brain already has a deficiency in a particular neurotransmitter and you take an SSRI, which does not address the cause of the deficiency, the brain will continue to make less and less of the neurotransmitter. Eventually, the brain's capacity to make the neurotransmitter stops working altogether.

Consider this analogous example: you see the "low oil" light on in your car because the engine is leaking oil; rather than put motor oil into the engine, you put vegetable oil into the engine, which makes the oil light go off, but does not fix the leak. The light goes off because it is sensing enough oil. However, the engine cannot run for long on vegetable oil, because it is not the correct type of oil. You may have "fixed" the low oil light from staying on, but the leak has to be fixed. In our practice, we frequently prescribe GABA to addicted patients to help their brains normalize. It works slower, but it is more natural and far safer.

Another reason that addicted brains lack neurotransmitters is stress, which makes the brain use up these chemicals very quickly. Toxins, infection, poor nutrition, lack of the proper vitamins and minerals, and generally poor health can also lead to deficiencies of these neurotransmitters. If someone has a genetic deficiency of any of the cofactors, enzymes, or vitamins that are needed to manufacture these neurotransmitters, this makes them likely to develop the deficiencies. It is our belief that one of these issues is not enough to cause someone to be addicted. For instance, a genetic deficiency does not make one become addicted. A genetic deficiency, coupled with stress, toxins, infection, etcetera, may be enough to cause the person to cross the threshold of dependence and addiction when he or she is exposed to an opiate. Psychological and spiritual causes of addiction and how we treat them are also significant factors. The point is, any one of these in and of itself may not be enough to cause dependence and addiction, but combine three or four of these factors and you have a serious problem. Another way to describe this would be, say someone has a genetic deficiency of one of the precursors needed to make GABA. In addition, he or she is in an abusive relationship and has poor self-esteem. This combination together would cause the individual to have a higher incidence of dependence and addiction. As you can see, treating only one aspect of the addiction, for instance the biochemical part, will not be enough to elicit improvement in the ability to stay clean. You have to have a multifaceted approach, including proper substitution therapy, such buprenorphine, supplements, diet, psychological counseling, social support, and spiritual counseling. The more of these you are able to utilize in your treatment, the more likely you will be able to stay in remission.

In our treatment protocol, we also recommend a number of supplements in addition to a healthy diet to help the person recover and increase his ability to make the necessary neurotransmitters that he or she is lacking. We will discuss this after we look further at stages of behavioral change, opiate receptors and the biochemistry of the brain.

STAGES OF BEHAVIORAL CHANGE

As providers, we frequently see people fail in their treatment and ultimately relapse. When we first encounter some patients, we sometimes get a sense that they are not ready to go through the treatment process. This is especially true if they have been mandated to get treatment through a court action. In addition, parents will sometimes ask, "why can't my child stay clean?" They will ask how we know if they are ready to change. To better understand this, we need to look at the stages of behavioral change. There are five stages of behavioral change.

Stage I is the precontemplation stage. This is when the addicted person has no intention of taking action within the foreseeable future, which usually means in the next six months. The person is usually unaware of the need to change and he or she may overestimate the cost of change. In addition, he or she tends to underestimate the benefits. The individual may be reluctant to change because he or she is rebellious, overwhelmed, or demoralized by the idea of change. That person is unable to rationalize the consequences of the addiction behavior. This is especially true in teenagers who do not have a fully developed sense of right and wrong in their neurologic hardwiring, and especially if responsibility for actions is not taught and enforced in early childhood. There is also a significant amount of denial in this stage. They may feel that all the issues and consequences really do not apply to them because "they can change at any time." The bottom line is, they are willing to put up with the negative aspects of addiction rather than make the necessary changes to achieve sobriety. When addicts contemplate the positive aspects of staying clean, versus continuing to use, they choose to continue using opiates because they are *unconsciously* not ready to change. Tension breeds change. By changing the dynamics of the situation, in a sense upping the ante, we can sometimes accelerate them into the next phase. A situation like being arrested for dealing drugs or for a DUI or other criminal activity may move them into the next phase. Nothing like spending a few nights in jail to encourage desire to change! For some of the younger people, just the possibility of jail time will move them further along in their desire to change their behavior. We find that older addicts who have been in and out of jail do not have this same desire. They are desensitized to the experience of being in jail, and for some, it is better than their present living situation. For a younger teen, facing jail time is scary enough to make him or her seriously consider changing their addiction behavior. It is not uncommon for an impressionable teen to spend a night in jail and have an "epiphany," which changes his or her behavior. Unfortunately, parents have a tendency to bail out the teen, in some cases, before they have felt the full brunt of incarceration. It is difficult for parents to imagine their teen in jail, without having the urge to bail them out as soon as possible. There is also a fine line between enabling and helping. This will be discussed when we look at the psychological counseling. In the precontemplation phase, teens generally are somewhat aloof when they come into the office. They really are not focusing on the negative aspects of their addiction; they don't ask questions about treatment, they don't seem to understand the negative consequences, and they usually do not adhere to the program for more than a few weeks. Part of the protocol for treating addiction is that they are regularly drug tested and have to stay clean. People who are not out of the precontemplation phase tend to fail their first drug or second drug test. They are not that upset when they are told that they are being dismissed from the program. To them using drugs and all that surrounds the behavior is more desirable than the work it takes to stay clean. And it is work. These teens usually either spiral out of control and end up with bad outcomes, or something happens to negatively impact them and move them into the second stage of behavioral change. This is usually an event such as getting arrested, being thrown out of school, losing a girlfriend or boyfriend because of the addictive behavior, experiencing the death of a schoolmate or friend from an overdose, or getting a serious illness. It is not that they suddenly wake up and realize that this is leading them down the wrong path in life. That does not occur because their brains are not mature enough to suddenly have this thought process. The hardwiring that is installed when we realize right from wrong can be accelerated by negative events, but usually it is a process of time and life's events that mature our brains.

Stage II of behavior change is the contemplation phase. In this phase, the addicted person is considering change within the next six months. At this point, the addicted person is ambivalent about change, but he or she perceives the costs equaling the benefits. The addicted person is fed up with the negative aspects of trying to buy drugs and using drugs, and the negative aspects of being caught and constantly feeling ill when they do not use. The addicted person is starting to realize that his or her life is spiraling in a negative direction. When these kids come in for help, often they are the young teens whose parents caught them using for the first time; the shock and turmoil created by the incident is enough to get them at least into the office. Generally in our experience, they will stick with the program for a short period of time. They will attend the counseling sessions for several weeks or even several months. They may even have clean urine for the first few months. Unfortunately, they usually end up coming in with excuses, like they are not being relieved by the dose of the medications we are giving them, or they will miss the appointment with counseling, or they will have any number of excuses for not adhering to the program. As with the precontemplation phase, it usually takes a serious negative event to move them into the next stage of behavioral change.

Stage III of behavioral change is the preparatory or preparation phase. In this phase, the addicted person has a definitive action plan, which will usually be initiated within the next month. They may have already taken steps toward change and they are often concerned about the possibility of failure. In the case of teenagers, it is usually the teen that calls for an appointment, and not the parent. It is always worrisome to us when a parent calls and we are unable to speak to the teen. We usually can get a good idea about a teen's motivation by speaking to him or her about what it takes to complete the program. If he or she hesitates when we say they have to stay clean, be drug tested regularly, have regular visits, and attend counseling, it is a bad prognosis. If, on the other hand, they say, "I will do whatever it takes," it is generally a good sign. If he or she makes any comment such as, "Do I have to stay off of all drugs, including alcohol or marijuana?" the addicted person predictably will not make it through the program. If they say, "Alcohol is a legal drug," or "Marijuana is not a hard drug," or "Everyone smokes marijuana," he or she predictably will not make it or not show up for the first appointment. In this phase, teens generally will look for a program that suits their needs, but the critical point is they have a plan, and they have initiated a part of the plan. At this phase, there is no guarantee they will complete the process. Usually, though, the teens are ready to initiate it. In our experience, these patients usually are enthusiastic at their first visit. Typically, they last two or three months and will follow the rules during that time. Subsequently, they begin to have difficulty and either drop out or have to be dismissed. They find that the treatment does not fulfill all of their needs, or their social structure, and their support system is not good enough to keep them abstinent. Typically we find that they either drop out of the program or are dismissed. Some will call within a six-month period, and ask to be reinstated in the program. It is extremely rare for us to accept a person after they have been dismissed, unless a very unusual set of circumstances intervenes. In our experience, if they fail in our program the first time, they will likely fail subsequent times. We also, are restricted to one hundred patients, (we will explain this restriction later), and we always have a lengthy waiting list of patients eager to get treated. For instance, we once took a seventeen-year-old girl back into the program because she had a baby, and when she called to be reinstated she had a much more mature attitude about dealing with the addiction. The baby was also a huge motivation factor for her as well. She did very well the second time in the program. If the support system has not changed and the teen has not enrolled in school, worked at getting a GED, started a job or done something else to show some signs of maturity, we will not take them back.

Stage IV is the action phase. In this stage, the addicted teenager actively changes and works hard in the first six months to make changes. In this stage, the teen needs vigilance, support, and encouragement to keep the momentum. In this phase, we actively involve parents, girlfriends or boyfriends, siblings, teachers, and support staff in encouraging the teens to hold their gains. Although they are much more diligent and ready to stay clean, they need constant encouragement and monitoring. Once they have stayed clean for about six months, the positive reinforcement of a clean lifestyle seems to take on a life of its own. They usually are actively enrolled in school, getting along better with their parents, or have a decent job. They find that working for a nice apartment, nice clothes, or decent car is enough to prevent them from going back to their old lifestyle of addiction. In the meantime, they have been learning new coping skills for anxieties and stressors in life. Although they struggle in this phase, they are finally realizing that some of the positives they got from drugs are now received by being independent and self-sustaining.

Stage V is the maintenance phase. Usually teenagers have been clean for more than six months and have changed some of their negative behaviors and created new and positive ones. They benefit from reminders about high-risk situations and are looking for ways to cope with situations that tempt them to use. They are discovering their own inner power and control over the drugs. Anyone who has quit smoking knows how good it feels to have accomplished overcoming that addiction. These young adults are maturing neurologically and starting to realize the negative aspects of the addictive lifestyle. Although they are not out of the woods, they are much less likely to relapse when they reach this stage. Traditional drug counseling discusses people, places, and things; they talk about avoiding people with whom they used drugs, as well as where they use drugs, and what they were doing while using. Obviously, people who dealt drugs with them should be avoided, and this includes avoiding places where they used to do drugs or bought drugs. More important is to avoid triggers that make an individual want to use drugs. In this case, the counselor discusses more rational and acceptable ways of dealing with anxiety-provoking situations. When someone is in the maintenance phase, he or she is much more open to this type of counseling. Discussing people, places, and things with a person who is not ready to hear it or who is experiencing craving and withdrawal has very little effect on the outcome of his or her addiction. Assuming the person is ready to start the counseling, we must first deal with the physical craving and withdrawal that occurs when the drugs are stopped. It is difficult for parents to understand that dealing with the craving and withdrawal may be the most difficult task in initiating drug treatment. Some parents do not appreciate how hard it is to stop drugs because of the awful craving and the horrible withdrawal symptoms that occur when the drugs are stopped. In addition, they do not realize that these symptoms can occur for weeks or months after quitting the drugs. No one, teenager or adult, is able to do any meaningful counseling when he or she is constantly thinking about the craving and withdrawal symptoms. The best analogy for this is being told you cannot eat for three weeks. Then you come back to me and I put your favorite food in front of you, and we discuss ways to not eat that food. You would not be able to resist the food. If you magnify that tenfold, it is closer to what an addict feels when he or she is craving an opiate drug. Craving is very similar to hunger but much more intense. It is very difficult to describe, but addictive people tell me it is many times more intense than hunger craving. To deal with the counseling, you have to deal with the craving, but before the craving, you have to deal with the withdrawal.

THE CHEMISTRY OF ADDICTION

To understand craving and withdrawal, you have to look at the biochemistry of addiction, and you have to know a little bit about opioid receptor pharmacology. In opioid receptor pharmacology, there are agonists, antagonists, and partial agonists.

Agonists are substances that bind to the receptor and produce a full biologic response, a stimulator, if you will.

An *antagonist* is a substance that binds to the receptor and will not produce a biologic response, a blocker, if you will.

A *partial agonist* is a substance that binds to the receptor and produces a limited response, less than the full response produced by an agonist. It is a partial stimulator.

So if sitting by a fire is considered a heat agonist or stimulator of your heat receptors, a blow dryer set on low would be considered a partial agonist or partial stimulator of your heat receptors. On the other hand, a heat shield or insulator that blocks the effect of either the fire or blow dryer would be considered an antagonist or blocker of the heat receptors in your skin. If the heat shield is between you and the heat source, your receptors for heat in the skin cannot feel the heat.

To understand opioid receptor activity on the cells, which are very similar to the GABA receptors in function, you have to understand affinity, intrinsic activity, and the concept of dissociation.

The concept of a receptor is somewhat of a misnomer. A receptor is more like an electrical trigger point or a biochemical switch. The history of receptor sites comes from research in diabetes. Years ago, endocrinologists knew that if you ate a carbohydrate-rich meal, your blood glucose (sugar) went up. When the blood glucose rose, it "triggered" the pancreas to release insulin. The glucose attached to "receptor sites" in the pancreas, which caused a biochemical switch to turn on the cells that release insulin. The more glucose molecules that attached to these receptor sites, the more switches were turned on. The insulin and glucose then traveled together to receptor sites on the muscles, which turned on the switch for the muscle to move. After the endocrinologists described these "receptor sites," other specialists, including gastro-enterologists, cardiologists, and lung specialists (pulmonologists) started to describe receptors in each of their areas of expertise. When the psychiatrists got in the act, they described receptor sites in the brain, which were triggered by chemicals that attach to the receptors in our brains and spinal cords. These chemicals modify mood and sense of well-being and cause addictive behaviors, by triggering switches that fire in our nervous system. These receptor sites are designed to accept naturally occurring chemicals (neurotransmitters) that are synthesized in our bodies. If we have a shortage of these natural neurotransmitters, the ingested drugs will fill the receptor sites and cause the biochemical switches to fire. Unfortunately, drugs of abuse can cause problems because they may modify these receptor sites to prefer the drugs of abuse to the natural neurotransmitters. If someone has an inherent lack of a neurotransmitter, the abused drug may be quite acceptable to the receptor.

Another problem occurs because many drugs of abuse quickly get metabolized to other drugs that are readily taken up by the receptors, and may be closer matches to the natural neurotransmitter. Worse, the metabolite may be more potent than the normal neurotransmitter, making more receptor (switches) fire. For example, heroin is metabolized to morphine within 120 *seconds* of being ingested in our bodies. We really do not have heroin addicts, we have morphine addicts. Since some of these drugs are toxic, our bodies try to get rid of them quickly. If we cannot get rid of them quickly, they can be stored in our fat. This allows the body to slowly release them and slowly detoxify them. This can prolong the withdrawal and craving, even after stopping a drug. I believe a young brain may actually morph the endorphin receptors to prefer opiates to the normal neurotransmitter. This is especially a problem in teens since they have more plasticity and ability to change their brains' hardwiring than an adult's brain would have.

To understand withdrawal, you have to understand a little bit about opiate activity and receptors in the brain. A brain receptor, in addition to being a biochemical switch, is like a lock on a door. For the door to open, you have to have a key to that lock. A receptor in the brain is like a biochemical lock. However, cells contain a number of these biochemical locks. Until all of the locks have keys, a cell cannot function. Assume, for example, that a cell has a hundred biochemical receptors. If you only have eighty keys for these biochemical receptors, the cell will not function properly. In the case of a nerve cell, it will not fire and stimulate the next nerve in line to ultimately satisfy parts of the brain that need to be satisfied. So if someone is anxious, he or she needs the GABA receptor nerves to fire to decrease the anxiety. If only eighty of the one hundred biochemical receptors/locks have keys, the GABA receptors on the cell will not have enough chemical keys to make the nerve fire. This causes the person to have extreme anxiety, or in the case of opiate addiction, extreme withdrawal. We discussed earlier how severe withdrawal can be. Unless you do something to satisfy these receptors in the withdrawal process, the craving will start.

This is similar to our hunger for food when our blood glucose drops between meals. The glucose receptors are not filled enough to satisfy our energy needs for muscle movement. This causes us to crave food or sometimes more specifically, sweets.

Let's look at some of the characteristics of receptors. We will start by describing some terms.

Affinity is best described as how tightly the drug binds to the receptor.

Intrinsic activity is how much the drug or chemical stimulates the receptor.

Dissociation is best described as how fast the drug leaves the receptor.

A neurotransmitter or a chemical, in this case, an opiate drug, has several characteristics that will predict how well it satisfies the receptors on a cell. The chemical has an inherent affinity to the receptor. The affinity is described as how tightly that particular drug or chemical binds or sticks to the receptor. A chemical or drug with a high affinity is like a key that fits well and is difficult to remove.

The second characteristic of a drug or chemical is its intrinsic activity on that receptor. In other words, it describes how much that drug or chemical stimulates the receptor. A drug that stimulates the receptor to a large degree will cause that nerve to fire vigorously when all the receptors are filled.

A drug that only partially stimulates the receptor will satisfy the receptor but not make it fire as vigorously as a drug that has a much larger stimulating capacity. An example of this would be a woman getting hot flashes during menopause. If you give her estrogen, the receptor feels better with a fairly low dose and the flashes cease. If you give her an herbal remedy, such as black cohosh, it only has 1 or 2 percent of the inherent activity of her own estrogen, but it will cause the flashes to diminish nonetheless. Another way to look at this is if you are thirsty and you cannot get water, if someone gave you coffee or tea, your thirst would be satisfied but not as well is if you had what your body needs, which is water. Although opioids have a very high intrinsic activity, they are not what your cells need. So although the GABA receptor will be satisfied by the opioid, in the long run, the receptor really wants GABA. The other problem with the opioids is that because they are so potent and they stimulate the receptor aggressively, sometimes the cell receptor will actually mutate or morph into a receptor that "likes" the opiate better than its inherent substance, such as GABA. This is a severe issue especially with teenagers, as we mentioned previously. If they subject themselves to long-term use of opiates, they will actually develop receptors on their cells that like the opiate more than the original neurotransmitter. This is also a significant danger in children born to addicted mothers. Because the child was exposed to opiates in utero, they probably developed opiate receptors. This will likely predispose them to addiction problems later in life. Because they have these receptors, if they expose the brain to opiates as a teen or adult, the receptor will "wake up" and crave the drug once exposure occurs. Increased intrinsic activity is a negative in the case of opiate drugs. This is because although it is not a perfect match for the receptor because it has a very high stimulatory or intrinsic activity, the receptor will prefer this over the inherent chemical the receptor was designed for, in this case GABA. It is only after the opiate is removed that the receptor will slowly evolve to its original biochemical structure were GABA becomes the preferred substance.

The third characteristic of the receptor or a neurotransmitter is its ability to dissociate from the receptor. In other words, this relates to how fast the drug or the chemical leaves the receptor. A chemical that does not leave the receptor quickly can be an advantage if you're looking for the stimulatory effects. For instance, if a chemical has a poor ability to dissociate from the receptor, it would somewhat protect the receptor from an outside stimulatory agent like the opioid. If, on the other hand, the dissociation was poor and it was an unwanted chemical such as an opioid, this would not be a good characteristic. Originally methadone, which is a long-acting synthetic narcotic, was used to treat opioid withdrawal and craving because it had a very long half-life (it is difficult to metabolize and stays in the system a long time), and this was viewed as a positive. For addiction treatment, it could be given once a day and prevent the withdrawal symptoms. However, because it is not what the brain really needs, in the long run this is a negative aspect of the drug. In addition, methadone has a very high intrinsic activity, meaning it stimulates the receptor fairly aggressively, and it is a fairly high affinity, so it binds to the receptor fairly tightly.

As you can see, a drug or a pharmacologic treatment for treating the receptor that is lacking GABA can be challenging because of these characteristics of affinity, intrinsic activity, and dissociation. The question comes up as to why we don't just use GABA or a pharmacologic drug that mimics GABA to treat addictions. The reason we don't use GABA is that it is not strong enough to displace the opioid from the receptor. In other words, if someone is using morphine or another opioid, the GABA will not be able to push it off the receptor and therefore it cannot be utilized by the cell. If a person has been off the opioid and is in withdrawal, it takes tremendous doses of GABA to calm down the receptor because it is so used to the very high stimulating effects of the opioid. Generally, the person either is unable to take the dose needed or does not get enough stimulatory effect from the GABA to make it a worthwhile treatment in the early stages of withdrawal. It is, however, a good way to maintain someone once he or she has gone through withdrawal and is in a maintenance phase of treatment. The dosages needed for someone in maintenance would be anywhere from 1000 mg to 5000 mg per day of over-the-counter

GABA, in order to keep their receptors happy and avoid craving and withdrawal. In the early stages of withdrawal, it is not practical to give doses that would be needed for GABA to achieve this. The benzodiazepine drugs such as Xanax Valium, Ativan, and clonazepam will achieve enough control to help the person get through withdrawal. The reason for this is that they have fairly high intrinsic activity in doses that are usually prescribed. It is not unusual for an opiate addict to actually need some Xanax, Valium, or another drug to help him or her through withdrawal while on other substitution therapies that will be discussed later.

This is a very controversial aspect of treating the opiate addict, because many people who treat addicts believe no prescription drugs should be given. It has been our experience that the occasional patient who has a tremendous GABA deficiency will experience some benefit from the benzodiazepine drugs. However, these have to be monitored closely because there is some dependence and addiction potential from these medications. It is always preferable to try to rebuild the neurotransmitters using a more natural substance like GABA or the precursors to GABA, including the vitamins, minerals, and supplements discussed later.

In discussing substitution therapy, we're talking about something that substitutes for what the brain is lacking to get the person through their withdrawal and craving. Originally substitution therapy was done with low-dose opiate drugs, which were slowly tapered. As mentioned earlier, this does not achieve a good outcome. The next phase of substitution therapy was the use of methadone, which is still in use today. The advantages to methadone are that it can be given once a day, it is administered through a methadone maintenance center, and the dosing is somewhat controlled. Because it has a long half-life (it stays in your system a long time), once-a-day dosing is sufficient. The main issue with methadone maintenance is you are still giving the addicted person an opiate drug, except you are controlling the dosing to some degree. The negatives to methadone maintenance are: you are still giving an opiate, and there is tremendous stigma associated with going to methadone maintenance. Also, it makes it very hard for someone trying to get his or her life back. It is difficult to go to methadone maintenance on a daily basis if you're trying to go to school or trying to work. In addition if you go on vacation or do not show up for your appointment, you do not get your dose. Most methadone maintenance programs require some sort of counseling, which is a plus.

Other substitution therapies have been developed that are superior to methadone maintenance. The drug buprenorphine has been used in the treatment of opioid addiction in the United States since 2002. It originally was prescribed as a lower level pain reliever. It was used in Europe for years before it was used in the United States for treating addiction. It is a synthetic opioid drug, meaning it has the characteristics of an opioid but it is manufactured in a lab. It has some interesting and useful characteristics, which make it a very good drug for substitution therapy.

BUPRENORPHINE AS SUBSTITUTION THERAPY

Buprenorphine is a partial agonist, or partial stimulator, of something called the *mu receptor* of brain cells. The *mu receptor* is the receptor in the brain cell that is responsible for the sense of feeling high or euphoria that occurs when using opiates. In other words, if you stimulate the *mu* receptor with low doses, it causes you to have a sense of well-being, and with higher doses, it causes a sense of euphoria or feeling high. Without going into sophisticated cell bio-chemistry, suffice it to say the *mu* receptor is similar to the GABA receptor. The *mu* receptor responds best to endorphins, which are chemicals that make us feel good and help relieve pain. If you stimulate the *mu* receptor of the cell, the GABA receptor also seems to respond positively. Because buprenorphine is a partial agonist of the receptor, it does not have as much stimulatory effect as the opiate does. This is good news from a treatment standpoint, but not such good news from the standpoint of the addicted person trying to get high. Because it is a partial agonist, the person can only get so much of a high sensation from it. It also has something called a *ceiling effect*. A *ceiling effect* is best described as being able to take so much of a drug and after that it has little or no effect. It's like saying that if I take two aspirin for a headache, taking five is not going to relieve it much more.

Opiates have some unique properties. In low to moderate doses, they are pain relievers, at high doses, they cause euphoria or a sense of feeling high, and at very high doses, they cause depression of your respiratory center in the brain and will cause you to stop breathing. This is best demonstrated by the graph below.

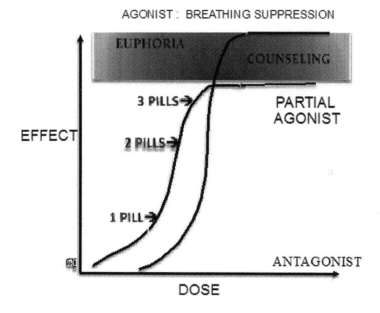

AGONIST : BREATHING SUPPRESSION

The ceiling effect is demonstrated along the partial agonist line to the left. As you can see when you get up to just beyond three pills, no matter how many you take, the effect levels out. This is the *ceiling effect*. It protects the person from overdosing and it prevents him or her from getting into the "euphoria or feeling high" zone. The lack of euphoria, or in some cases, numbing of the brain from negative thoughts, is the reason addicts need counseling. They need to learn how to live without numbing the brain. They need tools to deal with previous trauma, because the buprenorphine cannot give them the numbing or euphoria. With a full agonist, the line to the right, such as an opiate drug, as you can see, the more you take, and the more effect it has. Also, as you increase the dose of a full agonist or opiate, you go through the euphoria range until you hit a breathing suppression. At that point, the brain stops sending signals to the lungs and breathing stops. Obviously this is a life-threatening problem. If an individual is not immediately given an antidote through either emergency providers or the hospital emergency room, he or she will die. Since buprenorphine is a partial stimulator, you do not get this life-threatening effect. Buprenorphine is usually safe when used properly.

Originally buprenorphine was sold as a drug called Subutex, or in combination with naloxone, as a drug called Suboxone and was manufactured by Reckitt-Benkeiser. We do not have any connection or financial ties to Reckitt-Benkeiser. Other companies now make buprenorphine and the buprenorphine/naloxone combination, but Reckitt-Benckiser was the original manufacturer. So as not to confuse the reader, we use Suboxone and buprenorphine/naloxone interchangeably in reference to substitution therapy. Subutex and buprenorphine are also used in a similar way. Suboxone and Subutex were the first commercial patent drugs used as partial agonist substitution therapies. It is similar to people using Kleenex interchangeably with tissue. Generics for Suboxone and Subutex are on the market, but not widely used at this time.

The statements that follow are based on our experience with their products and policies. The pure buprenorphine form of the drug is only used if people have significant side effects to the combination of buprenorphine and naloxone found in the drug sold as Suboxone, made by the same company. You will recall that naloxone is an antagonist and is added to the buprenorphine to prevent patients from trying to inject the buprenorphine to attempt to get high. If you inject naloxone intravenously, it causes immediate withdrawal by blocking the *mu* receptor. This prevents the opiate from attaching and stimulating the receptor. This will be discussed later. Initially, when the drug came out it was only in pill form. Reckitt-Benkeiser is a company that seems concerned about safety and effectiveness. They also make Lysol, which has been around for years and is a very effective and well-known household cleaning product with antibacterial properties. When cases of toxicity or poisoning occurred in young children who mistakenly took Suboxone, from on adult prescription that was left unprotected, the company wanted to make it safer and to prevent these accidents. In addition, there were a number of reports of Suboxone and Subutex pills being diverted or sold on the street. We will discuss this diversion problem later and how we deal with it. Because of these things, Reckitt-Benkeiser decided to make a safer form of Suboxone, and came out with Suboxone film. It is extremely difficult to process or modify the film so that the active ingredient can be injected. Also, young children are less likely to ingest Suboxone film accidentally. One of the problems with the pills is that they were orange and looked a little like candy. The film, however, is clear and looks like breath-freshening filmstrips. When the film came out, providers were encouraged to switch patients from the pills to the film. After about a year and a half of this transition, the company decided only to make the film to prevent any of the pills from being mistaken as candy by young children. In addition, they made the decision to stop making Subutex, because they felt that this drug was diverted or sold on the streets much more than Suboxone. They also tried to educate providers about not switching patients to Subutex, unless they had severe reactions to the Suboxone. Although this was a small segment of the population, the drug company made the decision only to make Suboxone, and only in a relatively safe delivery system, which was the film. Buprenorphine without naloxone is still made by companies other than Reckitt-Benkeiser, and it is only made in pill form not film. Providers are usually suspicious of patients who demand the Subutex because it is much more likely to be diverted to the street than Suboxone film. Addicted patients will grind up the buprenorphine, and inject it to get a slight high or euphoria. Although this is not as intense as injecting an opiate drug, to some it is more desirable than the oral effect.

The question always comes up as to why someone would sell or divert a drug that blocks the craving for opiates. The answer is complicated, but it can be summarized by saying people will buy Suboxone or buprenorphine to stop their withdrawal or because it is the only drug available on the streets. We also believe that some people can "convince themselves" that they get a significant high from these drugs. The scientific studies and experience of providers prescribing these drugs counters that belief. However, you cannot discount the power of the mind in these situations. If someone is convinced the drug will get them high, they are likely to get a high even if the drug does not have the properties to do that.

In addition to being a partial agonist or stimulator of the receptor on the cell, buprenorphine has a high affinity for the receptor. This means that it binds more tightly to the receptor then the opiate or full agonist or stimulator. This has clinical implications because two things occur. First, if any opiate is on the cell and a person takes buprenorphine, the buprenorphine will displace or replace the opiate off the cell receptor. Second, because it has high affinity for the receptor once it is bound to the receptor, the opiate is not able to move it off the receptor, so in a sense it protects the receptor with his blocking action.

The third characteristic of buprenorphine helps make it a good substitution therapy. It has a very slow dissociation from the receptor. In other words, it does not like to leave the cell and stays attached to the receptor for a prolonged period. This is a good when you're treating addictions. The reason for that is because if it does not move off the receptor quickly, you do not have to take it frequently. Usually once or twice a day dosing is enough. This protects the person from withdrawal because there is always some buprenorphine attached to the cell receptor sites. In addition, because it is tightly bound, it will prevent an opiate from stimulating the receptor and causing a euphoria or high.

In summary, buprenorphine is a very good substitution therapy for opiate addiction because it does not stimulate the receptor enough to cause a high and it has a ceiling effect, meaning that after you take three or four pills per day, it does not have any increased effect to make you feel high or to suppress your breathing. In addition, because it has a high affinity for the receptor, it binds tightly to prevent opiates that might be introduced from stimulating the cell, and it does not dissociate or leave the cell quickly, which prevents withdrawal from happening with once or twice daily dosing, and it has a significant long-term blocking effect. Because this drug has these effects, it helps the biochemical aspects of addiction, craving and withdrawal, from interfering with the psychosocial and spiritual counseling that needs to be done to improve the outcome.

There is another aspect of buprenorphine that makes it a relatively good treatment option. When buprenorphine was used as a painkiller, it was usually given by injection. The reason is it is not absorbed very well orally. When it is used for addiction, it is given under the tongue. This again becomes an advantage in addiction treatment. Since it is not absorbed well orally but it is absorbed well under the tongue, it can be combined with another drug, naloxone.

Naloxone is a drug that is used to treat opiate overdoses. The reason naloxone is used to treat opiate overdoses is because it is something called an *opioid antagonist.* An antagonist is a substance that binds to the cell receptor but does not produce a biologic response. It is a key that will fit into the lock but cannot open the lock. Because it fits into the key or receptor but cannot open it, it blocks the effect of keys/chemicals that can open or stimulate the receptor. So if someone has overdosed on an opiate and is unconscious and you give naloxone intravenously, it will displace or push the opiate out of the system and cause the person to wake up. It does this because it has a strong affinity for the receptor, and it has the ability to displace the opiate out of the receptor site. Although it has a very strong affinity, it has little or no intrinsic stimulating activity. Even though it would be a good treatment for an overdose, it is not a good treatment for someone whose cells are craving some intrinsic stimulatory activity, because it has to be given by injection. Naloxone has been used for years in emergency room settings for opiate overdoses. The advantage is that when given intravenously, it works almost immediately. Its disadvantage for treating overdoses is that it is minimally absorbed when taken orally. However, this is an advantage for addiction treatment. Naloxone was originally combined with buprenorphine in a pill as a treatment for addiction. Suboxone is the brand name of the pill, as stated previously.

The interesting thing about Suboxone is the way that buprenorphine and naloxone complement each other. As I stated, when given under the tongue, the buprenorphine is absorbed fairly well. The naloxone, which is not absorbed orally or sublingually, is actually added to the buprenorphine as a type of insurance. As you will recall, buprenorphine originally was a painkiller administered intravenously. It has moderate pain-killing activity when administered intravenously. Although it has the characteristics of high affinity, slow dissociation, and only partial intrinsic activity to the cell receptors when used sublingually, intravenously it increases stimulation of the receptor in the cells so the person will feel some pain relief and a slight euphoria. The naloxone was added so that the addicted person would not be tempted to try to grind up the Suboxone and inject it. If an individual injects Suboxone, the naloxone will be absorbed and activated, and the person will experience immediate withdrawal symptoms. This is because the naloxone will displace any opiate or buprenorphine from the cell and precipitate withdrawal. Addicted people know this property and will never inject Suboxone to try to get a high from the buprenorphine. Interestingly, naloxone could be added to virtually any opiate drug, which would help prevent addicts from grinding up an opiate pill to inject intravenously. Naloxone is not well absorbed orally; intravenously it has a pronounced effect.

We do not see manufacturers of potent painkillers adding naloxone to their drugs as insurance so people will not try to inject that drug to get high. It is unclear why the drug companies refuse to add this drug. It is my opinion that they know a significant portion of the prescribed drug gets diverted to the streets. Adding the naloxone would negatively affect the diversion and cut into their sales. Many addicts will grind up prescription drugs and inject them to get high. Adding naloxone would discourage that behavior.

Buprenorphine, on the other hand, has a moderate stimulatory effect intravenously, a significant affect sublingually, and a minimal effect orally. By giving Suboxone sublingually you get a moderate effect from the buprenorphine and no effect from naloxone. If you inject Suboxone by grinding up the pills and mixing this with a solvent, you get an immediate withdrawal because the naloxone is absorbed very well. In effect, the buprenorphine stimulatory effect is neutralized or blocked by the naloxone. Frequently parents ask why someone would grind up a pill and inject it. The answer is some addicted people will grind anything up and inject it, snort it, or insert it rectally to get a high. They know that intravenous ingestion gives you the quickest absorption, that nasal or rectal application gives you fairly rapid absorption because these are mucous membranes, and that oral ingestion gives you the least rapid absorption. When Suboxone was formulated, the makers used the characteristics of buprenorphine and naloxone to maximize the novel characteristics of each of these drugs; this is an interesting synergy and a very effective treatment.

Prior to Suboxone coming out in the United States, it was used for many years in Europe. Before Suboxone, substitution therapy almost always involved methadone. Methadone is a synthetic opiate drug that has a very long duration of action or half-life. It is, however, a full agonist and has all of the properties of opiate drugs, including that in higher doses it can cause euphoria and in very high doses breathing suppression. The reason it was used in treatment was it could be given once a day. When methadone maintenance centers were started, the protocol was to have addicted patients come in once a day for their daily dose. This way, the dosage could be controlled, patients would not have withdrawal, and they could be monitored. In addition, counseling and medical treatment were available at the methadone maintenance center. However, if someone was trying to work, go to school, or go on vacation, he or she would not be able to get their dose, or it was very inconvenient. These methadone maintenance programs were proliferating at a time when thoughts about addiction causes were not the same as they are today. There also was a significant stigma attached to going to a methadone maintenance center. Whether you were an executive, student, housewife, professional, or homeless person, you all went to the same program and got the same once-a-day dose. This prevented people who did not want to be associated with that setting from getting proper treatment through the methadone maintenance program.

DRUG ADDICTION TREATMENT ACT OF 2000

When Suboxone was approved in the United States in 2000 for addiction treatment, stipulations were added to the approval, which limited the number of patients treated by an individual provider. It is not totally clear why some of these were put in place. We will look at some possible explanations below. A significant percentage of Suboxone providers believe it was the methadone lobby that put some of these restrictions on Suboxone providers. Since Suboxone could be done in a private doctor's office and prescriptions could be given for up to thirty days, it seriously threatens the methadone maintenance programs for a large percentage of the population.

The Drug Addiction Treatment Act of 2000, the DATA 2000 Act, outlined the requirements and restrictions for physicians to prescribe Suboxone, once Suboxone was approved for addiction treatment in the United States. The stipulations included:

- The physician had to have a current state license and have an active DEA number; this is a number that allows physicians to prescribe controlled drugs.

- The physician prescribing Suboxone had to hold specialty boards in either psychiatry or addiction medicine.

- If the physician was not a psychiatrist and/or addiction medicine specialist, he or she had to complete a training course of not less than eight hours, which outlined the treatment and management of addicted patients using buprenorphine.

- The physician had to have the capacity to refer addicted patients for appropriate counseling.

- Physicians could not have more than thirty patients in active treatment at any time in the first year. After the first year, they could apply for a waiver to increase that number to no more than one hundred patients.

During the training for physicians in the use of Suboxone and Subutex, guidelines for patients in the addiction program are stipulated. They include: a prescription could be given for a supply of thirty days or less, and the addicted patient would be drug tested on a regular basis. An addicted person also has to be involved in a counseling program, in addition to medical visits for the prescriptions of Suboxone. All addicted patients had to sign an agreement that outlined these requirements. As you can see by the DATA 2000 Act and the guidelines, physicians have significant restrictions on not only what they are allowed to do, but also the number of patients they are allowed to see. This is the only form of treatment in medicine where the government restricts the number of patients that can be seen with a given diagnosis. It is not clear is why this restriction is tied to the DATA 2000 waivers, which allow physicians to prescribe buprenorphine. If such a restriction were, for example, mandated to cardiologists and the number of angiograms performed in a given year, the cardiologists would be up in arms. In some ways, this discriminates against the number of opiate addicts able to get treatment, and it causes a significant gap between the number of patients needing treatment and the number of patients able to get treatment. In our area of western New York, we probably only have enough physicians to treat 10 to 20 percent of the population that is opiate addicted. This is because virtually every physician who is Suboxone-certified has a full practice of one hundred patients. It is not uncommon for us to get five to six calls per day requesting treatment. Prospective patients are told that our program is full because we have reached the hundred-patient maximum.

Why are doctors limited to only treating thirty or one hundred patients at a time? According to the *National Alliance of Advocates for Buprenorphine Treatment, (NAABT)* the DATA-2000 act was amended twice; once in August 2005 and a second time in December of 2006. The 2005 amendment allowed every certified doctor to prescribe to up to thirty patients regardless of whether they were in a group or solo practice. Prior to then, a group practice had the same limit as a single practitioner. This was very restrictive for large practices. The 2006 amendment allowed physician who had their DATA-2000 certification more than one year the option of increasing their maximum to one hundred patients. Despite aggressive recruitment, as of April 2014, only 24,726 of America's 800,000 potential physicians have become certified, but only about one third of them actually prescribe the drug. According to NAABT, "without knowing the abuse potential and social impact of these yet to be discovered drugs for addiction safeguards were built in the law," thus the limits. This was probably a good idea when the drug was first approved. However, we now know the drug is very safe compared to opiates. The restriction makes little sense after over twelve years of experience prescribing buprenorphine in the United States, and even more experience in Europe. As you will see in the last chapter, approval without restriction of much more dangerous drugs is occurring without any restrictions.

The NAABT lists fifteen reasons why the patient limits on prescribing buprenorphine should be lifted. They are listed below:

1. Forty to forty-five people die a day from prescription overdoses. This does not include heroin or illicit drug overdoses.
2. Access to treatment is severely limited for addicted patients seeking effective treatment.
3. It forces patients into less effective treatments, and many times these are costlier treatments.
4. The limit disproportionately affects the poor. Many physicians do not accept Medicaid, or only accept cash for addiction treatment with buprenorphine. If the limit were lifted, more physicians prescribing buprenorphine would create competition for patients. This in turn would encourage more physicians to accept Medicaid for addiction treatment.
5. The limit prohibits the evolution of experts. Limiting the number of patients treated per physician discourages and even prevents physicians from devoting their entire practice to treating opiate addiction.
6. Stable patients are sometimes forced off treatment prematurely to make room for patient with more urgent needs. This is discouraged, but unfortunately happens.
7. Limiting fosters more diversion of the drug. Patients are sometimes forced to buy the drug or opiates on the street to prevent severe withdrawal..
8. Waiting lists occur, which prevent patients from obtaining treatment when they are the most ready and willing.
9. One hundred patients may not be enough for physicians to recoup the cost of extra regulatory compliance and staff to effectively treat patients in an environment that is not prejudicial.

10. Buprenorphine is safer than the drugs the limit forces patients to remain on.
11. Even though buprenorphine is occasionally diverted, (mostly to prevent withdrawal), and exceptionally desired on the street, rationing exacerbates the diversion problem. Better to obtain the drug from an experienced prescriber than on the street. What possible reason is there to ration this lifesaving treatment to the arbitrary limit of thirty or one hundred patients when others in the community desperately need it.
12. It limits patient choice. In some areas the number of certified physicians is so low it forces patients to see a physician they would not otherwise select as a provider. Also, some unscrupulous physicians are more likely to survive in an environment where supply and demand is so out of proportion.
13. Methadone clinics are allowed to control their own dispensing schedule for buprenorphine. This means they can allow take home doses with more discretion than methadone. A methadone counselor can have 500 clients or more, but a buprenorphine certified physician has the thirty or one hundred limit. Methadone clinics are mandated to dispense methadone daily. A patient can only get a single day's dose. If an administrator of a methadone clinic had a choice they might not want to switch patients off methadone and onto buprenorphine, because of the loss of revenue and the limits. Methadone versus buprenorphine will be discussed later.
14. Once providers can distribute the fixed costs of medication assisted treatment practice over a much larger patient base, economics of scale should reduce the prices they charge for everyone.

15. It is unethical. Limiting the number of patients treated actually promotes addiction. If one in ten patients become dependent, and one in four patients become addicted after taking prescribed opiates, limiting the number of patients treated is a problem. In addition for every one hundred physicians who can and do prescribe the opioid drugs, we only have one active prescriber treating the disease.

The question comes up as to whether this is something that is enforced by the DEA. We can only tell you from our experience that officials do come to your office unannounced. When this occurred in our practice, we were told that we have to have charts of a different color or a different designation for the hundred patients, so that they can be distinguished from our medical patients. This is impossible with electronic charts. In addition, the charts have to be on a separate shelf. We are mandated to keep a running list of active patients, and we are asked to produce the list when the inspectors from the DEA come to the office without any warning or notification. During our unannounced inspection, the two DEA agents told me that they would need "forty-five minutes of my time during office hours." I was also told that if I did not give the permission for agents to come at that time, they would be back with a search warrant, and I would have no choice at that point. Obviously I did not want the latter, so I took forty-five minutes out of my busy day to answer questions. During the questioning, they asked to see my patient list, which I presented. They asked whether I drug tested patients in the office, which I do, and the inspector asked if I "followed patients into the bathroom" or if I had a staff member follow them into the bathroom when they give us a urine sample. I replied that that was not our practice, as I believed that the patient had the right to some dignity. They asked me if I was sure it was that patient's urine, and I told them I was relatively sure it was a patient's urine and not some substitute. They subsequently asked if I knew if any of my patients were selling Suboxone on the street. I replied that I did not know of any patients that were selling it, but if I found out, they would be immediately dismissed. I asked them, "How would I know that someone was selling the Suboxone on the street, without having a tip from someone," and they did not reply. They asked about some of our procedures for handling the patients and told me I could not exceed the hundred-patient limit. When I inquired what happens if I exceed the hundred-patient limit I was told "If you go over the hundred-patient limit, there is a $10,000 fine." In addition, I was told that if I was at the hundred-patient limit and I dismissed a patient, "I had to wait until that dismissed patient's prescription ran out before I could accept another patient."

I later found out that the tactics of these two DEA agents are certainly not what should be expected when there is an inspection. It is true that inspectors are allowed to come unannounced. However, visits are meant to monitor and not to intimidate providers. Again, this is the only area where the DEA is allowed to come in unannounced, unless there is a report of negligence or an abnormal behavior associated with prescribing, such as a patient complaint, a complaint from another provider, or overprescribing of a controlled substance.

It is because of the general misconception about addicted patients being people who will try to steal or intimidate providers for medications that make most providers unwilling to deal with them. That is not to say that dealing with addicted patients is not difficult. Couple this with the fact that you have to be certified to use Suboxone, that you are limited to either thirty or one hundred patients, and that the DEA can come in your office without warning and intimidate you. This is why most providers do not expressly want to deal with Suboxone or addicted patients.

Addicted people can be difficult to deal with and represent a significantly greater amount of time per visit than other patients.

However, there is a need to treat them and we now have effective means of treatment, which makes addiction treatment an area that is deficient in our system.

Suboxone has dramatically changed addiction treatment for opiates and has improved the success dramatically. I am in full agreement with patients being mandated to counseling, regularly drug tested, and monitored closely. If, however, we are trying to bring addiction treatment into the office setting rather than into a hospital or methadone maintenance center setting, I do not understand why government agencies discriminate against addicted patients by the DEA requiring us to separate their charts and segregating them from other patients. When addicted patients come into our office, people in the waiting room do not know whether they are there for routine medical treatment, holistic care, counseling, or addiction treatment. That is the way it should be. If someone goes to methadone maintenance, it is clear why he or she is going there. Suboxone treatment has allowed patients trying to get their lives back on track to come to an office setting for treatment and get excellent results.

To summarize buprenorphine:

- It blocks the effects of withdrawal from opioids.

- It has a maximum effect at relatively low doses.

- It has a ceiling effect at about 24 mg.

- It does not make you high or euphoric when used sublingually.

- It can be used in addiction treatment as an outpatient.

- Physicians using it must be certified.

- Only thirty patients are allowed per physician in the first year, and then one hundred patients if the physician applies for of another waiver.

- It is part of a comprehensive program that includes counseling, drug testing, and regular visits to a physician's office

To better understand how Suboxone works, I will quickly review its characteristics.

- The buprenorphine works when placed under the tongue, though very little naloxone is absorbed when the medication is placed under the tongue.

- Naloxone works when injected, because it attaches to the receptor faster than the buprenorphine, and it is able to displace virtually any opiate or buprenorphine from the receptor.

- Naloxone has poor oral and sublingual absorption, but high IV absorption.

- Buprenorphine suppresses withdrawal and craving.

- Naloxone causes withdrawal when injected into an opioid dependent person. It pushes the opioid drug off the cell receptor and does not stimulate the receptor; instead it antagonizes the receptor and does not satisfy it.

To better understand Suboxone, versus Subutex, we will review the two drugs.

- Suboxone is buprenorphine and naloxone.

- Subutex is buprenorphine only.

  o Occasionally patients need Subutex due to nausea or side effects with Suboxone.

  o Subutex is indicated during pregnancy, which we will discuss later.

- Subutex is more likely to be abused.

- As of March 2013, Suboxone is only made as a film by Reckitt-Benkeiser. A generic form does exist as a pill; however, its effectiveness is not generally felt to be as good, and it is more easily diverted or abused.

- Subutex comes as a pill but not a film.

- Both are administered sublingually.

It is important for someone considering buprenorphine in treatment to compare it to using methadone, which has been the preferred substitution therapy prior to 2000. It is also important to note that methadone is still used as a very potent opiate pain reliever. In pain management it is a useful drug, especially for severe pain or terminal pain such as in a terminal cancer patient.

It is important to compare and contrast buprenorphine and methadone. The following table highlights the main issues:

BUPRENORPHINE	METHADONE
• Partial agonist	• Full agonist
• Sublingual dosing	• Oral or IV (intravenous) dosing
• Ceiling effect	• Increased effect until breathing suppression
• Low addiction potential	• High addiction potential
• Moderately long half-life (duration of action)	• Very long half-life (duration of action)
• Little or no euphoria at high doses	• Euphoria at high doses
• No breathing suppression at high doses	• Breathing suppression at high doses
• Monthly visits, 30 day supply	• Daily visits, only one day supply
• Private office outpatient	• Methadone maintenance center
• Can detox with it as outpatient, whole process several hours	• Cannot detox with it, only get methadone after detox while on maintenance
• No need for inpatient detox	• Must be detoxed before getting prescription
• Low level analgesic (pain reliever)	• Potent analgesic

WHAT SHOULD PARENTS DO IF THEY HAVE AN ADDICTED TEEN?

Before we discuss the actual treatment process, it is important to discuss what to do and what not to do if you are the parent or friend of a teenage addict. Since the bulk of our patients are young adults or teenagers, we have a lot of experience in dealing with this population.

What NOT to do:

- Do not hide or throw away drugs hoping the teenager will stop. This is not going to happen. The teen will find other ways to get his or her drugs, and he or she will only be angry and rebel.
- Do not attempt to punish, threaten, bribe, or preach. The teen will agree to anything as long as you stop badgering him or her. Threatening and punishing do not work, because this is a biochemical process that is beyond his or her control, and the addiction can be much stronger than the teen's willpower.
- Do not take over responsibilities, leaving the teen with no sense of importance or self-esteem. A big mistake is to say, "you don't have to go to school or go to work or do your chores around the house," hoping that the teen will have time to reflect and rest, and finally come to his or her senses. This will never work. It just gives the teen more time to acquire drugs. A big part of addiction is low self-esteem; if you take away all responsibilities, it lowers self-esteem further.
- Do not argue with a teen when he or she is high. First of all, he or she is not able to absorb what you are saying, let alone assimilate the information in an intelligent

manner. You have to remember that the teen's sense of right and wrong is already disconnected, and when he or she is high, this is magnified a number of times.

- *Do not take drugs with the teen thinking it will teach them self-control by showing him or her you have control.* A hallmark of addiction is the lack of control. Your control over taking an addictive substance has absolutely nothing to do with the teen either learning self-control or exhibiting self-control. As we have stated previously, having your son or daughter smoke their first joint with you or have his or her first drink with you as a way to share the experience is a huge mistake. Doing the same once they are addicted is profoundly worse and achieves nothing.

What to do:

- Get professional help. Addiction treatment requires multiple professionals, including physicians and skilled counselors with experience in addiction. This is not something you can tackle on your own. Even with professional help, treatment is ongoing and intensive, especially in the first few months.
- Look for the possibility of abuse. Abuse may be perceived abuse on the part of the addicted person, but it can be from family, friends, babysitters, and so forth. Many times it is not "true" abuse but is perceived to be an abusive interaction. However, in our experience, the majority of addicted teens have experienced some sort of behavior that they perceive as abusive. Abuse is high in our society. The prevalence of abuse, coupled with the availability of drugs, and a biochemistry that is vulnerable to addiction, is a bad combination.

- Educate yourself about addiction. Much of addiction is biochemical and it helps to understand that teens cannot control their behavior without help. This is not something that you can beat out of them, talk out of them, or will out of them. Before addicts can begin to heal, they first need to detoxify from the drug, then get substitution therapy, and rebuild their brain chemistry. They need to understand their addiction, get counseling for psychological issues, and rebuild self-esteem. This is something that's going to take a long time, a lot of work, and facilitation by professionals.

- The latest treatments use substitution therapy, mostly Suboxone. Attempting therapy without substitution therapy statistically gives much poorer results, and is extremely difficult and painful for the teenager. It is state of the art is to use substitution therapy, get the brain under control, eliminate withdrawal, decrease cravings, and then go to counseling. You cannot counsel someone who is constantly craving and you certainly cannot counsel someone who is in withdrawal.

- Be supportive, but do not enable. It is sometimes difficult to tell the difference between supporting and enabling, but this will be discussed in our counseling section. Some things are very clear. If your teen has a cell phone and you are paying for the cell phone, stop paying. If they have a car or insurance that you are paying for, stop. Helping your child requires you to withdraw financial support until he or she gets treatment. One of our patients was a sixteen-year-old male who was arrested for dealing heroin. His parents had no clue that he had an addiction problem. When he was referred to us for treatment, he admitted to using eight to ten bags of heroin daily, intravenously. His habit cost anywhere from $80 to $100 a day. Because of the cost, and the fact that he was unable to earn this kind of money, he had to deal drugs. When he was arrested, his parents were shocked. After their son was evaluated in our office, we discussed the situation with his parents. Our policy is that anyone under eighteen years old has to have the parents involved or we will not accept him or her in the program. After we explained the severity of the problem, the fact that he had been addicted since he was thirteen years old and had used alcohol and marijuana from the time he was ten years old, they were even more embarrassed and surprised. When we explained that this is going to be an ongoing problem and that it would require intensive therapy and constant supervision, his father asked if he should continue paying for his son's cell phone. We were somewhat surprised that he would have to ask. Sometimes parents do not realize that things need to be earned, and privileges are not something that should be granted to children simply because they want them. Our reply was "What would your father or mother do?" They always come up with the right answer, such as, "My father would have never paid for a cell phone in the first place unless we got good grades or did our chores." Today some parents think that a cell phone, or paying for car insurance or a car, is a privilege that comes without responsibility. This is clearly an example of enabling rather than supporting. What we suggested is using the cell phone as a reward for him staying clean for three or four months. Since a teenager's sense of right and wrong is not fully developed in their mid to late teens, teaching him or her that the privilege of a cell phone comes with responsibility helps to install the software in their brains. The hardwiring is not fully developed so it is sometimes difficult to install this sense of responsibility once kids are teens; it is not impossible, just more difficult.

- Look for therapies and medical professionals that believe in and use substitution therapy. It is clear that state-of-the-art treatment for opiate addiction utilizes substitution therapy, most often with Suboxone. If you do not use substitution therapy, the chance of improving and staying clean for one year drops from about 80 percent to around 20 percent. It is even more critical in this age group because the lack of neurotransmitters is sometimes magnified over an older addicted person's. We still encounter counselors or agencies that tell the addicted teens "Suboxone is a drug, and if you're using Suboxone, you are still addicted." The truth is, Suboxone *is* a drug, but it is substituting for what your brain is lacking. Because of its characteristics of not being able to cause euphoria and blocking the receptor that is crying out for the opiate, it enables teens to at least be able to assess the situation, learn some self-control, and develop the life skills needed to overcome their addiction. In our opinion, not using substitution therapy is an anachronism for treating opiate addiction.
- We also run into situations where the counselor insists on not using any drugs, including Suboxone. In addition, some places require counseling three times a week. They also require addicts to go to group sessions two to three times a week, in addition to private counseling sessions. For a teenager, these demands make attending school and/or working extremely difficult or impossible. It is our belief that helping teens function in society by finishing school and/or working is an important part of treatment. When they come in for the induction at their first visit for Suboxone treatment, we discuss this. We will discuss this further when we go into detail about the actual treatment process.

THE TREATMENT PROCESS

The actual treatment process begins with a phone call. Since we are limited in the number of patients we can have in our program at any given time, we have to screen the patients before they come in, assuming we have openings. The initial phone call usually comes from a worried parent, or in some cases from the patients themselves. Usually they have decided to come because of a significant event that triggered them to seek help. They could have been stopped for a DUI, arrested for possession or sale of illegal drugs, or a school official could have informed their parents. The least likely is for the teenagers themselves to call us for help. This is usually because they have not reached the third stage of behavioral change, where they are preparing for expected change by stopping drugs and seeking help. Many young people have contemplated change because they inherently know this is not rational behavior. But because they are young and have not had enough experience with the negative consequences of these behaviors, they are really in stage one or two, where they either have not thought about change or they are just starting to think about it. Because most physicians have very limited openings, the screening phase is most critical for getting people into Suboxone programs who are likely to do well.

If a parent, patient, school official, psychologist, or other healthcare provider calls requesting that we accept someone into our program, we insist that a phone conversation occurs between the physician and patient, and/or parent, first. If the child is under eighteen, I will discuss the issue with the parent first. If the child is over eighteen, I will discuss the situation with the teenager or young adult, and strongly recommend that a parent be involved. If the teenager is living with his or her parents and is dependent on them, I make it a requirement to speak to and have them involved. If he or she refuses to involve parents, I will not accept the teen into the program. If he or she is under eighteen and there is an issue of abuse on the part of his or her only parent and the teen lives with that parent, it becomes a much more difficult situation. I will still push for at least one parent to be involved, but I may not discuss the abuse issue directly with the parent and leave that to the counselor. If just the parent initially calls and the teenager is not available, I tell the parent I have to have a discussion with the patient. There are several reasons for this: Many times the teenager is not being truthful with the parent about how much he or she is using, and many times the teen will not inform the parent that he or she is using heroin because of the significant social stigma associated with heroin use. I can usually tell if the teenager is being relatively truthful in that conversation. If I do not get a phone call from the patient, I will not enroll them in the program.

When I speak to the teen, I inform them that there are rules that go along with being involved in the program. The first is, he or she has to be in withdrawal when they come in. By law, the first dose has to be given in the presence of a physician, and the patient has to be in withdrawal. If he or she is not in withdrawal, the Suboxone will precipitate a rapid withdrawal, which can be severe. I once had a patient who did not admit that they were injecting heroin at a rate of twenty bags per day, a large dose. On the phone they told me they were using two to three bags per day. When he came into the office, he was in withdrawal; however, he had taken some heroin about four hours prior to the visit, to decrease the severity of the withdrawal symptoms. When I administered the first dose of Suboxone, within twenty minutes the withdrawal intensified dramatically. The patient was sweating profusely, vomiting, had severe anxiety, walked out of the room, and immediately went outdoors. I thought he was going to leave; however, he went out to his car. After about twenty minutes he started to feel better and came back into the office. It sometimes takes 8 to 12 mg, one to one and a half pills or film, of Suboxone to alleviate the withdrawal symptoms. It is rare to give more than that. If patients are not truthful about how much they take or not truthful about abstaining for twenty-four to forty-eight hours prior to coming in, they are likely to have severe withdrawal with administration of the first dose of Suboxone. In addition to being truthful about how much they take and what they are taking, I tell them that they have to be off for at least twenty-four hours, preferably forty-eight hours for most opiates, except for methadone. Methadone is a quite different because it is an opiate that lasts for a long time in an individual's system. I strongly recommend patients abstain from methadone for forty-eight to seventy-two hours even though they are going to have fairly severe withdrawal during that time. If they are on methadone and abstain less than forty-eight hours, they are more likely to have severe withdrawal in the office and may require prolonged observation and a significant amount of Suboxone, in the 16 to 20 mg range. It is important that individuals understand that the opiate has to be out of their system, and they have to be truthful about what they take so we have an idea of how much Suboxone they are going to need and how precipitated the withdrawal will be.

If on the phone the patient agrees to arrive in withdrawal and he or she is truthful about what he or she is taking, I explain the rules of the program: He or she must stay clean of all drugs while under treatment, participate in some sort of counseling, undergo urine testing on a regular basis, avoid all illegal and legal opiates and narcotics, and come in at least once per month. Initially, I tell patients we may see them more often, sometimes twice a week in severe cases, but usually every one to two weeks after their first dose. After a time, we start spreading out visits depending on how well a patient is doing. If he or she hesitates at any of the requirements, I will not accept him or her in the program. If, for instance, the patient asks, "Does that mean I can't drink alcohol or smoke marijuana?" I tell him or her that it is true. Sometimes a patient will say, "Alcohol is legal, why can't I drink?" I tell the patient that alcohol is a substance that affects the thought process, and it has addictive properties itself. While on Suboxone, opiate addicts will substitute alcohol or marijuana for the euphoria. They try to replicate the sensation they felt with the opiate. The DATA 2000 Act, which mandates the rules for using Suboxone, specifically states that the patient must stay clean of all addictive substances, and must only take prescribed substances from the addiction-treating physician or primary physician, as long as the Suboxone-treating physician knows about these drugs. If a patient continues to argue about the alcohol or marijuana, I will not accept him or her into the program. This is a sign the individual is not really serious about making the changes needed to get better. The teen is informed that his or her parents will be involved in the treatment process. This means that if he or she is under eighteen, the parent will be with him or her when he or she comes in at the first visit. If he or she is over eighteen and living with their parent, I tell them that my rules are that the parent will be involved or they can't get into our program. If the teen balks at this, I will not accept them. Although they can legally be treated on their own, it is my feeling that if they are living with the parents, the parents have a right to know what is going on; they are also a major part of the treatment and social support system. In addition, if the parents are actually paying for the program because they do not have insurance, I insist they be allowed to call me at any time to see how their child is doing. If the teen does not agree, I will not accept them into the program. I do not get involved with dependent teens that refuse to have the parents involved in treatment. The vast majority of addicted teens agree to have the parents involved, and in many cases, they are relieved. I do use discretion if a child has severe addiction problems and has done things that he or she is ashamed of to obtain or use drugs. I will not share all of the details with parents. Many times this information is destructive for both parents and teen.

Suffice it to say that the parent should know that their teen is being treated, and that he or she has an addiction problem. When the teenager is ready, they will share the details of the behaviors with their parents. Sometimes the teen does not share them at all.

It is extremely important for parents to be involved in the treatment process. I remember a sixteen-year-old boy I will call Johnny who was addicted to heroin. He had been using drugs for about four years and was snorting heroin when he called for the appointment. He lived with his grandfather, and his parents were never involved in his upbringing. Although I spoke to the grandfather before he came in, and explained that he should be involved in the treatment process, when the teen came to our office, his grandfather was not with him. Johnny already had severe issues of abandonment from his parents, and the fact that his grandfather would not accompany him to the appointment was devastating to him. When I asked him where his grandfather was, he told me, "He's waiting in the car." This only reinforced the underlying abandonment issues. I did not think he would do very well in the program. He came for one other appointment and never returned.

Involving the parents at the first visit helps them to learn about what addiction is, and that it is treatable. They also learn that their child does not want to be this way, but it is a disease, just like diabetes or heart disease. Most times they are relieved, and almost universally feel better when they leave the office knowing that there is hope. A big part of treatment is education, support, and giving the patient and parents hope that this can be treated.

If I do not have openings in my Suboxone program, I do not return phone calls to prospective patients. Nothing is worse than raising expectations and not being able to deliver on these expectations. If the program is full, it could be months before another opening occurs. As stated previously, the penalty for going over the hundred patients is very stiff. In fact, if a physician is penalized and loses his or her buprenorphine certification, it not only punishes that physician but also the hundred patients in his or her program who have to subsequently find another physician; this is not an easy task. Although it is rare to lose certification, it is a distinct possibility and constantly hangs over the head of the physician. If I do have an opening, and we all agree to the rules and to arrive in withdrawal and involve the parents, I will give the teen an appointment within one or two days. If I delay the appointment for more than that, we have a very high no-show rate, because many times you have to catch people at the right time for them to initiate treatment. If they are referred by the court system, school, or the parents, they are more likely to fail. If another health provider refers them, I have a higher success rate, however the best situation is if the person really wants to make some changes.

During the initial phone discussion, insurance always comes up as an issue. Most insurance will cover buprenorphine induction in the office and subsequent treatment. However, some insurance does not cover the actual prescription for Suboxone. This can be very expensive, running anywhere from $8 to $10 per pill, and patients can need from one half to three pills per day. If they do not have insurance coverage for the visit, most physicians charge in the range of $200 to $350 for the first visit. They are in the office for anywhere from an hour and a half to two hours and require significant observation time and time to discuss the program. Follow-up visits are generally charged at either the office rate or slightly higher than an office visit. Another problem is the need to be regularly drug tested; if patients have no insurance these visits can be significantly more expensive because they have to pay for the drug test. Luckily, most people have insurance coverage for either the office visits and/or the prescription. Some insurance companies will not pay for the in-office drug testing even though it is mandated. This is shortsighted, because physicians will be reluctant to accept these patients for treatment and many times they end up in long-term rehab. The long-term rehab still requires addicts to be on some sort of substitution therapy, such as buprenorphine or methadone, after they leave long-term rehab. The other option is that they go to inpatient detox for three to four days, and again will need the substitution therapy with buprenorphine when they leave. It is important to check if your insurance carrier covers the treatment, the in-office drug testing, and the prescription.

If the insurer does not cover in-office testing, we are forced to send patients to an outside lab for the toxicology testing. This has a number of issues associated with it. When patients are sent to these agencies, they usually are not known well by the agencies and may not give their own urine. Sometimes, they bring someone else's urine with them, or they may try to dilute their urine, hoping that an illegal or unauthorized drug does not show up. The drug testing in office is much more cost-effective because if a person is stable and doing well, we generally will not send his or her urine out for verification at an outside lab at a significantly higher cost, if their urine is negative in office. Many patients are in this category once they have been stable on the Suboxone or buprenorphine.

The new types of in-office testing strips or methods are much more accurate than they were in the past. In the past, urine could be adulterated, allowing the patient to "pass" the test. The new tests work under a different principle. They have antibodies to the particular drugs being tested. If those tested have any traces of the drug, it will be positive. We also are able to test whether it is valid urine by checking the temperature of the urine to make sure it is body temperature. We can also check the specific gravity and whether it contains the normal chemicals that urine would always contain. It is easy for us to determine whether urine has been modified. Occasionally a patient will get through with adulterated urine. We ultimately discover later that they have given us a dirty urine sample. When this occurs, they usually are dismissed from the program, so who wins and who loses? In some cases, a significant other will warn us about a person adulterating his or her urine. One of our patients came in and we had been suspicious that his urine was adulterated. While in the exam room, his girlfriend, who was angry with him for not following the program rules, told me he had a urine container strapped to his leg. I asked him to pull up his pant leg, and sure enough he did have a container filled with urine. We also have situations where a patient will bring one of their young children in the bathroom and collect the urine from the child. Once I had a seventeen-year-old male who tested positive in the office for THC, the active ingredient in marijuana. When I confronted him, he was very angry. I asked him why he was angry. I assumed he was angry that he had been discovered. He told me he was angry because the urine was from his fifteen-year-old brother, and he had no idea his brother was using drugs. In the past, an addict could purchase substances that would "block" the urine drug screen or make it appear negative for drugs. Those days are over. The new tests have sophisticated methodology that is virtually impossible to interfere with drugs. If patients have drugs in their urine they will be detected by the new tests.

When teens arrive at the office for their first visit, we check their vital signs and get an initial observation of how severe they are experiencing withdrawal. As stated previously, the first dose of Suboxone has to be given in the office; however, we are not allowed to keep the drug in the office. This is inconvenient, for the patient and the office, because we have to write a prescription for one or two of the film strips of Suboxone and send them to the nearest pharmacy to get it filled. They have to return and we administer the dose. Initially, we thought some people would arrive, get the prescription for one or two film strips and never return. This generally does not happen. In fact, it is rare.

To assure that patients will return, we tell them if they do not return, they will forfeit their copayment and will not receive any more appointments. If they are paying cash, they will forfeit their cash amount, since we collect it before they are seen. When we first started doing Suboxone, we allowed people to pay after their visit, only to find that a good percentage of them did not have the money, and we never saw them or the money after the visit. This behavior causes prices to increase and is not fair to other patients. We now collect the copayment and/or the visit money before the patients are seen and before they get a prescription. Because we do not want to single out addicts, we collect payment from all of our patients prior to their appointments.

During the initial screening phone call, I cannot tell you how many times I have told people who do not have insurance coverage that the cost is $265 for the first visit. Many patients will say, "that's expensive," or, "I don't have the money." When I remind them that their drug habit was costing them $100, $200 or $300 a day, it does not seem to faze them. When I tell them that this is like one or two days of buying drugs on the street, they seem oblivious to that. At that point I tell the prospective patient I will not take them on as a patient. This is another example of the lack of connecting the negative consequences of addiction with the behaviors. Although at a conscious level, they understand that the first visit is only slightly more than a day's worth of drugs, and it may give them significant relief from their addiction, they do not seem to grasp the value of treatment. I will ask them if they tell their drug dealer that they think the price is too high when they buy drugs. They usually say, "I would never tell my drug dealer that because he wouldn't give me drugs." They do not seem to have the same value system for health professionals and treatment that they do for drug dealers and buying illegal drugs. This is a major reason for telling them what the program requires and the cost of the program. If they argue about the cost of the Suboxone film because they have no prescription plan, I do not accept them in the program because they have a distorted view of value for their health. I also tell them

I have no control over what their insurance company covers and does not cover. It is unfortunate that many of these people feel more comfortable in the drug culture and appear to be more comfortable stealing and dealing drugs to keep their habit going than they are paying a physician for treatment. This is a sign of addiction and a behavior that is manifested by the addicted person. I do not take it personally. Sometimes, as a physician, I have to be very blunt with those I am treating.

After an individual returns from the pharmacy with the film, he or she gets a history and physical. The detailed history is obtained after we administer the first dose of Suboxone. It is extremely hard for us to get any cogent history from a person who is in full-blown withdrawal. After we check the patient's vital signs, we give him or her the first dose and tell them that they may get worse before feeling better. This is because the Suboxone may precipitate withdrawal by forcing the opiate in the system off the receptor before replacing it. During this short time, the patient experiences what is known as "precipitated withdrawal." This is when the Suboxone, or buprenorphine, replaces the opiate on the cells, and finally the cell stops "crying out" for the opiate. In our experience, most patients do not experience this worsening. Usually within twenty to thirty minutes, the patient starts to feel significantly better. If, however, the patient has been using methadone or heroin prior to our visit and has not been in withdrawal for at least twenty-four to forty-eight hours, he or she may experience this period of worsening. I have not seen this worsening as much with hydrocodone and oxycodone, and most of these patients do very well with the initial treatment.

The patient is checked every ten to fifteen minutes to make sure that they are not getting a severe withdrawal reaction. After forty-five minutes to an hour, if the withdrawal is getting significantly worse, I may administer another dose of Suboxone, either 4 or 8 mg. By forty-five minutes to an hour, the vast majority of people feel significantly better and are able to give a more complete history. We are also able to examine the patient more completely. I have performed over four hundred of the initial inductions and have yet to see a person who did not feel significantly better after he or she had the Suboxone in the office.

WITHDRAWAL TREATMENT

If a person goes through withdrawal as an inpatient, it can take anywhere from two to four days before he or she is feeling better. Until recently, inpatient withdrawal consisted of observation and giving the patient benzodiazepines such as Valium, Librium, clonazepam, Ativan, or the drug Clonidine. Clonidine is a drug used for treating high blood pressure, but it helps alleviate opiate withdrawal symptoms, and is commonly used in the treatment of withdrawal. When an individual is released, he or she has to have substitution therapy, preferably with Suboxone, or they will start to crave and get withdrawal within a few days of release. Many inpatient detox programs are now using Suboxone or Subutex, the pure buprenorphine for inpatient detox. This shortens the hospital stay by a day or two, but the patient still needs the substitution therapy when he or she leaves.

I have seen a significant amount of resistance by inpatient detox centers to use the Suboxone for detox. I am not sure why this happens. Suffice it to say, detoxing as an outpatient, in an office setting is the preferred way to start the process of treatment. It compresses the three or four days of detox down to a half hour or an hour and allows the patient to do it in the dignity of an outpatient private office setting. It also allows patients to have comprehensive one-on-one interaction with a physician familiar with treating addictions. Along with feeling physically better, most patients feel mentally better when they understand that much of addiction is not under their control.

After the first dose is given, most patients have calmed down and are feeling much less withdrawal. We then discuss addiction in detail. I tell our patients and/or their families about the characteristics of opiates, causing first pain relief, then euphoria and breathing suppression. I explain that if you give one hundred people an opiate for the first time, ten out of the hundred will not like it at all, and will feel somewhat ill after taking it for the first time. I also tell them that eighty out of a hundred people will say, "I can take it or leave it." They cannot understand why people get addicted to the drug. I subsequently tell them that ten out of a hundred people will really like the medications. Of those ten, four will become dependent on the drug and start all of the behaviors associated with addiction. Since some people will get the opiate for the first time from an injury or as pain relief for surgical or dental problems, they still could be in the four out of a hundred who are prone to addiction. If you are in that four out of a hundred prone to addiction and you have a good support system and no issues of abuse, self-esteem, or serious psychological problems, you are less likely to get dependent than someone who has one or more of those problems.

If you are in the four out of a hundred prone to addiction and you have, for instance, self-esteem issues, or a history of abuse in your past or present situation, you are very likely to become dependent and addiction could follow. We talk about the fact that this propensity for addiction is biochemical and most likely has a genetic basis. I also discuss that much of this is out of the individual's control and how addiction is more like a medical problem such as diabetes or hypertension. Most people, who have never heard this before, are extremely relieved to know that this is a disease and not a serious behavioral issue manifested by a weak or immoral person. I also tell patients that addiction is a *disease* manifested by behavioral problems, but a disease nonetheless. We talk about the other characteristics of opiates and how dependent and addicted people have a different way of handling these medications. I describe the concept of tolerance, of needing more of the drug to get the same effect. I explain how addicted people tend to exhibit tolerance much more often than non-addicted people, and the difference between dependence, in which stopping the drug causes withdrawal and crossing the line to addiction. Addiction is a process of compulsion to use a drug, including continued use of the drug in spite of knowing it is bad, and loss of control of the dosing. To demonstrate this loss of control of the dosing, I ask patients, "If you were to get a hundred hydrocodone, how long would they last?" They admit they could never make it last more than a few days. They start to see what how this loss of control is a part of their problem. We also talk about how the drug has really controlled them, and how they have lost control over their lives. I tell them about our patients who use the drugs for pain relief; they generally do not build tolerance and are able to use only three or four a day, sometimes less, to control their pain, without completely using up the drug before their next prescription is due. I describe people with pain using it to relieve pain, not trying to get a high or euphoric, so they at least see the contrast. It helps patients understand how the addicted brain chemistry differs from the brain that utilizes the opiate only for relief of pain.

After we talk about the characteristics of opiate medications, I discuss how Suboxone works. We cover how it has a strong affinity for the opiate receptor. It also has a very long duration of action, so that they only have to take it once or twice a day, and finally, how it is only a partial agonist or stimulator of the receptors so that it should not cause euphoria and will not cause death except under extremely unusual circumstances. Death has been reported taking very large doses intravenously. Serious side effects such as breathing suppression can occur if the Suboxone is taken with large doses of sedating tranquilizers. These side effects are more common with pure buprenorphine. These side effects are very rare compared to full agonist opiates. We talk a little bit about the history of drug treatment, and how we have changed our thinking to treat it more like a disease process. There is also the use of substitution therapy and the difference between Suboxone and methadone and how Suboxone therapy is now becoming the preferred treatment method. Then there are the mandates of using Suboxone and being in a Suboxone program as outlined by the legislation in the DATA 2000 Act. I tell patients about the mandate of only thirty patients per physician waiver, and the restriction of one hundred patients per physician after one year if the physician applies for another waiver. We also outline requirements that mandate that patients being treated with Suboxone have to be in counseling and have to stay clean while on Suboxone. Patients are told that these are mandates, not my rules, and they will have to follow them if they want to stay in the program. I reinforce the positive points about Suboxone, such as being able to do this as an outpatient in a private office setting and not having to go every day to get medication as a patient would in a methadone maintenance program. We also talk about the requirement of signing an agreement, which outlines all of the rules. I have never had a patient refuse to sign this after I explain the reasoning and rationale for doing it. At this point in the process, I will answer any questions they or their parents have. Sometimes I will see the teenager alone and then bring the parents in, especially if they have some issues such as legal or other sensitive issues that they don't want discussed with their parents. At some point, however, the parents come into the room and will hear what I have told their son or daughter.

The next step in the process is to cover the reasons people get addicted. We discuss the fact that the vast majority of these people have a biochemical propensity for addiction. We talk about issues of abuse or perceived abuse in their present or past situations and how this has affected their self-esteem and how we have to work on these issues for them to get better and have a "normal" life. This topic usually brings up a lot of questions. For some, it is a relief to know that they will be able to discuss their issues of abuse. For most of them, it is a time when they finally realize that someone understands how they feel inside. This is a time when many of these kids share stories of how they have disappointed their parents, teachers, and family. Many express the feeling that disappointing their parents is the worst part. Usually this is when they share their first experience with opiates. Most did not feel high, but it was the first time they felt "normal." It was only after they started using increased doses of the medication that they started to feel the euphoria. They all describe the downward spiral of needing more of the drug to get same effect and not feeling high but using the drugs so they do not feel the awful symptoms of withdrawal. They talk about how they accelerated their use to the point where they had to go to stronger drugs and finally to snorting the drug. Many reveal snorting then injecting heroin after the "pills" no longer relieved the withdrawal symptoms. The low cost and availability of heroin make it a drug used frequently after teens have used high doses of Oxycontin or hydrocodone. As stated previously, almost all of these teens started using drugs sometime between age nine and fourteen. Most start by sneaking alcohol from their parent's supply. After a year or so, they start smoking marijuana with their friends, and then accelerate to ecstasy, cocaine, and/or mushrooms. Most do not like those three, and when exposed to hydrocodone, which is almost universally the first opiate they try, they describe a feeling of normalcy. Ecstasy, cocaine, and mushrooms exacerbate their anxiety because they are deficient in calming neurotransmitters. Within six months to a year of using hydrocodone, many are using so much that they have to go on to oxycodone, then OxyContin, and within a year, they are usually using fentanyl patches or morphine.

Addicts find innovative ways to use fentanyl patches by either snorting it or scraping off the gel and smoking it or inserting it rectally. When first introduced to heroin, they usually start by snorting, with few exceptions. A few actually start by injecting the heroin before they snort it, but this is an exception. As stated previously, over 90 percent of these young teenagers start with legally prescribed opiate drugs, usually hydrocodone, from either a family member or a friend. Sometimes it is prescribed for them after a dental or surgical procedure, but rarely for a pain issue not related to a dental or surgical problem. Most start to realize they have a serious problem when they get to the heroin stage. Luckily, some get intervention before this because they have legal issues or their parents discover they have a drug problem. This is another point where they are relieved to know they are not that much different from other teenagers, except for the biochemical issue and the fact that they are self-medicating to cover up a negative thought process.

As mentioned earlier in this book, I discuss the facts of trying to treat addiction with no help. For instance, if they try to quit cold turkey, they have about a 3 three in a 1000 chance of staying clean for one year. If they go to inpatient rehab for 30 or 60 days, they have a 17 to 20% chance of staying clean for one year, about an 80 to 83% chance of failing and not staying clean. On the other hand, statistics for Suboxone treatment reflect that 80 to 85% stay clean after one year if they follow the protocol of substitution therapy along with counseling.

WHAT WILL HAPPEN IF THEY DO NOT STOP DRUGS?

At this point, usually in front of their parents, I discuss issues that bring the most emotional response. After I have explained the program, how opiates work, how addicted people get addicted, how substitution therapy works, and that there is hope for them, I will tell them the following: If you do not stop using drugs

within the next five years, there are only six possibilities of what
will happen:

1. You will deal drugs. You will never have enough resources
   to support your habit without dealing drugs.
2. You will be in jail or prison. You will eventually do something illegal that will get you incarcerated.
3. You will develop a serious infection like AIDS, endocarditis or hepatitis. Usually it will be from using a dirty or
   infected needle. I tell them the story about the young
   man who ended up with the infected heart valve, had a
   stroke, needed a pacemaker, and was partially paralyzed.
4. You will become a prostitute. When I tell them this, many
   of the females get emotional and start crying, sometimes
   because they are already prostituting, have seriously considered doing it, or have been pressured to prostitute. For
   some, they had not even considered this as a possibility and
   now are faced with that down the road. It is not uncommon in a addiction practice to have a young female prostitute end up dead from an overdose or violence against
   them. This has, in fact, happened in our practice more
   than once, an extremely emotional issue for young female
   teens. When I say this to males, many get a little smile on
   their face, sometimes saying, "that wouldn't be so bad." I
   follow up by saying, "you will not be prostituting yourself
   with good-looking young women. It is more likely you will
   be doing it with pedophiles or dirty old men." I add, "You
   will likely despise what you're doing."
5. You will end up dead, most likely from an overdose, violence, or infection. The life expectancy of an intravenous
   heroin user is very short; after an addicted person starts
   injecting, he or she has a life expectancy of fifteen to
   twenty years.

6. You could end up in a vegetative state. You may also be left with a serious traumatic brain injury from the drug. The only thing worse than death is wishing you are dead. I tell the story of a young college student, Gregg, who was very bright. Gregg was not a full-blown addict; he "dabbled" in heroin—a "social user," so to speak. He was home from college and used heroin while his parents were away at dinner. When his parents came home, they found him unconscious, and he was rushed to the hospital. When he got to the hospital, he was comatose but they were able to resuscitate him. Unfortunately his MRI showed severe damage to the white matter in his brain, which is the area relating to higher thought processes. This occurred because of the prolonged period of anoxia or lack of oxygen to the brain. Initially his parents hoped he would have a complete recovery. He spent months, then years, in rehab facilities and now has limited capabilities. Gregg is now unable to walk and is in a wheelchair. After years of intense rehab, he will likely be someone with limitations for the rest of his life. He is extremely courageous and never gives up. His parents have devoted their lives to helping him regain normal function. It is unfortunate that his extreme courage and effort couldn't be used to better his life, rather than regain basic functions. He has found unbelievable strength and resolve from his drug addiction, which is a positive.

We had a similar patient in our practice who was resuscitated and was on life support for weeks. After initially hoping for a full recovery, the parents began praying for her to die. They knew their young teenage daughter would have a life of institutionalization and reliance on aides for even her most basic human functions. Ultimately she died. In both cases, whether a child lives and has limited function, or whether a child dies, the family is changed forever. The death of a child is among the worst experiences a human can have. Sometimes after the death of a child parents feel they have to contribute something to make up for that loss.

One of our most touching experiences occurred after one of our patients died from an overdose of fentanyl. Alison was eighteen years old and was actually doing well on Suboxone. She was addicted to fentanyl prior to seeing us. One day Alison decided to stop the Suboxone and "get high" with a friend. If Suboxone is stopped, addicted people know they can get high after about twenty-four hours. What many do *not* know is the receptors for the opiates become sensitized after they have been on Suboxone. It takes much less of an opiate to give them a high than previous amounts. Alison did not know that. She apparently used the same dose of fentanyl that she used prior to Suboxone treatment. Unfortunately, after one dose her breathing suppressed to the point where she was unresponsive and was found by her parents. She did not make it to the hospital. Alison's parents came to my office about two weeks after her death to explain what had happened. I thought they came to share the grief and inform me of their daughter's passing. They were there to inform me of her passing, but they were more concerned about opening up a spot in my Suboxone program for another teenager in need of treatment. They did not want another parent to go through what they went through with their daughter and wanted to expedite another addicted teen getting in our program. This is just one sad commentary on the horrors of addicted teens and a system that only allows a hundred patients to be treated by each physician.

After I explain to our young patients and their parents what could happen to them if they do not quit, we talk about counseling. Counseling is mandated by the buprenorphine program guidelines and with good reason. We discuss the types of counseling available. Patients can do drug counseling through an agency, they can counsel at our center with one-on-one counseling, or they can do counseling through a private psychologist or social worker. I am somewhat biased about agency counseling for teenagers, because of their unrealistic demands as mentioned earlier.

SPECIAL DEMANDS ON ADDICTED TEENS

There are several problems with these demands for teenagers. For one, many of them still go to school or are working, which helps build confidence and responsibility, something often lacking in the addicted. Is difficult to work and/or go to school if you are going to counseling several times a week and attending three group sessions. Even if kids could attend all these appointments, it interferes with homework and the normal socialization. This does not include socializing with known drug users or dealers, which is who make up these groups; one of the easiest places to obtain drugs is at a group meeting for addicts. Some of the groups and agencies have a negative view of using Suboxone or any substitution therapy as well. They have, in my opinion, an antiquated belief that you can only recover if you do not use any drugs during your recovery and maintenance phase. The fact is this is old thinking and not nearly as effective as substitution therapy. It shows a lack of understanding of the biochemical nature of addiction and the acknowledgment that this is a disease not a behavioral issue. Behavioral issues are a manifestation of the biochemical disease. Also, when teens attend group sessions, they are generally mixed with all age groups and all addictions. Some agencies do specifically have teenage or young adult groups, and we will discuss these later.

By attending a group session and being mixed with all age groups, addicted teens see a different spectrum of addicted people, many of whom are alcoholics and not opiate drug addicts. When a teenager attends a group where older alcoholics or opiate addicts are part of the group, a different message is delivered that they cannot relate to and may have a counterproductive outcome. Many of these older alcoholics and addicts believe, "once an alcoholic, always an alcoholic," or "once an addict, always an addict." Teens have difficulty relating to this for several reasons: They do not see themselves continuing in their present lifestyle and ending up the way these older alcoholics and addicts have ended up with their disease. Also, we teach kids that addiction is a treatable disease and that it goes into remission for long periods of time, sometimes for the rest of their lives. We are of the belief that addiction can be effectively treated to the point where patients consider themselves no longer addicted, even though they always have to be cautious about using opiates for any reason. We are also of the belief that if you help to rebuild the brain chemistry through counseling, lifestyle, and supplements, you can reverse some of the biochemical abnormalities of addiction, especially in young people.

When addicted teens hear that alcoholics and addicts believe that they will always be an alcoholic or addict, this is a contradiction to them. Because their brains are still developing, they can be confused as to what the truth really is. It is also difficult for them to relate to older "burned out" addicts who attend these groups and really have not improved as far as getting on with their lives. The groups sometimes take on the role of their socialization and support and replace career, education, and family, which is contrary to what we try to teach our young addicted patients. We want them to become independent, not dependent.

The problem with age-matched groups for addicts is that other young addicts will try to convince them to use drugs with them after the meetings. In addition, not everyone is on Suboxone, and if someone finds out you are on Suboxone, he or she may try to buy some. Additionally, many young teens are mandated to be in these groups through agencies and are not serious about getting better, so they can be a negative influence on a teen that is serious about quitting and is in a Suboxone program. We hear complaints from our young teens about people trying to score drugs and trying to buy Suboxone from them. When addicted teens even hear about using drugs, it reminds them of how they used to feel. If they are not far along in their recovery, it can initiate craving again, even if they are on Suboxone.

We talk about people, places, and things to avoid when teens are being treated for addiction. Sometimes these addiction treatment groups will have a negative effect on their craving and treatment instead of a positive effect. That is not to say that these groups are ineffective for all people. It is our opinion that they may not fit the needs of teen addicts and we have had better success with one-on-one counseling. I will also state that Alcoholics Anonymous has done remarkable things for many alcoholics and is very useful for many people. However, their model does not quite fit as well for teenage opiate addicts.

We strongly recommend one-on-one counseling, preferably in our office, because we get the best results when we are keeping a closer eye on the counseling. We work together for the best interest of the kids. Suffice it to say that counseling is an integral part of the recovery program, and even if it were not mandated, it is extremely important. If you recall the curve of Suboxone versus full agonist opiate, the euphoric area is what we are trying to treat with the counseling. Since addicted teens cannot get into that euphoric or numbing state with Suboxone, they need counseling as a substitute therapy.

We often get the question of how long someone has to stay in counseling. The answer is, it depends. It depends on the individual's social support network, whether significant abuse is an issue, whether the individual still craves drugs after being on Suboxone, how soon the individual has developed the tools to deal with issues of anxiety or stress, whether they have rebuilt self-esteem and relationships, and a multitude of other factors. These skills do not happen quickly. In general, if people have put their lives together, have had a minimum of six months to a year of no relapsing, and the counselor believes that they have completed a reasonable course of therapy and do not need further monthly therapy, we will allow them to continue in the program without the counseling. However, people who can maintain sobriety with only six or twelve sessions of therapy are usually those who have become addicted through prescribed medications for pain. Kids who become addicted because they wanted to get high usually take longer. Many patients continue counseling even after they are off Suboxone. They feel that they get good advice and enjoy the benefits of the counseling. If a person does not like the counseling or the counselor, he or she will not want to continue the counseling for any reason. Some teens want to quit because of the cost, especially when it is not covered by insurance. We are mandated to have people in counseling in the beginning of treatment, but they can "graduate" from regular counseling if they have resolved most of their issues and stay clean. As a matter of fact, we do not mandate "drug counseling" for teenagers. Instead, we mandate psychotherapy. The reason is that psychotherapy addresses the deeper issues that cause kids to want to alter their minds and emotions. These kids do have to be in some type of counseling, but for many, the drug counseling does not fit the needs of their treatment nor does it address their emotional needs, and we get better results with one-on-one counseling. We discuss counseling in detail in an upcoming chapter.

We get questions about how long individuals will have to be on Suboxone. In our experience, even under the best circumstances, we recommend being on Suboxone for at least six months. After that time, if patients have been able to taper down to no more than a half a film or 4 mg per day, we will start a final taper process. If patients are in need of 8 to 12 mg or one to one and a half of the 8 mg film per day, it is unlikely that they will be able to taper, due to craving or withdrawal. If they are able to maintain themselves on one half or less of the film per day (4 mg), we can begin the taper process. I generally recommend patients decrease by no more than 2 mg every two weeks. At some point, if they cannot taper further they will get withdrawal and/or craving. When they reach that point, they have to maintain that level for several weeks to several months before they try to taper further. The reason is that the receptors reach a point were the inherent manufacture of the neurotransmitters they are lacking cannot keep up with the taper process, so they have deficiencies and start getting craving and/or withdrawal. We will discuss ways to rebuild these neurotransmitters later. We have a number of patients who taper down to very low doses, sometimes as low as ½ mg or a sliver of the film per day. If patients go below that, they get craving and withdrawal, so they maintain themselves on that dose. This seems to be the endpoint for a large segment of the population. We justify staying at ½ mg by explaining that if these patients were diabetic and were on insulin, they may need to stay on the insulin indefinitely even if they watch their diet and exercise. Since the biochemical aspect of addiction is similar to diabetes, they seem to understand and accept it as reasonable.

A smaller segment of the population begins a taper process after three months and these individuals are able to get off of the Suboxone completely. We do not recommend this before three months and usually recommend at least six months of treatment. This gives the receptors a chance to recover from the opiate dependents. Typically these are patients that became addicted after an injury or surgical procedure and do not have a lot of the psychosocial issues of many addicted people. These are what I would call "biochemically addicted people." They usually do not have the social or psychological issues of the more addicted patients. That is not to say that they can safely use opiates in the future. If they use opiates in the future, it essentially triggers the whole process again. It's like clicking the icon on your computer. It could be inactive for years and if you click it once, it starts a whole cascade of events that leads to dependence and addiction.

IS ADDICTION BIOCHEMICAL OR BEHAVIORAL?

An ongoing debate is occurring about how much of addiction is biochemical and how much is environmental. In my view, the answer depends on the person. All addicted people have biochemical and environmental issues. Some have more biochemical than environmental, and some have more environmental than biochemical. It is not always easy to tell where an addicted person falls on that spectrum. Dr. Cherie Santasiero mentions this briefly later on. It becomes much clearer after an individual has had substitution therapy and counseling for at least six months.

As a holistic provider, questions usually come up about ways to restore the brain's biochemical imbalances. For many people, lifestyle, diet, and supplementation will help to restore these imbalances. Many of these imbalances are due to lack of vitamins, minerals, essential fatty acids, amino acids, or other nutrients. We recommend regular exercise, which helps to restore endorphins and a good diet, which includes lots of fruits and vegetables, preferably organically grown, and avoidance of junk food and processed foods. We recommend B vitamins, a good multivitamin, and vitamin D-3 after checking vitamin D levels. We like to keep a patient's vitamin D level somewhere between 40 and 60, which has to be checked by a physician or other health provider. In addition, a patient needs to eat nutrient dense protein. This includes fish, organically grown chicken, and grass-fed lean beef. We like to keep the vitamin B 12 level in the high normal range, generally between 800 and 1000. We also recommend the supplement GABA, which can be bought over-the-counter. The one we sell is a wafer form, which is chewable and gets into the system fairly quickly; it is a form of GABA called PharmaGABA. Several vitamin companies sell it. It is a form of GABA that can get into your brain more easily because it can get through a natural barrier called the blood-brain barrier. Over-the-counter GABA is identical to the neurotransmitter GABA and will calm down the receptor that is sometimes crying out for this calming chemical.

We like to assess the neurotransmitters with a questionnaire that gives us an idea of what brain chemicals are deficient. We previously mentioned the questionnaire by Eric Braverman, MD, which we find very useful. It closely matches what we have found by doing blood sampling for neurotransmitters, and we almost never do the sampling after they have done the questionnaire. Blood sampling can be tricky because the levels of the neurotransmitters fluctuate so much in a day. It is like taking a snapshot of something that really needs a video to get a good understanding of what is happening in the patient. It would be impossible to give an entire list of supplements that we recommend because every person has a different chemical makeup. When patients take the Braverman questionnaire, we can tailor the supplements to their needs.

It is important that sleep is reestablished; it is an imperative part of recovery. We like to use herbal products such as melatonin, 5-HTP, GABA, L-theonine, passionflower, and Valerian. These can be found in combination at health food stores and at our center. These are to be used with caution when a patient is on other psychotropic drugs, including antidepressants and antianxiety drugs. They should be used only under the supervision of a health provider who is familiar with the use of holistic approaches to treating disease. If someone has severe anxiety, we also use other proven modalities such as meditation, hypnosis, and acupuncture.

Acupuncture can be useful with addicted patients, especially for the withdrawal phase. There is no substitute for a healthy lifestyle and diet in the treatment of addiction. It is rare to see someone come off Suboxone therapy without doing the holistic approaches as outlined above. Many people deplete their body of essential nutrients by being exposed to toxins that could be chemical or emotional. Chronic stress will deplete our bodies of these calming neurotransmitters so replenishing them is only half the story. A toxic relationship can be just as damaging as exposure to chemical toxins and junk food. It is important to deal with these toxic relationships through counseling.

Smoking is probably the worst thing you can do to yourself. It is very difficult to restore the brain's normal balance of biochemicals and neurotransmitters if you smoke. We cover the restoration of sleep, lifestyle changes, dietary optimization, removal of toxins, emotional and chemical aspects, exercise, and supplementation for patients that want to make major changes in their lives and control their addictions. It is the holistic approach that results in the best outcomes. To think that substitution therapy with Suboxone and some counseling resolves the addiction is a simplistic and unrealistic paradigm. Optimization of all the elements mentioned above achieves the best results.

THE DAY OF TREATMENT AND THE TREATMENT CONTRACT

On the first visit, after a patient has had the induction with Suboxone, he or she almost invariably states that they feel better than they have in a long time. This is after the very first dose in the office. At this point, if the patient has no questions, we have him or her sign the agreement for treatment with a buprenorphine contract. In the contract, he or she agrees to the following:

1. Ongoing counseling. This can be a 12-step recovery program, a faith based program, a formal drug treatment program, or one-on-one counseling. I have discussed my preferences above.

2. A physician will coordinate the medication switch from the opiate to buprenorphine, which we do during the first visit.

3. The patient will come to his or her first visit while in withdrawal, which we outline in the initial telephone conversation, and he or she receives their first dose of Suboxone or buprenorphine in the office under the supervision of a physician.

4. Take-home doses and frequency of visits will be determined by how well the patient is doing, as determined by the physician.

5. The patient will not allow anyone else to take the buprenorphine. We are extremely strict about this one. If we find the patient is selling the buprenorphine or giving it to another person, he or she will be dismissed immediately.

6. The patient shall not to take any other medications with the buprenorphine without prior permission from us. This is particularly important for medications like Librium, Valium, Xanax, Ativan, or any other benzodiazepine. Although rare, combinations of benzodiazepine with buprenorphine or Suboxone can be fatal. This is especially dangerous if the patient injects pure buprenorphine without the naloxone. I have yet to see a serious reaction taking sublingual buprenorphine with an oral benzodiazepine.

7. Buprenorphine is an opiate-like drug and can produce physical dependence that is similar to other opiates. If the patient stops the buprenorphine, he or she will experience some withdrawal, although not as severe as with full stimulation or full agonist opiates such as hydrocodone, oxycodone, morphine, heroin, or fentanyl. If the patient has been compliant with the supplementation, the withdrawal symptoms are usually less intense.

8. The goal of treatment of opiate dependency is to learn to live without drugs of abuse. However, buprenorphine

treatment shall continue as long as necessary to prevent relapse to opiate abuse, dependence, or addiction. This is added to assure the patient that we cannot dismiss him or her from the program as long as he or she follows the rules. However, when the patient is ready to come off of the buprenorphine, he or she has to be cautious about using any opiate, as it may cause relapse.

9. Periodic drug testing is done to detect early relapse and to document the progress of treatment. This will be done at the discretion of the provider. We generally drug test patients every visit until they are stable, and then we may drug test them every other visit.

10. Buprenorphine will be prescribed in quantities that last from visit to visit. The frequency of visits is determined by how well the patient is progressing but cannot be longer than thirty days. We can prescribe up to a 30-day supply, if the patient is doing well.

11. Lost prescriptions are considered a serious issue and may result in discontinuation of the buprenorphine and dismissal from the program. I have heard every excuse imaginable, from "the dog ate the pills," "I left them in the overhead bin of the airplane," "the prescription flew out of my car when I left here, before I could get it filled," "a burglar broke into my house and stole only the pills," "they were on the windowsill over my sink and the wind blew the pill bottle over and they fell down the drain," "my babysitter stole the pills," "my boyfriend took them from me because he doesn't think I should be on medication if I'm an addict." Addicted people sometimes have very "innovative" excuses. One of the most novel was an addict describing how he found some hydrocodone in the pocket of a jacket he was trying on at a department store, which is why he failed his drug test. We could write a whole chapter on excuses. If the prescription is

lost or stolen, it will not be replaced, even with a police report, except under very extreme circumstances. It is not uncommon for a person to say the pills were stolen and produce a legitimate police report that does not prove anything except that they were reported stolen. The diversion of this drug and other opiate drugs is extremely common. We will discuss diversion later. However, I emphasize to patients that they should not even call if they have lost the prescription, and they will have to deal with withdrawal until they are due again. Although this sounds draconian and heartless, after dealing with addicted people long enough, almost all physicians feel the same way about lost or stolen prescriptions. It also helps patients to learn some self-responsibility.

12. For women only: if a woman becomes pregnant, she needs to let us know because we switch to Subutex or pure buprenorphine, which we will discuss later.

13. If the patient misses an appointment, he or she risks being terminated from the program, unless he or she has a very good excuse.

After the patient reads the agreement, he or she signs it, and I witness the signature. This formalizes what they agree to. I also will point out that they have signed this agreement when they violate the rules they agreed to, and have to be terminated from the program. The contract is created from a template provided to the physician during the buprenorphine training. The provider has little ability to waiver from the terms of the contract.

Termination from the program occurs approximately 15 to 20 percent of the time. If a patient gets through the first six months without being terminated, the rate of termination drops to about 5 percent. Most terminations occur because of positive urine samples for illegal or un-prescribed drugs or missed appointments. We tend toward a little more leniency with teens for the first two visits, and we will sometimes allow a single positive urine if we reinforce that this cannot happen again. It is been my experience that if the teen is serious about getting better, he or she tends to follow the rules fairly well.

Before patients leave the office they are told that they have to do three things. First, they have to make an appointment for follow-up, usually at one or two weeks from the initial visit. Second, they are told to call me the next day to let me know how they are doing so we can adjust the dose. I also tell patients they can take another ½ to 1 film later that night if they are still having withdrawal. I explain that if they are taking the right dose, they will feel relatively normal. If they take too much, they will get some nausea, and if they are not taking enough they will feel a little bit of withdrawal or craving. I also reinforce that not taking the right dose and taking either too much or too little is not in their best interest. If they are trying to recover from addiction, they have to take the correct amount to make them feel relatively normal. It is surprising that many of these people do not know what normal is until after they have been on Suboxone for several weeks. Third, patients are told to make an appointment for counseling either at our office or through an outside agency or provider. Before they return for the next visit, they either have to have seen a counselor or have an appointment with a counselor. If the counselor is outside our center, the patient will have to present a note from him or her, or a counselor will have to contact us verifying that the patient is in counseling. For the vast majority of teens, I also tell them that their parents are allowed to call me to check on their status as part of the agreement for being in the program. I rarely get complaints about this. I will not request this if I believe there is any evidence of abuse by a parent or caregiver. I will at that point discuss the possibility of abuse with their counselor so they are aware of the situation.

The next day, nearly all patients call to update me on their progress. Most patients tell me they feel much better on the second day, and I tell them to call me after the fifth day. When they call me at that point, they invariably say, "I haven't felt this good in a long time." When I first started treating addicted teens, I thought this was an aberration. However, I would say this is the rule rather than the exception. One of the nice things about Suboxone is that because it partially stimulates the receptor, it makes many of them feel better than they've ever felt before. It is truly a life-changing drug for many people. I can also say that many people have attempted to quit opiate addiction without Suboxone and were unable to do it. With Suboxone, they can lead normal lives, start working again, and go back to school or start a career.

DIVERSION

What about diversion? There is no doubt that Suboxone is diverted and sold on the streets. However, it is less diverted than opiates. It is purchased at the pharmacy for anywhere from $8 to $9 per pill, or with insurance, it might even be obtained without a copay. It is sold on the streets for two to three times that. It does not take a genius to figure out that people will sell this drug, and, in fact, it does occur. If the drug is supposed to stop craving and does not give a high, the question comes up as to why it is sold on the streets. The answer is not simple. Sometimes Suboxone is diverted because if a person is getting pure buprenorphine or Subutex and it is in pill form, it can be ground up and snorted or even injected. This gives the user a slight euphoric or high feeling but not nearly what is experienced with opiates. We also discovered that even though the film is less diverted than the pill form, it can be melted and snorted. This is less likely to occur because it is messy, not easily done, and contains the antagonist naloxone, which will get partially absorbed if snorted, making the person ill if they absorb enough. Treated patients will sometimes stop the Suboxone to get high with an opiate. Sometimes they will sell the Suboxone on the streets, and use the money to buy an opiate. The Suboxone film has diminished the amount of diversion on the streets, but it still occurs. Subutex, which comes as a pill, is diverted more frequently.

We are always suspicious of patients who say they become ill from the Suboxone film as opposed to Subutex, because we know Subutex is diverted more frequently. That is not to say some people do not need Subutex. However, some addicted people have difficulty leaving their previous lifestyle behind. They are constantly tempted to deal drugs and return to places where they used or dealt drugs. Even though they are on a legal substitution for their opiate, they sometimes will have relapses and get into that lifestyle or attempt to get high again.

In my opinion, even though diversion occurs, more so with Subutex and pure buprenorphine than Suboxone, it is much less of a problem than the diversion of prescription opiates. I believe that if people are buying Suboxone on the streets, they are likely buying it to prevent the withdrawal symptoms, and it is less harmful than buying an opiate such as heroin. Many people buy Suboxone on the street because it is available, safer, and often cheaper than buying opiate pills. It is simply a supply and demand issue. Some enforcement officials have magnified the diversion of Suboxone. It is much safer to have Suboxone on the streets than heroin or opiates because it is almost impossible to die of an overdose of Suboxone and much more likely to overdose on opiates. Although this does not justify the diversion, it is the lesser of two evils. It is difficult for providers and prescribers to prevent this diversion.

We also suspect diversion if patients request three or more Suboxone film per day to control their symptoms. Requesting Subutex rather than Suboxone because of side effects on Suboxone is another red flag. As providers we try to counteract this by resisting the switch to Subutex. We may also do a random urine tests and call for the patient to come in that day for the test. We will call patients into the office for a film or pill count on twenty-four hours notice if we think there is a possibility of diversion or selling the drug. Although we do this on a random basis for our patients, we can target a specific patient if we feel it is justified. Many communities of addicts are not the most loyal to each other. We sometimes get reports from other addicts that a patient of ours is selling the drug on the street. Although it is difficult to prove, we can do random pill or film counts as a way to counteract this possible illegal behavior. Providers should be alerted to the fact that addicts may have a network to address a request from providers for a random pill or film count. They may borrow from each other if they are diverting or using more than they are supposed to use. We sometime see pills that look like they have been handled a number of times or are even dirty because they have been passed back and forth. The random pill or film count is by no means foolproof for providers, but it is a deterrent. Sometimes patients cannot get the "temporary supply" from friends, and we will find them short on the pill or film count.

SPECIAL SITUATIONS

Anxiety

Severe anxiety while on Suboxone is not uncommon. Opiate-addicted patients may continue to experience severe anxiety even after being treated. This is most likely because of their deficiency in GABA, a calming neurotransmitter, which as stated previously, is mimicked by the benzodiazepine drugs Valium, Librium, Xanax, and Ativan. Although many of these patients feel better on the Suboxone, some still have severe anxiety and mistakenly believe it is craving for the opiate. We try to address this with supplements, including GABA or B vitamins with amino acids to help restore their own GABA. In addition, we try to convince them to do meditation, relaxation therapy, exercise, or to try acupuncture as a substitute. Because these patients tend to be used to immediate gratification, they often are reluctant to try these modalities.

If anxiety becomes a serious issue, we have occasionally prescribed a benzodiazepine like Ativan, Xanax, or clonazepam. It is not our first choice, but if the patient continues with to have anxiety, he or she may relapse. If it is not due to being underdosed on the Suboxone, we sometimes are left with no choice but to try one of these prescription medications. A number of psychotherapists recommend a drug called buspirone (Buspar), which we have also tried. I would say I have mixed results with this medication and more often than not end up switching to a benzodiazepine. As stated previously, it is not our first choice but relapse is a distinct possibility if we do not address the anxiety. Again, it becomes the lesser of two evils.

PREGNANCY

Pregnancy changes treatment. If a woman becomes pregnant while taking Suboxone, we will switch her to Subutex to eliminate the possibility of the naloxone causing problems with the pregnancy. Initially, when Suboxone came into the United States market, it was not known what effect Subutex or Suboxone would even have on pregnancy. It was the practice at that time to switch them from Suboxone to methadone, but this was quickly abandoned. After almost ten years of experience with Subutex, most providers believe it is safer to switch a woman to Subutex than methadone. Again, neither is a great alternative. If a baby is born to a mother on methadone, the baby almost invariably has a withdrawal syndrome and has to be in the hospital for a prolonged period of time to get through the withdrawal. When Suboxone first came out, if a child was born to a mother on Suboxone or Subutex, the child was treated as a methadone baby and detoxed for days to weeks with decreasing doses of methadone. It is my opinion that if a mother is on methadone while that child is developing, that child will develop methadone receptors and be at increased risk for addiction later in life. This coupled with the fact that the mother has a propensity for addiction could likely increase the chance of addiction for that child later in life. In my practice when we switch the mother to Subutex, we try to taper the dose as low as possible during the last trimester of pregnancy. If the pregnant woman tries to taper too quickly they experience withdrawal. I explain this stresses the baby, because they likely experience the same symptoms. It is important to taper at a reasonable rate for both mother and baby. We try to balance any withdrawal the mother might experience with tapering as low as we can get. If the mother is on 4 to 8 mg Subutex per day at the time of delivery, the chance of the baby experiencing significant withdrawal is relatively low. If she can get to 4 mg of Subutex, the chance of withdrawal is extremely low. There is no easy answer to this, but tapering the Subutex as low as possible and aiming for a goal of one half pill per day (4 mg) in the third trimester gives the baby the best chance of not needing treatment for withdrawal. After delivery, the mother can either increase the dose of Subutex or preferably going back to Suboxone film. If the mother is breastfeeding, we do not know if these drugs pass through the breast milk, so we do not recommend breastfeeding at this point. This will be a question that will be answered in the future. My experience to date with 4 mg Subutex at the time of delivery is very favorable. None of the newborns (approximately ten births) has required detox after delivery. All newborns left the hospital with the mothers. The numbers are low, but the results have been very good. I strongly advise new mothers on Suboxone to find a pediatrician familiar with Suboxone in newborns. Your newborn is less likely to be put on methadone if the pediatrician has experience with Suboxone. Also, new mothers are less likely to be treated with prejudice.

PAIN

There are sometimes pain issues while on Suboxone. Pain is a complicated issue for an addicted person. If I get a call from an addicted person who is on an opiate for pain, and they developed an addiction, my first question is what are they going to do for the pain if they go off the opiate? Many times, patients do not have an answer. If I suggest a modality such as acupuncture, and a patient refuses, I am reluctant to treat that patient and most likely will not accept him or her in the Suboxone program. If the pain is relatively minor, we can deal with it using non-opiate pain relievers, such as nonsteroidal anti-inflammatories, including Motrin, Naprosyn, Aleve, Celebrex, and so forth. We also have other drugs that are used, such as tramadol (Ultram). I have found tramadol to be relatively effective for mild pain, but not good for treating moderate to severe pain. Tramadol does not generally interfere with the Suboxone treatment. Sometimes a pharmacist will call to notify me about a patient on Suboxone getting a tramadol prescription. I have not found a problem using both. Suboxone and Subutex may block some of the effect of the tramadol, because part of the effect on pain with the use of tramadol is with the *mu* receptor on the cells. Apparently it does not affect the same part of the receptor that is affected by opiates. The actual explanation is beyond the scope of this book. Probably acetaminophen (Tylenol) and aspirin are as reasonable as prescription drugs for mild to moderate pain. Occasionally I have seen pain-blocking agents as gabapentin (Neurontin), helpful for mild to moderate pain. This is likely because Neurontin is also a GABA mimicking drug. Dental pain is another common problem. It is treated the same way as other pains. Most dental procedures require significant pain relief for one or two days and can be treated with non-opiate pain relievers. We must remember that buprenorphine is also a low-level pain reliever and was originally approved for that purpose.

If a person is scheduled for surgery or has severe trauma, such as a fracture from an accident we usually only have one choice. We usually stop the Suboxone, and give them a lower dose of an opiate that will help to relieve pain but will not cause the euphoria. It is been my experience that a person being treated with

Suboxone can be regulated with an opiate pain reliever if we stop the Suboxone and adjust the dose to relieve pain and not create euphoria. In an elective situation, we recommend stopping the Suboxone for twenty-four hours before the procedure and then using hydrocodone for pain. We prefer to manage pain medication for our Suboxone patients, but this is not always true for other Suboxone-prescribing physicians. Many are not comfortable prescribing pain medicines. After the pain has subsided, we stop the opiate painkiller and restart the Suboxone. This is done with a mini-induction method where we stop the opiate for twenty-four hours and substitute the Suboxone, usually with minimal problems. In an emergency situation with someone on Suboxone, in which an individual experiences severe trauma, such as in a car accident, it is imperative that emergency physicians know the individual is on Suboxone. The individual can get pain relief with parenteral, intravenous, or intramuscular opiates for pain if a physician, usually an anesthesiologist, who is familiar with Suboxone treatment, regulates them. In the inpatient setting, this can be done with good results. In my experience, most of the people with acute pain do very well with short-term opiates and are anxious to go back on the Suboxone because they have experienced what it is like to stay off the opiates. It's important to note that tolerance is developed to the euphoric effect of an opiate, and not to the painkilling effect. Therefore, relatively low doses of these drugs will give good pain relief.

Pain relief is a murky area with regards to Suboxone. There is a preparation called Butrans, which is a low dose of buprenorphine and naloxone that is used for pain relief. Although it is illegal for a doctor to use Suboxone for pain relief unless they have a waiver from the government, he or she can use Butrans for pain relief. Butrans only comes as a patch, and it is in a relatively low dose compared to Suboxone. This is very confusing to the average provider, because he or she may not be sure of the difference between Suboxone and the Butrans. It must be remembered that, as stated above, buprenorphine originally came out as a lower level opiate-like painkiller, which is why Butrans can be used for pain. You cannot use Butrans for opiate addiction treatment, and you cannot use Suboxone for pain relief. Even providers of Suboxone for addiction are not allowed to use Suboxone for pain relief because of the way the laws are written. In fact, if I were prescribing Suboxone for pain patients, they would count against the hundred-patient limit I am allowed to have for Suboxone. The use of Butrans for pain and Suboxone for addiction has been a complex area for most providers to comprehend. I suspect most providers avoid using Butrans for pain relief because of this confusion. To date, the use of Butrans for pain is a rare occurrence. In general, if confusion exists about a method of treatment, most doctors will revert to what they are comfortable with treating. The low utilization of Butrans for pain will likely result in the manufacturer's rethinking the strategy.

In my experience, a number of patients who are on Suboxone for addiction who have dental extractions or relatively minor pain are more than willing to try a nonsteroidal anti-inflammatory for pain relief and do very well with this medication. If these patients need an opiate for pain, ten to twelve pills are usually enough. I would discuss this issue with your dentist. If the dentist writes for more than that number, request a prescription for less, especially if it is for your child. When he or she needs the opiate painkillers for severe surgical pain or trauma, he or she also seems to do very well and rarely relapse if they are monitored closely.

HOLISTIC TREATMENTS

Diet

It is important that patients follow a strict very healthy diet when they are trying to get over any addiction. Many of these patients have protein or essential nutrient deficiencies. Without the proper diet and without the proper nutrition, they cannot make the normal neurotransmitters that are lacking. A large percentage of the opiate-addicted teenagers lack GABA. A significant portion also lacks serotonin, or the serotonin deficiency may be their most significant deficiency. If they are not eating enough protein or essential nutrients, they cannot make these two chemicals. When they use the opiate, although it isn't a perfect match, it is enough of a match to stimulate the receptor and will satisfy the brain's needs in the beginning. After teens use the opiates long enough, because they are much more potent than eating the right food and making the neurotransmitters in their own body, the opiates then become the preferred food, so to speak, for the receptors. It is important that teens follow a healthy diet, which includes lots of fruits and vegetables, preferably organically grown. If they eat red meat, it should be relatively lean and organic or grass-fed beef. Beef should be eaten only three times per week, preferably less. Chicken should be free-range and organic, and fish should be wild rather than farm raised. Without going into a lot of detail about organic versus nonorganic, suffice it to say the additives in the nonorganic foods can have negative effects on the brain chemistry. They stimulate hormone receptors that should not be stimulated and can cause early onset of puberty in females and weight gain or breast development in males, called gynecomastia. Other added chemicals also mimic hormones. For instance, some pesticides mimic estrogen. Estrogen and other hormones also affect our behavior. It is these pesticides, and other nonorganic additives, that may affect the behavior of addicted teenagers. A good diet does *not* include junk food, sugar, soda, artificially sweetened foods or drinks, or any processed foods.

Avoidance of alcohol is especially important because it may be substituting for the addictive substance, and it has no nutritional value. Although wine has some positive attributes, especially red wine, it is still alcohol and is forbidden when treating addiction. We rarely allow wine for older addicted patients, even in small amounts, after they are off Suboxone, because it is playing with fire. It is never allowed in treating teen addicts. The negative effects of alcohol far outweigh the positive benefits of drinking the red wine. Some patients argue that red wine has health benefits. Red wine contains small amounts of resveratrol, an antioxidant, but it does not outweigh the negative affects of alcohol. Besides, resveratrol is available in capsule form without alcohol. Virtually every physician who prescribes Suboxone does not allow alcohol while in treatment. Sometimes teenagers will argue that it is a legal substance, but we reply it is not allowed.

Junk food and table sugar can stimulate areas of the brain that will cause craving, in addition to the fact that they have no nutritional value, other than calories. Eating junk food, processed food, sugar, soft drinks, and foods exposed to pesticides is a huge problem in this population. If addicted patients are not willing to follow a healthy diet, everything else they do has limited benefits. You can only make up so much negative territory by adding supplements to a very poor diet.

Excercise

Exercise is also essential in recovery. It helps the body to make a quicker recovery, removes toxins through sweating, improves metabolism, burns off excess carbohydrate calories, and creates endorphins. Endorphins also help bind up opiate receptors to help the recovery process. I recommend that exercise should be something that the individual likes as opposed to recommending a specific exercise such as jogging or weightlifting. If someone does not like the exercise, he or she will not do it very long. A way to get individuals to exercise is to encourage it as part of building self-esteem. For instance, if an individual is slightly overweight, it can be used as a part of decreasing weight and resculpting body image. Self-esteem is critical for recovery, and exercise can be a good way to improve the physical self-esteem of an addicted person. Finding out what an individual likes to do is probably the most important part of getting him or her to exercise. If an individual does not like exercise, I recommend starting out walking just a quarter of a mile per day and increasing by about 10 percent every three to four days, until he or she is exercising at least thirty minutes three times per week. The patient should reach a point where it gets to be an accepted behavior, and he or she may even look forward to it because he or she will start to feel better physically, emotionally, and mentally.

Sleep

Reestablishing a sleep pattern is also important. Sleep is when we do most of our healing. In addition, it helps to balance some of the excitatory neurotransmitters that are created through stress. It also decreases cortisol formation, a stress hormone that is high in addicted individuals. Reestablishing sleep patterns helps the brain balance stress, and chemicals are manufactured that help the brain get into a pattern of homeostasis or balance. We do not generally recommend pharmaceutical sleep aids, especially as first-line treatment. None of them increases the deepest most restorative sleep called REM (rapid eye movement), a restful sleep needed by the brain. Most pharmaceutical sleep aids will put you asleep for a short time, but it is not a deep enough sleep to help the brain get a good biochemical recovery. Most also have very negative side effects, including, sleepwalking, bad dreams, or even a paradoxical stimulatory effect. If a patient has severe GABA deficiencies, we may put him or her on a benzodiazepine. I like to use clonazepam because it has a relatively long duration of action and it helps to calm patients down. Another drug called Trazadone (Desyrel) is an older antidepressant that seems to work fairly well as a sleep aid if pharmaceuticals are going to be recommended or prescribed. Trazadone is not ordinarily addictive, but a physical or emotional dependence can occur. It is best to use it short term, in the range of five to ten days to help reestablish sleep pattern, and then to slowly taper by using it every other day or by decreasing the dose. The preference is to use nonpharmaceutical aids for sleep and there are some good ones. These would include taking a hot bath with either Epson salts, ½ cup per tub, or adding oil of lavender to a warm bath. Epsom salts have magnesium, which is absorbed through the skin and helps relax many patients. This is effective especially for people who have chronic muscle aches, which keep them awake, especially if they have had fibromyalgia and have become addicted to narcotics because of the fibromyalgia. We also use melatonin in the range of one 2 to10 mg at bedtime. We usually start someone with 1 mg, use that for three days, and then slowly increase the dose by one to 2 mg increments until 10 mg is reached. It is our experience that if 10 mg does not help, it is not likely to be a good remedy for sleep. Melatonin can cause vivid and sometimes disturbing dreams in the beginning, but this will usually pass with time. Another remedy is 5-hydroxytryptophan (5-OH tryptophan), or 5-HTP. We start with 50 mg at bedtime, increase it the same way you would melatonin, but by 50 mg increments until we reach 200 mg. If 200 mg at bedtime does not help the patient's sleep we do not continue with it. 5-HTP is best taken a half-hour to one hour before bedtime so it can metabolize into serotonin, which is what makes you tired. Melatonin and 5-HTP should be avoided if the patient is on any of the SSRI antidepressants, such as Prozac, Paxil, Effexor, Zoloft, Cymbalta, or Celexa or any other SSRI. The SSRIs, as you will recall, cause serotonin to stay in the synaptic space longer, and 5-HTP can increase the total amount of serotonin that will cause a reaction. Use of 5-HTP with an SSRI requires intervention by a physician who is familiar with using them together. Usually we start tapering the SSRI while using the 5-HTP. We do not recommend you do this on your own.

You can also take GABA at bedtime. This is not well absorbed orally and has difficulty getting into the central nervous system or brain. To get around this, you can try a form of GABA called PharmaGABA in wafers that are chewable and absorbed through mucous membranes in the mouth. The dose is usually 500 mg to start and you can work your way up to 2000 mg at bedtime. We use a product called PharmaGABA made by Designs for Health, but it is made by other companies as well. The dose is 200 mg to start. You can increase the dose up to 800 mg. Some people respond very well to this, while some people do not absorb it very well or do not respond well to this treatment. We also have used an amino acid called L-theonine. The dose of this can be started at about 200 to 250 mg at bedtime increasing in increments of 250 until 1000 mg is reached. Also, the herb passionflower at a dose of 250 mg increasing to about 1000 mg is useful. Valerian root from 250 mg to 1000 mg at bedtime can be calming for many people. You can also get these natural products in combination. I have seen combinations that contain most of these in one preparation. Is has been our experience that they either work well or not at all.

The usual recommendation for reestablishing sleep patterns also holds here. Things such as only going to bed when you are tired, not watching TV before bedtime in your bedroom, and only using your bedroom for sleep, are critical. If you go to your bedroom while anxious, you may associate the bedroom with anxiety, which will inhibit sleep. It is important to avoid doing anything stimulating just before bedtime, such as computer work or activities that require a lot of thinking; light, from computers or other sources diminishes melatonin in the brain. Reading at bedtime can be helpful especially if after a short time it makes you sleepy. Is important to follow your body's signals and put down the book when you are tired, otherwise your brain will make excitatory chemicals that counteract the calming effect of the reading and you will not be able to sleep. Exercise before sleep can be very useful if it is done one to two hours before bedtime. Some people find this makes them tired, others find it stimulating. You have to see into which group you fall.

Supplements

Supplements are essential for restoring brain chemistry. Most addictive people in treatment need vitamin B-complex. Vitamin B-complex contains most of the B vitamins essential for normal nervous system function and production of neurotransmitters. The most important ones are folate and vitamin B12. A significant percentage of the population has difficulty metabolizing the form of folic acid that is found in many supplements. For some people, folic acid (folate) may not be able to be metabolized into the useful form of folate called methylfolate. We check patients for something called an MTHFR mutation. MTHFR stands for methyltetrahydrofolate reductase, an enzyme that converts folic acid to the more usable form of folate called tetrahydrofolate. If you have the MTHFR mutated gene for making the reductase enzyme, you are not able to convert enough folic acid to the usable form of methyltetrahydrofolate. Methyltetrahydrofolate is used in the synthesis of essential neurotransmitters utilized by the brain that modulates emotions, behavior, and general health. You can be checked for this mutation through a blood test. However, unless your physician is familiar with this mutation, he or she will not know what you are talking about. If you have the genetic mutation, you will need to take methylfolate or 5-methyltetrahydrofolate. These are forms of folate that are biologically active and usable for biochemical reactions, even if you have the gene mutation. Folate is essential for your health, repair of DNA, protein synthesis, and production of neurotransmitters, along with other essential chemical reactions in your body. It is also critical for treatment of addiction. If you cannot find a physician to check you for the MTHFR mutation, you can take methylfolate or 5-methyltetrahyrofolate instead of folic acid. The dose is 1000 mcg per day. Note that 1000 micrograms (mcg) equals 1 milligram (mg). A microgram can be abbreviated as mcg or *ug*. Many B-complex supplements already contain methylfolate or 5-methyltetrahydrofolate but not always in a sufficient amount.

In addition, virtually every addicted person needs a good multivitamin and mineral preparation. Make sure that the supplement says that the manufacturer has subjected it to quality assurance testing, which most will gladly display on their label. Good supplements will always tell you that they have been tested for quality assurance and will list every ingredient and how many milligrams each of the ingredients has. The bottle will say something like "independently tested for authenticity, potency, solvent residue, stability, bacteria, yeast and mold counts." Be aware that companies can add binders or fillers, wheat or gluten, milk/dairy, corn protein, soy protein, eggs, sugar, artificial coloring, artificial flavorings, or preservatives to their supplements. The good companies will verify they have none of these and that an independent company tested for quality assurance measures mentioned above. A good multivitamin will also contain vitamin A in the range of 5,000 to 10,000 units (IU), vitamin C 300 to 500 mg, vitamin D 400 to 1000 (IU) units, vitamin E 200 to 400 (IU) units per day. Most will contain some B vitamins but not usually enough, and you will usually have to supplement with B-complex. A good multivitamin should also contain zinc 10 to 30 mg, selenium 100 to 200 mcg, and usually some other essential minerals like copper 1 to 2 mg, manganese 3 to 5 mg and chromium 100 mcg. These are essential for manufacture of the neurotransmitters. You have to learn to read labels.

Ignore the percent of recommended daily allowance or RDA, as these levels are much too low. RDA can also be expressed as DV or daily value. Without going into a long explanation, the RDA is the amount of a supplement or nutrient the government has decided is needed in your daily diet to *prevent* a disease. Some of the studies on levels of RDA were done in the 1950s on very small populations. It is *not* the amount needed to promote health, which is what we are looking for, and it is not the amount for optimal wellness, which is an even higher dose. It is the amount of the vitamin that *prevents you from getting a disease.* A good example of this is vitamin C. To prevent severe vitamin C deficiency or scurvy, you only need 60 mg per day, which is the RDA. To promote health, you need much higher doses, in the range of 500 to 2000 mg per day. To achieve optimal wellness, the dose could be much higher depending on whether you have an illness or not. If you are acutely ill, for example if you have an upper respiratory infection, you may need much higher doses of vitamin C. These doses can be in the range of 5000 to 10,000 mg. If you take too much vitamin C, you will get diarrhea, so it is hard to take too much. Humans do not make vitamin C. All our vitamin C comes from our diet or supplementation. If you have a poor diet and do not supplement, you are likely vitamin C deficient.

Another trick used by the manufacturers is to say a serving size contains so many milligrams, IUs, micrograms, or a percentage of the RDA. It should be noted that all fat-soluble vitamins are expressed as international units (IU) instead of milligrams. This includes vitamin A, vitamin D, and vitamin E. A serving size can be anywhere from one to six capsules per day. Capsules per serving is usually identified at the top of the listings but in very small writing. For example: take two bottles of vitamin C. One cost $10 and contains thirty capsules. Each capsule is 600 mg, so one per day is a serving. The other bottle cost $18 and says "600 mg per serving" and has 180 capsules so people think they are getting a deal. The problem is that if each capsule is only 100 mg, you would need six capsules to equal just one serving. Many people presume the bottle with 180 capsules is a better deal, until they compare servings in milligrams for each bottle. With OTC brands, you do not always know what it contains besides the vitamin. Some contain heavy metals, yeast spores, or other unhealthy ingredients. You have to compare the actual serving sizes, costs, and how long each bottle will last. Become an educated consumer when you are taking supplements. Also, a vitamin may be listed as a percentage of RDA. The RDA for vitamin C is 60 mg. If the capsule contains 120 mg, it may be listed as vitamin C 200 percent of RDA. It sounds like a large dose, but it is really a small dose if you are trying to achieve optimal wellness.

Essential fatty acids are important for normal brain function. Omega-3 fatty acids are the most important in our culture because we do not generally eat enough of these. Omega-3 fatty acids come from either plant-based origin or marine-based foods. If you do not eat enough fatty fish such as salmon, you will not get enough omega-3 oils. Plant-based omega-3 oils come from foods such as olive oil. Unfortunately the Western diet is very high in something called Omega-6 fats. These are animal-based fats and are found in land-based protein sources such as beef and pork. Omega-3 fats are anti-inflammatory, which means they reduce inflammation, and they are essential for normal cell and nerve functioning. Our brains are predominantly made up of fat and protein. Omega-6 fats, on the other hand, are pro-inflammatory, meaning they cause inflammation. You might wonder if inflammation can be a good thing. The answer is simple. If you injure yourself, you need some inflammation to protect the area, but at some point the inflammation has to subside and allow the body to heal that area. If you have too much omega-6 fat in relation to the Omega 3 fat, you will get more chronic inflammatory diseases that are common in our culture. Imbalance of omega-6 fats to omega-3 fat is one of the main causes of inflammatory arthritis, cardiovascular disease, and degenerative disease. It also is an important aspect of addiction, because you cannot have a healthy nervous system unless you have enough omega-3 fat in our diet.

Generally, people in Asia eat a much greater proportion of omega-3 fats versus omega-6 fats, whereas Americans eat more omega-6 fats in relation to omega-3 fats. Think of omega-3 as the good guy and omega-6 as the not so good guy. Since our diet is lacking in omega-3, we have to supplement. We recommend 3000 mg of omega-3 fish oil or equivalent per day. This should be taken with food, as it is fat-soluble and better absorbed with food. We have to avoid another bad fat in order to be healthy, called trans fat, which is found in margarine. Trans fats are highly inflammatory. Typically we should use plant-based oils, either olive oil (extra virgin) or possibly flax oil, or canola oil as a backup. Extra virgin olive oil is by far the best oil for us. It contains a good amount of omega-3 but also a small amount of omega-6 and helps to complement the omega-3 fish oil capsules. In general, butter is much better than margarine. Although it is an animal-based fat, if the choice is between margarine and butter, butter wins hands down. If you have a choice, olive oil is better than butter. A good rule of thumb is that an oil is bad for you if it turns to solid form when refrigerated. An exception is coconut oil, which is semisolid until it is heated.

In addition to needing a good multivitamin and essential fatty acids, if an addicted person has a serotonin deficiency or a GABA deficiency, he or she also needs an amino acid called L-glutamine. The dose of L-glutamine is generally 1000 to 6000 mg per day. Although this sounds like a high dose, it is essential for rebuilding the neurotransmitters. Even in the rare case of a person lacking dopamine or another neurotransmitter, L-glutamine is essential to rebuild all neurotransmitters. In addition, L-glutamine is an essential nutrient to help reestablish normal intestinal flora. This is discussed this later.

If someone lacks serotonin in addition to the above supplements, we recommend 5- HTP, starting at a dose of 50 mg and working up to as high as 300 mg at bedtime. This has to be taken with the cautions mentioned above and adjusted under the supervision of a nutritionally oriented physician or provider. A physician or provider who is not educated or trained to use these supplements cannot do this. People who lack serotonin usually have difficulty with sleep and are anxious. Using 5-HTP at bedtime is the preferred way because it helps promote sleep.

GABA deficient patients also need the amino acid L-taurine in a dose of 1000 mg up to three times a day. They may also use the supplement GABA by itself. However, using GABA does not promote the nervous system to make GABA. By giving GABA to calm a person down, you are essentially signaling the nerve cells that there is enough GABA in the system already. This is a stopgap measure but can be useful. For some patients, giving L-taurine with the essential supplements mentioned above may not give them enough production of GABA to calm them down. As mentioned earlier, GABA deficiency is seen in the vast majority of opiate-addicted people and is especially common in teenage opiate addicts.

We try to test vitamin D-3 levels and vitamin B-12 levels in all patients being treated for addiction. Both of these vitamins are essential for keeping the nervous system and body in homeostasis. We aim for optimal levels of both, not just what is considered normal. For instance, "normal vitamin" D-3 levels are around twenty-five to thirty-five. We aim for levels of forty to sixty or even higher if the person has an acute problem or a propensity to serious diseases. Toxicity does not occur even at levels of about one hundred and likely does not occur until levels are above one hundred and fifty. Depending on the latitude where an individual lives, a healthy person needs approximately 4000 units of vitamin D per day to function normally and to replace quantities used. If we are deficient, we may need doses as high as 10,000 units a day to make up for the deficiency. If you are exposed to sunlight for twenty minutes to an hour without sunscreen in the summer in southern climates, your body will make up to 10,000 units. If you live in a northern climate from September to May, the sun is not bright enough to make enough vitamin D-3 needed through sun exposure. It is essential that you supplement to get your levels into the ranges mentioned above. This has to be done with a nutritionally oriented physician or provider.

Vitamin B-12 is an essential vitamin for treating addictions. Normal vitamin B-12 levels are reported by many labs to be two hundred or greater. We look at "optimal" levels of B-12, which are generally in the range of eight hundred to a thousand. Studies show that vitamin B-12 may not function in the central nervous system until you see levels of around six hundred. It is important that levels are checked before you start the supplementation and aim for a level between eight hundred and one thousand. Another problem with vitamin B12 is many people do not absorb it well orally. Exacerbating poor absorption, especially after age forty, are proton pump inhibitors, such as Prilosec (omeprazole), Nexium (esomeprazole), Prevacid (famotidine), and Protonix (pantoprazole). Proton pump inhibitors are used to treat indigestion and reflux symptoms, because they shut off the acid production in the stomach. Because the body needs some acid to absorb vitamin B12; proton pump inhibitors further prevent absorption. Vitamin B-12 deficiency is extremely common in people on these medications. Supplementation for B-12 has to be either sublingually, (under the tongue), or by injection. This would have to be done by your medical provider. To be absorbed and synthesized in your body orally, vitamin B-12 needs two cofactors: stomach acid and something called intrinsic factor, which is made in the stomach and bowel. In addition, a large portion of our population does not eat red meat, a major source of vitamin B-12. Optimizing vitamin B-12 and vitamin D is a critical aspect of a holistic approach to treating addictions. I also utilize vitamin B-12 as a sentinel vitamin. In other words, if vitamin B12 is low, usually other B vitamins are usually low.

Probiotics

Intestinal flora problems constitute a large part of nutritional problems seen in addicted persons. In our practice, about 80 percent of people with any kind of chronic medical problem have intestinal flora problems or what we call *dysbiosis*. When dysbiosis occurs, it could be from lack of enough beneficial bacteria, overgrowth of the pathogenic or disease-causing bacteria, or overgrowth of yeast, which should not be present in the bowel in large quantities. Dysbiosis can occur due to a number of factors. Overuse of antibiotics can kill off too much of the good bacteria and will promote bad bacteria to flourish. In addition, yeast, an opportunist infection, will also grow if you kill off too much good bacteria. Overuse of pesticides and additives can also be a factor. Eating too many carbohydrates, white starches, and sugar, will feed the yeast at the expense of promoting growth of the good bacteria. Environmental toxins also cause disruption of the normal bacteria in the bowel.

Bad stress can be an issue because when we are stressed, we make too much cortisol, promoting overgrowth of yeast and pathogenic bacteria, because it increases our blood sugar and inhibits our immune system. Our intestines contain seventy percent of the cells of our immune system. When our immune system is not functioning properly, it affects us physically and mentally. Think of the intestinal flora being similar to your lawn. If you like a particular type of grass, you might try to get rid of the weeds and the crabgrass. Think of the good bacteria as the preferred type of grass, the weeds as yeast, and the crabgrass as pathogenic bacteria. Antibiotics are not selective. They will kill any bacteria that come in contact with them, including the normal intestinal flora, which is not particularly resistant to antibiotics. If you take the antibiotics often, more than three times a year, and do not replenish the good bacteria, the hardiest bacteria will replace the good bacteria. In addition, antibiotics have no effect against yeast, so they will flourish if you kill off the good bacteria. The analogy is that if you lose some of your good grass due to drought or disease, weeds or crabgrass will replace the grass, which is resistant to drought or disease. The same is true if you kill some of the weeds or crabgrass with herbicide; a new type of weed or crab grass will grow unless you plant good grass seed. Therefore, if you have dysbiosis and do not have enough good bacteria, even if you kill off the pathogenic bacteria and yeast you have to replenish the good bacteria in its place. Acidophilus and bifidobacterium are two of the main good bacteria we utilize in replacing intestinal flora if we have dysbiosis. Replacing the bad guys with the good guys takes a little bit of science. We recommend thirty billion colonies to sixty billion colonies per day of the probiotic, or good bacteria, when you are trying to replenish the good bacteria. Many providers recommend eating live culture yogurt or yogurt specifically designed to replace the probiotic bacteria. However, even if it is live culture or yogurt specifically designed to replace intestinal flora, the numbers do not add up. Most of the live culture yogurts only contain about one billion colonies of probiotic, hardly enough. Yogurt that has been pasteurized has none of the live culture needed, so it is worthless for this particular purpose. And if it is not sugar-free, you are feeding a yeast problem if you have one. If you do the math, you can see that you would have to eat thirty to sixty yogurts per day to get the same amount of probiotic in a good probiotic capsule. Capsules can range anywhere from two billion colonies up to thirty or forty billion or more colonies depending on the brand name. These are capsules of live bacteria, or dormant bacteria, that will flourish in the right environment. Eating thirty to sixty yogurts per day may give you the right amount of probiotic if you could eat that much, but you could have severe reactions to the amount of dairy in that amount of yogurt. Probiotic capsules are usually refrigerated, which slows down their ability to reproduce and also keeps them alive. The newer probiotics do not require refrigeration. When swallowed, they flourish since the intestinal environment is dark, warm, and moist, which is what they like. If you do not take enough of the probiotic, you will not get good regeneration of good bacteria. It would be like planting too few grass seeds on a bare lawn. The probiotic bacteria in your intestine serve multiple functions. They create a barrier for toxins to prevent them from being absorbed into your system. It also helps to manufacture essential nutrients and vitamins including the B vitamins. The bacteria also aids in digestion by helping to break down food. Bacteria are also essential for the immune cells in your intestines, as these bacteria aid in their normal function. You can see that, without proper intestinal bacteria, you cannot have normal bodily functions, including production of essential neurotransmitters that are lacking in addiction.

If you take probiotics, it is best to take them at night. There are several reasons for this. First, your intestines tend to rest at night, which gives the probiotic bacteria a better chance to grow and take hold. If you take any antibiotics during the day they are nonselective and will kill off the probiotic even if it is given as a capsule. I recommend probiotics for all patients after they have taken an antibiotic, and sometimes even during the course of antibiotics. If you take the probiotic at night, you can take the antibiotic during the day and get a reasonably good effect. In addition to taking them at night, the dose of the probiotic is important and thirty to sixty billion colonies is the common recommended dose per day. You also need to take what we call prebiotics, which are nutrients or cofactors that help the probiotic to grow, essentially acting as a fertilizer for them. The one mentioned above, L-glutamine, is essential, because many of the probiotics in our intestines use glutamine as their energy source, not sugar or glucose. Yeast, on the other hand, almost exclusively uses sugar as its energy source. You can see that if you have yeast in the intestine and your diet is poor, with increased carbohydrate and sugar intake, you are essentially fertilizing and feeding the yeast at the expense of the probiotic bacteria. Suffice it to say bowel dysfunction has to be corrected to get optimal results in treating addiction.

Removal of Toxins

Removal of toxins from the environment is essential. These can be heavy metal toxins, including lead, mercury, cadmium, and arsenic. The main source of mercury is the amalgam fillings in our teeth, and the main source of cadmium is from cigarette smoke. Lead is ubiquitous in our environment and it is difficult to control. Testing for these toxins by a physician who is trained to deal with them is important. If you have some toxic exposure to heavy metals you have to be treated to have them removed. Many people do not know they have high levels of toxic metals in their systems, which also destroy cells in the brain.

Toxins may also come in the form of relationships. A toxic relationship, which is a relationship that is detrimental to your well-being, should also be mitigated, eliminated, or dealt with in some way. A good therapist can help you work with toxic relationships. Sometimes it is very difficult to get out of a toxic relationship, so you have to look at ways to balance or reframe the relationship.

Acupuncture is an important part of treatment and should be utilized whenever possible. Auricular or ear acupuncture is something that has been well studied as a way to increase the release of calming endorphins for people who are going through withdrawal or still craving. Ear acupuncture is the placement of four or five tiny needles into the external ear at points that are known to stimulate endorphin release. The treatment protocol called the NADA protocol has been studied for over thirty years. It is extremely effective at relieving craving and withdrawal symptoms during addiction treatment. This protocol requires the person to have the needles placed in the ear externally for approximately forty-five minutes. During that time the person experiences significant relaxation and relief of symptoms.

The NADA protocol is utilized in over two thousand clinics worldwide with good results. This protocol should be used in conjunction with substitution therapy involving Suboxone, counseling, diet, and lifestyle. It is sometimes used with people who are trying to come off of Suboxone in order to stimulate the production of calming endorphins while their brain is recovering from the addiction.

As you can see, treatment of addiction is multifaceted. We will look at counseling, which is an essential part of this approach, in the next chapter.

Chapter 8

COUNSELING WITH "DR. CHERIE"

Spiritual Psychology in Addiction; Touching the
Human Soul

*"Every form of addiction is bad, no matter whether the narcotic
be alcohol or morphine or idealism."*
- Carl G. Jung, from *Memories, Dreams, Reflections*, 1962

I met Glenn in the office. He was accompanied by his grandmother,
who had raised him and his seventeen-year-old sister, Alba. Their
mother left them when they were one and two years old. Glenn was
eighteen years old when he first came to our office. Since then,
his mother had started another family and never looked back on
her "old" life with Glenn and his sister. His grandmother was in
tears because Glenn was addicted to heroin. She found him shooting up in his room one day while cleaning. Glenn's grandmother
worked full-time to provide him and Alba a home, because their
father's job took him on the road much of the time. She pleaded
with me, crying, "Please help my grandson. He means everything
to me! I will do anything to help him get better."

As a grandmother myself, my heart ached for this kind woman who should be enjoying retirement but had to work to raise her grandkids. I promised her that if Glenn was serious about quitting drugs, I would do my very best to help him. The healing, however, was completely up to him. He is the one at the helm. Dr. Ron and I are only healers; *being* healed is completely up to the patient. A healer does not heal people. A healer either speeds up or slows down the healing process. You are the only one who can heal yourself. When a surgeon removes an infected appendix, the final healing occurs from within the patient's own healing system. Removing the infected appendix helps the process. On the other hand, if the surgeon removes a gallbladder filled with stones and the person gets a post-op infection from the surgery, the healing process is inhibited and slowed, depending on the strength of the patient's immune system. Psychotherapists can have a similar effect on healing emotional wounds. If their advice and guidance are contrary to their patient's beliefs, and if there is no rapport, they may make the problem worse. Ultimately, the final healing comes from within and is modulated by the healer, the persons' innate healing capabilities, and the motivation of the person needing healing.

Glenn later came into my office, head down, looking like he had not slept in days. He was a polite young man and very shy. I had a strong sense that Glenn was a good kid who was led down a dangerous path and did not know how to get back on track. One of the biggest deterrents to healing lies in not understanding why and how you got to where you are. *No one plans on becoming an addict.* As I sat with him, I saw the boy he was, the baby without a mother, who preferred her new family. I also saw the man he might one day become if he won this battle. After getting to know each other a little, I went over the four causes of addiction and its successful treatment and gave him a copy. This is something he can look at every day. Chris Prentiss, founder of Passages Of Malibu, has one of the highest success rates in treating addiction to alcohol and drugs. I usually begin our sessions by going over Prentiss's four causes of addiction. It is very powerful to show someone that there is a cause to addiction and that there is also a "cure," or at least a hope, in being able to live free of addiction.

It is also important for patients to know that they did not become dependent or addicted on purpose. When our young patients first see me, they are anxious and do not know what to expect. Being comfortable in the office and with a therapist is critical. The main goal in my practice is to reframe specific patterns of thinking to show people that they can change all unwanted behaviors by changing their beliefs of themselves and the universe. They need to know that they are never alone and that help and guidance can be found right within themselves. Once they know that they have the power to change themselves, they will be able to beat their addiction. During our journey together, I remind them often that they have all the abilities and capabilities they need to achieve anything they want and that we are on their side. The Braverman neurochemistry profile, explained earlier, is another motivator for teens. I can show them on paper that there is a reason for their anxiety. I tell them, "It's in the brain!" Most are relieved, because there is something tangible to work with. I go over the four main reasons for addiction, the first of which is brain chemistry, which we look at right away. This is the easy part.

The following are points I explain and discuss during counseling.

- I explain the four causes and cures of addiction.

- I define and explain psychological patterns or anchors.

- I discuss what abuse means to the patients personally. The concept of this abuse is not always what we *consciously* think.

Especially in children, abuse is what they perceive, not what his actual, and it is different for everyone.

- I explain NLP (Neuro-Linguistic Programming) in healing, including Ericksonian hypnosis.

- I look at boundaries and how to build them.

- I examine possible toxic relationships.

- I discuss and develop self-responsibility.

- I discuss spiritual awareness (self-awareness, working with a higher power, achieving inner peace)

I teach kids how to help themselves, which builds self-esteem. When we esteem ourselves, we do not try to alter our minds to make our problems go away; we are confident that we can change our lives. As Chris Prentiss says, "you can't change past events, you can only change how you think about them."

DISCUSSING THE FOUR CAUSES OF ADDICTION

We owe the following concepts to the work of Chris Prentiss, his son Pax, and his staff at Passages in Malibu, California, who so clearly outline the main causes of addiction. His concepts fit our beliefs better than any we have seen. I strongly recommend his book, *The Alcoholism and Addiction Cure: A holistic Approach to Total Recovery*. The causes he outlines are:

1. Neurological chemical imbalance

2. Unresolved past events

3. Beliefs held true that are inconsistent with what *is* true

4. The inability to cope with current conditions

1. Neurological Chemical Imbalance

Dr. Ron Santasiero previously explained the biochemical role in addiction. Biochemical imbalance is probably responsible for over 95 percent of addiction problems. The brain lacks an essential chemical that controls behavior. There was probably a deficiency to begin with, which is why these individuals have been "self-medi-cating." In the case of opiates, most often the opiate takes the place of GABA or other calming neurotransmitters. I go over this with my patients. As we look over their Braverman Assessment, I talk to them briefly about their imbalances. We concentrate on dopa-mine, acetylcholine, GABA, and serotonin and how supplementa-tion and proper diet can help resolve these imbalances, especially in young people.

I am saddened, however, that the importance of rehabilitating the brain seems lost, not only on the youngsters, but also on their parents. When I ask if they are taking the supplements prescribed for brain health, I hear complaints about the initial cost of the sup-plements. They say, "I can't afford it right now." Supplementation costs more in the beginning of treatment because you are buying everything you need at once. However, you will not run out of everything at the same time. Even after explaining this to par-ents, they will still insist that they cannot afford the supplements. "Mrs. Smith," I say, "your kid was stealing from you and others for his $300 per *day* habit. You have paid thousands of dollars to lawyers and lost work because of this habit, and you think $100 or $150 worth of high quality supplements, brain food, which last three to six months is expensive? Really? Will you please think about this?" This is a struggle for me, but some do listen and a few end up liking the idea of being healthy, especially after a couple of months when their brain wakes up. By the way, though my language may seem harsh to some, it is a part of my NLP training, to send the wake-up call, so to speak, which is similar to a slap on the face, only nicer.

I first addressed the issue of brain chemistry with Glenn and gave him the assessment that would show him how addiction is not just psychological, but also physiological. Nothing is 100 percent. However, the vast majority of patients with dependency problems experience high anxiety, often to the extreme. Do not be fooled by exterior behavior. Most seem quiet, shy, or calm even, but under that calm exterior is a kid with high anxiety. When I told Glenn, he immediately smiled and said, "Oh my god, that's so true! How did you know?" There is relief at this point, because something "clicks" between us, one of many "clicks" to come. A large part of the relief is due to being told by a professional that there is something tangible contributing to the addiction. Rather than let him think I was a genius at mind reading, as tempting as that was, I told him that it was simply an educated guess. So here is the beginning of our therapy together.

The simple reason that people alter their awareness through drugs of any kind is to feel better. The question is, "*feel better than what?*" This is difficult at best for most people to explain to themselves, let alone to someone else. How many people do you think have ever asked themselves this question? A quest for *feeling better* leads to the second cause.

2. Unresolved Past Events

When presented, people automatically begin to wonder what "unresolved past events" could mean. We do not always consciously know. If we did, it most likely would not be a problem. It is the *unconscious* mind and its beliefs that create our behaviors. At the beginning of most sessions I ask again, "So why do you think you started drugs?" My patients know that I am not trying to be difficult, but that I am trying to tickle the unconscious mind and bring it to the surface, because when patients are ready to make a change, when they are ready to be able to deal with the deep painful issue, the cause will pop into the conscious mind. This unresolved traumatic event is not always what adults might think. However, to children, it could have been the biggest trauma of their lives. Sometimes it is something that we may think of right away, such as physical, sexual, or emotional abuse. Although it can be one of these things, it is not always—not even most of the time.

For example, Maggie, a sweet, bright, hard-working nineteen-year-old, first started seeing us two years ago. She was addicted to opiates, OxyContin, in particular. She lived at home with her parents and a sister and was close to her grandparents. It was a tight-knit family, a good family, and all members were hardworking. Whenever I asked Maggie why she did drugs, she would smile and say, "I keep thinking about it but I don't know." I would tell her to not think about it, that it will come to her when the time is just right.

I will never forget the day she came in with her answer. She was all smiles and eager to tell me something. Excitedly she said, "I know why I started doing drugs! I know what it was! I couldn't see before now!" Maggie went on to tell me how she had been jogging one day. Then, at the point when she entered "the zone," that meditative or hypnotic state I jokingly call the "duh" state, she began thinking of how I kept asking her why she started doing drugs and she began to "wonder" about it. Suddenly she saw a picture in her mind of her little cousin. She then did what I taught her to do when something came to mind, whether a picture or feeling, and asked herself, "What does this mean? Why am I seeing this?" She waited patiently and trusted her unconscious mind. Until just a few years ago, Maggie was the first and only granddaughter. She was beautifully spoiled and extremely close to her grandparents, especially her grandfather. Maggie spent most of her free time with her grandpa. He taught her many things. He taught her how to fish and bait her own hook. He even taught her how to build a tree fort. They often took long strolls in the park, played ball, and watched birds. Interestingly, her grandfather suffered from chronic back pain for years and would take hydrocodone while they were together. This alone does not seem like a reason to start an addiction or dependency. However, remember the little cousin's face that came to her mind. After her little cousin was born, her grandpa's time was now split between her and the new baby cousin. She quickly realized that she was not his only "special one." Although she loved her little cousin very much, she had difficulty dealing with the loss of her grandpa's full attention on her. Grandpa would pick up the new baby boy and coo and kiss and make him laugh. Maggie was confused. She did not understand her jealously and sense of loss and loneliness and felt guilty. How could she express what she did not understand? These jumbled-up emotions cut deep and continued to grow. Who wouldn't do anything to feel better in that state? Grandpa always felt better after taking a hydrocodone. So Maggie tried it too. As a child she connected the taking of hydrocodone with the emotion of feeling good. She did not understand the pain-alleviating properties of the hydrocodone. To a child, "pills make you feel good." She snuck a couple of from her grandfather and tried one a couple of times; she did feel better for a while. She also stopped thinking about her internal struggle, but only for a while, which led to her addiction. Maggie did not know it, but she also had a chemical imbalance that can lead to addiction, and taking the hydrocodone started the cascade of events that ultimately lead to her increasing the dosage of the opiate. Once Maggie received this "aha" from her own unconscious mind, she was ready to go into more self-exploration and looked forward to it. She had begun to see this self-exploration as quite interesting.

3. Beliefs You Hold That Are Inconsistent With What Is True

I could go on and on and on about all the negative beliefs that limit people when they are not in touch with reality. Something that you truly believe on a deep level becomes your reality. If you believe that God punishes you for your mistakes, then your unconscious mind will lead you to situations and people that justify the negative belief. For instance, if there is an underlying deep unconscious belief that you "are not good enough," then you will be attracted to people, whether friends or lovers, who mistreat you in some way. You may have known people for whom things simply seem to go wrong no matter what they do, and they think that it is because they are being punished. As children, our parents punished us for bad or unacceptable behavior. As adults, we are no longer punished by our parents, but we punish ourselves.

Another destructive belief is "I am alone in this world and without love." The actual truth of the matter is that there is an abundance of love that surrounds us. It is not love based on attachment but *agape*, or unconditional love. When we begin to recognize a sense of being connected with something bigger and more powerful than all there is, then we can recognize a sense of being enveloped in safety and caring when we need it most. If our unconscious belief is that we are alone, we will not be able to see or experience the love of a higher power. How could we if we do not look for it? Why would we look for it if we do not even believe it exists? This is why daily meditation is so important. It helps us reach a state of deep and inner awareness that connects us to all there is, which gives us a sense of camaraderie with an omnipotent power on whom we can rely during times of despair. This is one of many reasons that I teach meditation. We cannot afford to *not* to meditate every day.

4. The Inability to Cope with Current Conditions.

We are often at a loss as to how to cope with traumatic or even deeply emotional problems when we are very young. If we do not learn coping mechanisms for deep pain and loss, the inability to cope becomes a pattern into adulthood. When that happens, we can become dependent on something that artificially and only temporarily makes us feel better, such as drugs or alcohol. The brain will eventually become dependent or even addicted. We first have to recognize the emotional and traumatic event or events in our past of which we never learned to cope. If we go back to the example of Maggie, she was hurt, yes, but she was also confused because she loved her little cousin and consciously knew her grandfather still loved her very much. However, she still felt cheated somehow, and this led to a deep sense of loss and loneliness. She was grieving, a process which she was unfamiliar with, and she had no coping skills for the loss she experienced. She did not know how to deal with these unfamiliar emotions. There was a part of her deep inside that replayed the message, "people I love only love me until someone better comes along." In RoHun psychotherapy, this is called a *faulty thought pattern* or FTP; Carl G. Jung called it a *complex*, which is discussed later. Maggie took an opiate that helped her feel a little better for a while, and helped her to balance or cope with her FTP. I helped Maggie learn different coping mechanisms for difficult situations, now and in the future. She also learned different ways of looking at events in her life. We cannot change past events, but we have power to change how we think about them. It takes patience and it takes practice, and sometimes we need to fall down and get right back up again and learn from the fall.

Glenn's Journey

The most interesting and enjoyable part of my practice is working with motivated, compliant young adults who are open-minded and eager to learn about the universe and their place within it. So we talk about the psyche, the human mind, the soul, emotions, God or a higher power within the universe, and Spirit, in simple and straightforward terms. "Glenn," I said, leaning toward him with a conspiratorial smile, "Working together with me, you will learn about the psyche, the universe, and how to get access to the power of your mind on your journey to wholeness." Glenn became engaged. "You also have some negative beliefs about life, yourself, and others that are untrue. I am here to help you discover what you can know about the universe. You will learn how to become your own therapist." He smiled. I could see in his eyes that I had reached a deeper level of him that yearns for this knowledge. It can save his life, and his soul knows it.

Glenn told me his mom left him before he was a year old (abandonment issue 1). When he found her years later, she did not want him to "bother" her (abandonment issue 2). She had a new life and other children. This hit Glenn hard because she was choosing her younger children over him. These are kids who are his siblings and were living with her, growing up with her. "Why not *me*?" he wondered. "Oh, well," he said, "I don't really care. She's a jerk." As a protective mechanism, Glenn spent years telling himself how bad his mother was. At an unconscious level, however, he believed something was wrong with him. He did not know what he had done in his short life for her to turn him away and forget about him but not her other kids. Young children take on the blame for abandonment. They cannot comprehend that it could be something defective in the parent. Their brain has not yet developed that concept. This is not Glenn's only negative belief that affects his thoughts and behaviors, but it is huge. It is most likely what contributed to his anxiety about leaving the house other than for school; by staying home, he could make sure his family was there and would not leave him and his sister.

I told Glenn about the conscious mind and the unconscious mind. The conscious mind includes everything that we are consciously aware of. The unconscious mind holds all experiences, forgotten memories, thoughts, and feelings of which we are unaware; they are hidden behind a veil. It is the unconscious mind and its negative beliefs that cause most of our problems, I explained. As children, traumatic experiences cause a part of us to take on a negative belief about that experience. That small part of us becomes a subpersonality, what RoHun therapy calls a "Reactive Self," and creates a negative belief or Faulty Thought Pattern (FTP).

"Glenn, everyone has issues and problems," I told him. "They play out in many ways, but the unconscious mind is always trying to help us when it no longer needs to protect the conscious mind. It is as if the unconscious mind protects the conscious mind when it is necessary. Now it says it is time to be aware of those things behind the veil that you have forgotten. In other words, the unconscious mind says it is time for awareness of something important so that you can heal it; once we are aware of (conscious) past events and the insecurities, fears, and sadness they caused, they no longer negatively affect us. A time eventually comes for awareness of beliefs that otherwise hurt us and prevents us from achieving our goals." At this point, Glenn let me know that he is interested but a bit confused, and I realize that this is a lot of information, so I explained further. "At first the unconscious mind protects the conscious mind but it also knows when it is the right time for us to understand how these negative beliefs were born and how they prevent us from realizing our true spiritual selves. Our true spiritual selves know that we are powerful, loving, and lovable and have the capability to heal. Our true spiritual self, the soul, knows that we already have all the abilities and capabilities we need to be anyone and achieve anything we want." I waited until this sunk in, then I continued. "We are not humans who sometimes have a spiritual experience, we are spiritual beings having a human experience." It is the human side of us that holds fear, anxiety, loss, anger, hate. Your soul, the essence of who you really are, knows this. So let's look at where your unconscious mind leads you, deal with what it is trying to tell you, then move on from there.

"All the confusion and other negative emotions that were experienced and internalized while growing up without any conscious knowledge, are *psychological;* this is why you experimented with drugs. The addiction to drugs is *biological.* In other words, you didn't know how to handle the intense and confusing emotions of loss, anger, abandonment, sadness, and aloneness, because they were unconscious. You could not put the labels on your emotional pain," I explained.

Glenn sat with his head down, which is what we do when we access our feelings and said, "I never knew what it was that I felt all the time, and still don't. I just know that whatever I have been feeling, it is so sad, sometimes even angry. No matter what I'm doing or who I'm with, it's always there, like a nagging worm in the pit of my stomach. I never want to go out anymore or hang with friends, which I know I can't anymore anyway. That's why I tried to go to college and then quit. I'm so nervous when I'm not at home. And when I'm home with my gram and Alba, I still feel lonely and nervous. *Really* nervous." Glenn's wrist and hand started fidgeting, like a small tremor. I learned early on that this is a sign of an unconscious clue coming to the surface, though he does not connect it...yet. I noticed this unconscious sign during our first meeting, whenever he started getting deeper into his innermost thoughts, so I encourage and listen. "I don't know why it does that," he said, while watching his hand. "It's like it has a mind of its own." It is beginning to dawn on Glenn that there would soon be another loss in his life: his life-long friends. He tells me stories about them, some funny, some sad. Thus begins another grieving process. It is imperative that he no longer hangs out with them. I felt bad for him, and all the others who have to make this choice. These are best friends from early childhood. Making new friends while still in school is nearly impossible. The old friends still try to hang on, and the kids who don't do drugs don't want to hang with the kid who did drugs. Like Glenn, these kids cannot switch schools, so they must face this lonely time. If they make it through this, they will be stronger than ever before.

Another Day In Therapy

"Glenn," I said, wanting to reinforce what he had learned previously about addiction causes and the mind, "these emotions are internalized and jumbled up. You don't even know what it is that is bothering you to such a degree. After a while you no longer remember why you have these intense emotions. You just want them to stop. *That's* psychological. The first time you smoked pot, it helped you to forget the unpleasant and confusing feelings, if only for a little while. But that little while of forgetting felt a lot better than none at all. It is time to change your way of thinking so you look at your problems differently; then you will be able to discover the answers you need. These emotions are information. They want healing. But first you have to understand what they are and how they came to be. We will give them names, so we both know which ones you are dealing with at any given time."

As with so many people who start pot at a young age, after a while the pot no longer relieved Glenn's emotional pain as well as it had in the beginning, so he began to smoke more. Then someone offered him hydrocodone, telling him how much better it is than pot. From there, the drugs became more frequent and more potent. Eventually he tried heroin because it was cheap. Not realizing he was chasing the first high, which can never be achieved, he ended up shooting heroin and that is how we met. His life was falling apart. Glenn felt a little better knowing that addiction was not entirely his "fault." This is a key concept in treatment. Your biochemistry is not your fault. However, how you deal with it is within your control.

I further explained to Glenn that this would be a tough battle and that he absolutely needed to do his best to trust me and to at least try to utilize the tools I would give to him. Glenn also believed that he had learning disabilities, because that was what he was told from an early age. Again, this is where understanding the aspects of our minds helps. I reminded him of the difference between the conscious and unconscious mind. The conscious mind is that part that holds the beliefs of others taught to us as facts. Many of my patients, of all ages, have told me that this is one of the most helpful concepts for them. It gives them room to look at their "own truth," which is like pulling away the proverbial veil to see far beyond the limited beliefs of others. The unconscious mind is all that we are unaware of and that affects most of our behaviors. We all have many beliefs of which we are unaware. Some are good, some negative. If you are not aware of the unconscious negative beliefs, they dictate negative behaviors. They are like negative recordings that play over and over. A simplistic example, using Glenn's experience, is *the Unworthy Self,* whose FTP is, "I am not as good as others, and therefore no one will ever want me." This was based on Glenn's abandonment issues and made worse by discovering his mother preferred her other children to Glenn and his sister. Glenn pays for his own visits and supplements. He will finish his bachelor's degree next year and is a happy, sober young man who helps his grandmother, at home and financially.

Kelly

Kelly is a beautiful girl of fifteen, whose mother brought her to me for counseling. I was one of several therapists who worked with Kelly. Up until the age of fourteen, Kelly had been a straight A student and involved in any sport she could play without interfering with her grades. During her free time she would join the boys in the neighborhood to play basketball and football. Determined to do as well as any boy, no matter what the game, she became obsessed with "being the best." Kelly is a petite girl and incurred several minor injuries. Kelly's injuries bothered her mother and father but she would not give in. As a matter of fact, it made her work harder at beating the boys. "I'm as good as any boy," she told me when I asked her. "I can do everything boys can, and better." Kelly eventually spent all of her free time with the boys and no longer hung around with her girlfriends, who thought Kelly was "weird." After a while, they stopped bothering to calling her to hang out with them. Kelly did not care. She had her boyfriends.

Jeff, an eighteen-year-old on whom Kelly had a crush, invited Kelly to a party that night. There would be loud music and beer and no adult supervision. Kelly told her mother she was going to a show with friends. There was a nagging little voice in her head that warned her that she could get into trouble or worse, but Kelly brushed the voice aside. After all, these guys were her buddies; she was one of the guys, so to speak. Besides, Jeff invited her so he must be interested in her, she thought. She was so excited she could hardly contain herself. She wore her best jeans and a sharp red tie front-shirt with a dark blue hoodie. She knew she looked good. She would meet Jeff at the basketball court and they would go to the party together. Life was wonderful.

Most of her male friends were there, as well as some older girls she did not know but they were friendly to her so she relaxed. After a couple of beers, she spotted some girls her own age, girls from school. But these were girls Kelly would never have hung out with. She had heard that they were druggies. She wondered why they were there with her buddies, but she did not dwell on that. Instead, she looked around for Jeff and found him talking to a pretty blonde girl. He had another beer in his hand. She felt a twinge of jealously and put her arm through his. He said good-bye to the other girl then pulled Kelly into his arms and kissed her long and hard. Her head was reeling with excitement. Here she was, with the most popular boy in school and he preferred her to all the other girls. Jeff said, "Follow me, Kell." Kelly gladly followed Jeff up the stairs into a large bathroom. "That's weird," she thought, but did not care. Jeff kissed her again. Then he pulled something out his pocket. "What's that?" Kelly asked. "It's something that will make all your troubles go away. You'll feel like you're floating in heaven. I promise. Everyone does it. That's why we're having this party." Kelly did not know if it was true that everyone was doing it, but she did not want Jeff to think she was a sissy-girl. The sissy-girl was Kelly's Reactive Self (RS), but she did not know about that at the time. The faulty thought pattern, or FTP, of the RS was, "if I don't go along with Jeff, I will not be accepted by him or anyone else." When Jeff took off her hoodie and put the tourniquet on her arm, she refused to let him suspect her fear. It was all she could think of. "Don't let him see you scared," she thought. She knew he really liked her and wanted to kiss him again so she cooperated. "Is this dangerous?" she asked. "Naw," he said. "I'm right here with you. It's something we can do together. Wait till you see. You're gonna love it, sweetheart. I mean, you don't wanna be the only buddy in our group who doesn't love to feel heaven, do you?" Kelly let Jeff shoot her up with heroin. It was her first time shooting heroin and she was immediately addicted. She remembered vomiting at first, but after a few minutes she felt the heaven Jeff told her about, but it was the beginning of the hell Kelly would live from that point on, until she got treatment. She would soon do *anything* for the drug, and the boy she loved knew it. Kelly's grades began to fall and she had to wear long sleeves during summer to hide the scars on her arms from the needle marks. She was argumentative with her mother and stopped helping out at home. Jeff began dating the blonde girl from the party. Kelly was heartbroken. When she confronted him, he told her that she was one of the guys. How could they have *that* kind of relationship? Kelly became despondent and her drug use increased.

Kelly was eighteen when we first met at our center. Dr. Ron introduced us after talking with her about counseling. He knew she did not have a positive experience with counseling. When I went into the exam room, she was lying down. Dr. Santasiero had given her the first dose of Suboxone. I introduced myself and asked how she was feeling. "I never thought I could feel normal again," she told me, with tears on her cheeks. "Can you help me? I can't take it anymore!"

"I can help you," I told her, touching her hand. "But you are the one who will have to do the work. I will give you the necessary tools to go inside yourself and find out why you started using drugs, and it's not just because of peer pressure. It is deeper than that, Kelly. You will have to go deep into your heart to find the answer. It is something that was buried long ago. Once you find it though, you'll be on the road to true recovery. And it will certainly not be easy, nor will it be a short journey." I let my words sink in. "But it will be perhaps the most interesting, fascinating journey of your life."

On our first *formal* visit, in my office, I asked Kelly, "Kelly, why do you think you started drugs?" I knew I would hear the same pat answers I usually hear: peer pressure, the other kids were doing it, I wanted to fit in, my boyfriend told me it was great, and so forth. I ask this question on many visits, knowing that one day, the true answer will just pop out. In the meantime, I start with the four causes of addiction and cures, then teach Kelly simple meditation and ask her to meditate for twenty minutes or more per day, every day. When she told me she could not find the time, I told her that time does not hide from us. We cannot "find" time. We have to carve it out from somewhere else. "We all have the same twenty-fours hours in a day and cannot afford to live without daily meditation," I said. "Besides, if you want to bypass the left-brain critical factor, the beliefs taught by others so you can find your own truth, then daily meditation is key." Kelly, like the others, had little idea what I was talking about, but she knew what she was doing was not working. Her life was a mess and she would try just about anything.

On some visits I ask about dreams, and we go over their symbols and how they relate to the patient's life. I want Kelly to experience the universe beyond her. We did guided imagery, hypnosis, and used other tools to help her find answers to her problems. Rather than looking for answers from the limited conscious mind, we begin to look into the unconscious mind; the answers are there. All of these exercises take Kelly inside herself, tapping her unconscious mind, where eventually she learns that she is never alone, and her capabilities exceed all her of previous beliefs, and more importantly, that there is beautiful love inside her. At some point, the FTP reveals itself. We each have many FTPs, but I concern myself with only those that are meant for Kelly to know at that time. As Kelly was talking after a meditation session, she said, "I guess I always wanted to prove I'm as good as any boy. Problem is, I don't even know why." Her eyes and head were down and looking to the right, a sign that she was accessing her feelings, her intuition.

"And why did you feel the need to prove that you were as good as any boy?" I asked her. "What part of you, what 'little self,' thinks that? Give it a name," I said.

"The Unworthy Self."

"Good. And what is the FTP, the negative belief that this Unworthy Self keeps repeating?"

"I don't know why I think this, but I think my mother wanted a boy instead of me," Kelly said.

I encouraged her to expand. "Try saying, 'The Unworthy Self says...' then say the FTP in a sentence."

Kelly answered quickly, "The Unworthy Self says that boys are better than girls!" Kelly's eyes lit up as if she discovered a great secret, which she had.

"This FTP of yours," I said, "'that all boys are better than girls' has prevented you from seeing the truth around you. For instance, you and other girls are better than *some* boys in many ways and not in others. You haven't seen the truth of what actually is, because this schema takes over." I had already explained to Kelly a shortened version of a *schema*, a collection of thoughts that forms an internal representation of the world around us, a condensed version of what actually is. Some are good, some not. A good schema is one that tells us that everyone is equal and good, no matter his or her color or religion. An FTP is an example of a negative schema. For instance, Kelly's schema of "I have to be like a boy or I am unacceptable" was a negative schema. Negative schemas prevent us from seeing the world as it really is and inhibits us from taking in new information. Kelly's healing had begun.

ANCHORS

An *anchor* is another word we use in Neuro-Linguistic Programing, (NLP), to describe neurological patterns. NLP is the study of the map of thinking and how that thinking affects our behavior. NLP describes the fundamental dynamics between mind (neuro) and language (linguistic) and how their interplay affects our body and behavior (programming). The more times we perform a behavior, the more deeply ingrained it becomes within the brain. This repeated behavior creates a neural synapse, or engrained pattern, in the brain. These synapses are a way for the brain to move information or to create an action or thought, based on a feeling or observation. Learning about anchors is important for staying off drugs or negative behaviors, be they opiates or cigarettes or gambling. An anchor is an association to something that has become so internally engrained that even hearing a song associated with the event can cause the original synapse, which can feel as real as the original event or memory of the event. There are several descriptions of an anchor, but Richard Bandler, PhD and John Grinder, PhD, developers of NLP, make it fairly simple in their book, *Transformation*: "Anchoring refers to the tendency for any one element of an experience to bring back the entire experience."

Even a one-time event can create an anchor. Let's say that an event is emotionally traumatic, and at the peak of the emotion, there is a song playing. Then the event connects to the song. Whenever that specific song is heard, it will trigger the same emotions. The anchor may not be conscious. For example, Jennifer feared certain women, but not all. She could not figure out why. She would shy away from certain women and literally shake with fear for no clear reason, even with women she just met. We looked at the commonalities of the women she feared versus those she did not. We discovered that the women she feared were tall and had deep voices. This was her anchor. I did an NLP technique to collapse the anchor, which helped, but Jennifer still remained fearful of certain women. Collapsing an anchor is when we disconnect the stimulus from the belief or behavior. EFT (emotional freedom technic) or "tapping" is my therapeutic choice for collapsing anchors. So where did Jennifer's anchor originate? You do not have to know where the anchor originated in order to collapse it. Often it reveals itself anyway. Sometimes we will never know, which is okay. We can still collapse the anchor. Jennifer suddenly recalled an event from her past during an EFT session. Her fourth grade teacher punished her for passing notes to her girlfriend in school by sitting her in front of the class, facing her peers. After pushing

Jenifer into the chair, she towered over Jennifer and with her deep voice, had warned her that next time there would be severe consequences. The teacher's voice "was like a man's," Jennifer said. Of course, standing over the fourth-grader sitting down, the height intensified Jennifer's fear. This traumatic event anchored her to tall women with deep voices. From that point on, any time Jennifer met a tall woman with a deep voice, her mind recalled that old frightening feeling.

Some understanding of anchors is important in therapy, especially when treating addictions. For example, we talk about "people, places, and things." It is imperative to stay away from people with whom drugs were used, places where drugs were used, and games played or television programs frequently watched, when doing drugs. The hardest part of abstinence is realizing how powerful anchors are. I talk with young people about anchors in relation to the addiction that they are trying to reverse or cure.

When I help people quit smoking, I ask them several questions about their smoking behaviors. They may tell me their first cigarette is first thing in the morning while they are sitting in a chair in the kitchen reading the news. They take their coffee with medium cream and sugar. They get in the car and have two cigarettes on the way to work. These are anchors. In the above case, I suggest they get up either ten minutes earlier or ten minutes later, delay making the coffee, forget the sugar, which is healthier anyway, and/or the milk. Some people would prefer drinking tea instead, especially if it is green tea, because that is doing something healthy. Rather than reading the paper in the morning, I suggest they either read it in the car or later and to take a different route to work. If they do things connected to smoking in a *different order or in a different way*, it breaks the pattern of behavior, the anchor. These changes are for thirty days. For opiate addiction it can take years. What we are doing is changing the anchors because anchors, once they are fired off, make it nearly impossible to change in the middle of that behavior. Creating a new anchor is the best way to avoid the unwanted behavior.

Caffeine is a drug, in other words, it affects the brain. Marijuana is also a drug that affects the brain. These chemicals either satisfy or create receptors in the brain. Once we have the receptors, whether they are inherent or created, they must be filled to be satisfied. Interestingly, most people know that drugs are addictive. What they may not know is that emotions are addictive as well. Have you ever known someone who seems depressed all the time? Some of these people come to me for a session, then call several days later saying, "Dr. Cherie, I felt great for a few days after I left your office, and now I feel depressed again." When these people feel positive, the receptors in the brain start screaming to be filled with depression, no different from any other addiction. This is called withdrawal. Their anchors are at home, so in order to make withdrawal easier, they need to change what they do for a while. Countering depressive thoughts with positive opposite thoughts, for example, smiling in a mirror or listening to comedy, will eventually ease withdrawal symptoms. So I help walk my addiction patients through their daily lives and the role that drugs have played. We work on developing and defining new anchors, at least until they are strong enough to handle the ones no longer wanted or needed.

Getting back to people, places, and things as anchors, let's turn to *people*. It is extremely difficult to expect oneself to break the habit of drug abuse when they have receptors in the brain that are empty and screaming out for more drugs. If you hang around with the same people who you were doing drugs with before it is just asking too much of oneself. A lot of my clients think they can handle it, until they find out, too late, that they cannot. It is just too strong.

Places form another anchor that is difficult when trying to set up new patterns. For instance, people who are trying to stop drinking alcohol need to stay away from where they drank their alcohol. If they enjoyed most of their drinking while going out with friends to bars, then it is wise to stay away from bars until a new pattern of abstinence is formed. I also help my clients learn how to reestablish new "places" when they are ready. Many times, even driving by a place you bought or used drugs will cause craving.

Things almost always involve patterns of what people were doing when they were using their drug of choice, such as being out with friends at a bar. If hanging out at a friend's house when the parents were out was the favorite place to do drugs, then being at that friend's house is out of bounds; so is the friend. Using drugs may also be a way to cope with "life." These anchors are more powerful than one might think, so we are strict about staying away from them. Of course we have had young people think that they can handle their anchors, especially if they have been doing well with recent short-term abstinence. Unfortunately, they almost always learn the hard way. In a sense it can be a good lesson in helping them to know better the next time they are tempted. Together we go over various imagined scenarios of how they would handle a situation when an anchor unexpectedly presents itself. The anchor can be running into a drug buddy from the past who still uses, or even playing a game they played when doing drugs. If the old buddy offers drugs, it can be especially hard to resist without having practiced what to do. They are to practice several different scenarios daily. Right after meditating is especially good, because the brain is relaxed, which helps to better install the desired behavior. Patients are to practice what they will do the next time they are faced with these situations. And there will be a next time. They ask what to do if they are faced with a situation that has not been thought of during our session. By practicing various scenarios often, the brain creates schemas, mentioned earlier, so that the mind will react in a positive and more desirable way, even when a new situation reveals itself. Now they are proactive and confident that they have the ability to turn away from a situation where drugs are offered. The thing to be careful of is if they drink alcohol and someone approaches them with drugs. Even one drink lowers inhibitions. If an addicted person drinks and is then approached with drugs, the old anchors reawaken; the temptation may be too much to refuse. The behavioral patterns involved in anchors become stronger with use. However, we can create new and more desirable patterns that we must practice in order to ingrain them deeply into our brains. These neurological synapses are stored. We cannot erase them. They are like icons on a computer screen. Clicking them activates the icon; the icon activates a behavior or old anchor, which activates the neural pathway to the undesirable pattern of behavior. Even if you delete the icon, the program is still in the computer. If you accidently click the program from somewhere else in the computer, the anchor fires off and the program pops open. The same happens with addictive behaviors. Drinking alcohol or smoking pot is the same as clicking the program from within the computer; you can't see the icon but the program is still there.

What we can do is create new and positive patterns that will hopefully become stronger than the undesirable ones. Addictions are about anchors to behaviors. The drug, whether nicotine or opiates, is connected to the anchor, in this case, altering the mind with alcohol. Changing or "overwriting" the anchor helps diminish the power of the addiction. No alcohol or pot or any other mind-altering drug allowed.

Behaviors are difficult to change, and changing behaviors of any type takes practice. It takes conscious awareness. Humans go into a meditative state many times during the day where their brains will often go into neutral, and behaviors seem automatic. For instance, recently I found myself walking to the cupboard to grab a cup for tea. I went to the wrong cupboard, the one used for cups thirteen years ago before we remodeled our kitchen! Who knows where my mind was at the time, but I know my brainwave was in a trance state; an old anchor had fired off. I do not know what triggered the old anchor, perhaps whatever I was thinking of while at the time I wanted tea. Creating new and healthier anchors, where the outcome of the behavior is more desirable than the one we are trying to overcome, makes breaking addiction easier. The first step is defining our goals and identifying which positive behaviors we prefer to have in any given situation.

WHAT IS ABUSE TO *YOU*?

Abuse, just as stress, is about one's perception. What abuse is to one person, it may not be to another. Much of our perception is acquired from those who have raised us and those who are most prominent in our lives. There are the obvious abuses, such as sexually fondling a child, which is more common than some people think. There are child-beaters and those who scream at their kids. Some kids are called "stupid, no good," and told things such as, "You will never amount to anything." But what about the not so obvious? Did you ever wonder why some parents smoke pot with their kids? Or do cocaine with them? Some parents say the kids were doing it anyway. "Better to have them just do it with us, while they are home." Seriously? Do people *really* have themselves convinced that if they do drugs with their kids, then their kids will *only* do drugs when they are with their parents? Nonsense. So why do some people fool themselves like this? Why would parents risk their children's lives? Why would they lose the respect of their children and others? Can it be so that they can freely do drugs themselves, without needing to hide their own drug use or to wait until the kids are out of the house? This behavior is not only abusive, but it is selfish. This is also very confusing to children. Furthermore, a parent may smoke pot once in a while. To a kid, the parents "smoke dope," which to them justifies smoking dope every day.

Another form of abuse is what I call "guilty parenting." Guilty parenting is when mom and dad work all day and come home tired. Dinner is often late and not always healthy. Small children are geniuses in psychology; they have perfect timing, too. They know their parent's behavior patterns, perhaps better than the parents themselves. When little Billy refuses to eat dinner and has not eaten all day, Mom or Dad give in and let him have what he wants, as usual. Usually what Billy wants is something sweet and unhealthy, like candy, plain white bread, mac & cheese, or other carbohydrates. He flatly refuses vegetables of any kind, let alone healthy protein, so parents give in because they "feel bad." I hear, "At least he's eating *something*." This reminds me of the woman on TV who continued to feed her three-year-old son his favorite sweets because she loves him and just cannot refuse him. The boy, at three-years-old, weighed in at 114 pounds, almost four times heavier than normal. He could not walk and had to roll around on the floor. There are too many of these real-life tragedies, where parents no longer parent, and the children suffer the most. When you look at these kid's parents, you cannot help but wonder what goes through their minds. These are kids who eat what they want, when they want it, and what they want is unhealthy, even deadly. Often these kids are allowed to go to bed when they want and stay on a computer or smartphone for as long as they want, diminishing natural serotonin in the process. The parents "feel bad" about disciplining their children because they "aren't home much." The parents treat their kids as if they are their buddies, rather than being parents. Children prefer their buddies to be their own age; they do not want parents as buddies. Children are born to us because they need guidance and wisdom. No one needs to learn how to become addicted to drugs. Parents are failing their children and society by trying to please their children rather than doing their job teaching their kids how to survive in the world as adults. When children become adults, they will need skills to exist in our society. Once they are adults, who will give them anything they want, when they want it? How will they understand responsibility?

There are many forms of abuse, so many in fact I cannot list them all here. Abuse may be as simplistic as calling your child "stupid." As a child, I remember my father telling me "you don't know what's good for you," whenever I did not want to eat something new. A young impressionable child may carry that through life as a belief. If I do not know what is good for me, I might grow up insecure in my decisions and depend on others for my needs (I might even let Dr. Ron boss me around). It took me years to learn that I do know what is good for me. The important thing to remember is that it is the *perception* of abuse that creates "painful issues" that can cause behaviors that lead to addiction, even if it is not the intent of the parents.

NLP (NEURO-LINGUISTIC PROGRAMMING), EFT AND ERICKSONIAN HYPNOSIS

NLP is the study of the map of thinking. It works with people's perception of their environment. How people perceive their environment is based on what representational system is used, for example, visual, auditory, and/or kinesthetic or feeling. In simplistic terms, some of us learn and perceive by seeing things (visual), some by hearing things (auditory), and some by doing things (kinesthetic, feeling). We all have favored representational systems, but we utilize all three. I use NLP and EFT to reframe negative or unwanted behavior, to help someone who desires certain goals and does not know how to achieve them, or to collapse anchors to negative experiences. There is a plethora of information on NLP and EFT, including Ericksonian Hypnosis, used frequently in an NLP therapeutic setting. Milton Erickson, MD, founder of the American Society of Clinical Hypnosis, brought hypnosis into the clinical setting and made it legitimate as a therapeutic tool.

Dr. Erickson was a genius at using metaphors during the hypnotic state, hence bypassing the "left-brain critical factor." He could put people into a trance state simply by speaking to them is a certain way. NLP and EFT are two of the most useful tools for changing limiting behaviors and for achieving goals that I have used, professionally and personally. EFT (emotional freedom technic) uses acupuncture points and talk therapy to collapse anchors. I will not go into great detail about either of these processes, but just mention them as powerful therapeutic tools that can cut the time of therapy by years.

BOUNDARIES

What are boundaries? Why do we need them? Boundaries are lines in the sand, so to speak, that do not permit crossing, or that permit it, but with consequences. We are taught some boundaries, and some are imposed upon us. There are societal boundaries that a child is exposed to and then needs guidance acting on those boundaries. For example: how does a child behave in a restaurant? If parents do not teach acceptable behavior, the child has no boundaries when in a restaurant. This leads to unacceptable behaviors. We see parents who refuse to set boundaries, and the child does not know about the concept of cause and effect. This leads to behaviors that can lead to addiction. Boundaries help children feel secure.

There are many types of boundaries. Jane is not allowed to come home after 9:00 p.m. on the weekend and 8:00 p.m. on school nights. This boundary is because Jane's parents want her to get all her homework and chores done. Her parents also know that for good health, in mind and body, Jane needs a good night's sleep. Why are boundaries so important? They promote healthy behaviors and teach children the concept of cause and effect. Negative behaviors lead to negative consequences. If parents do not teach their children boundaries, they will learn them the hard way when they go out into the world. That might include a punch in the nose or worse. Many young people have trouble in their first job, because they do not follow the directions of their boss, and they may end up getting fired. They have no clue that their behaviors are unacceptable in the outside world. This can be a major factor in addictive behavior. When they see that bowl of unknown pills at a party, they do not think that swallowing a handful can be dangerous. Unfortunately, many teens have no clue, because parents have been too permissive.

SELF-ESTEEM, SELF-WORTH

When we uncover the initial root cause of the use of mind-altering drugs, we have to examine a person's self-esteem and self-worth. How much self-worth do people have when they take a handful of pills they knows nothing about? People who value themselves do not need to follow the crowd or do something dangerous because someone tells them to.

When you have a high sense of self-worth or self-esteem, you do not feel the need to alter your mind. However, someone who has deep feelings of unworthiness, loneliness, shame, deep unexplained sadness, fear, or feels their life is pointless, *will* want to change or bury that negative feeling. Taking drugs can do that, but only temporarily. The reason for these intense negative feelings about the self and life is buried in the unconscious mind. That is why I show kids the many ways that they can reach that deeper part of themselves, where all the answers lie. Building self-esteem is a critical part of the treatment and recovery if we expect long-lasting results. I look for an aspect of the teen that is "worthwhile" and build upon that. Jennifer is great with the elderly; I watched her with some of our elderly patients in the waiting room. I told her how they mentioned it to our office staff. They thoroughly enjoy her company.

She did not see this herself. I told her that there are a lot of old people who are lonely. Since then Jennifer sees how much our older patients enjoy her presence. She since started visiting a local nursing home and reads to or just visits with the patients there. She feels good about what she does; she loves helping people. Her self-esteem has grown and continues to grow. Now she knows that she just might possess other qualities about which she never knew.

Everyone has a worthwhile or positive aspect to himself or herself. Discovering qualities and cultivating them can be challenging. When parents set boundaries for their kids, they are the best builders of self-esteem in their children. Parents get insights into positive aspects of their child, so that together, the therapist and family can build upon them and reward positive behaviors.

TOXIC RELATIONSHIPS

It is common knowledge that toxins are poison and can kill us at worst, or at the very least make us extremely ill. What about toxic relationships? Relationships that are toxic not only make us sick, they can kill us. They kill us by slowly taxing our immune system. Toxic relationships are stressful; stress, which is the *perception* of not having control, compromises the immune system's ability to fight disease. Eliminating toxic relationships is extremely difficult, especially for young people. It can be difficult to change jobs or relationships if they are the source of the toxic relationship. We can change where we hang out, and if desperate, we can even change our jobs. As kids, it's almost impossible to change schools. This is another very stressful situation. For example, we explain that in order to heal, in order to overcome addiction, teens have to stay away from all associations with people, including longtime friends, who use drugs. However, for kids going to school, staying away from friends and acquaintances associated with drug use can be extremely painful and difficult. In addition, the kids who do not use drugs are likely not going to hang out with former drug users either. This is usually much more difficult on a teenager than it is for adults. For teens and young adults, they and their friends are the center of the universe. In my experience working with these young people, changing friends may be the hardest part of the process of curing addiction. Many times the teen addict becomes a loner. Socialization becomes a major problem. They will some-time gravitate to being a "homebody," where they feel safe and wanted. Socialization with new no-drug-using friends is a very slow and methodic process. We need to constantly reassure them that things will get better. We encourage them to try to focus on having one or two good friends that do not use drugs, rather than a group of friends.

SELF-RESPONSIBILITY

Treating teens and young adults can be extremely rewarding but also exasperating. For me the reward of watching a strung-out junkie turn into an educated, responsible adult who gives back to society far outweighs any frustrations. It often takes a while and a lot of tough love for these kids to finally understand that there are consequences of their actions, but most of them do, with love, understanding, and strong support.

There are many reasons kids start drugs. None of them thinks, "Hey, I'm gonna get high and become an addict!" Taking a drug to "feel" good or better is psychological; becoming addicted is physiological. In my experience treating kids, it is easier to treat the brain first, then the psyche. If teens do not address the unbalanced brain chemistry, then understanding and working with the under-lying psychological reasons for altering their minds and emotions is much more difficult. I often wish I could see them every day for a couple of months. They do not believe, not deep inside, that they can quit drugs, let alone stay off drugs. In large part, it's because they do not trust themselves to handle their emotions. They do not believe they are strong enough. They do not believe they will know how to have fun without drugs. Most of these kids don't remember how to have fun without drugs, usually because they started drugs at such a young age, often when they began smoking cigarettes. In other words, they have no self-confidence, no self-worth. It is usually desperation that brings them into our office. They have run out of money or a place to go for help. Maybe they experienced a stay in jail, or their families have given up and they are homeless. They finally realize that there is only one first high, no matter what they poison their bodies with. Most have watched someone die of an overdose or worse, or at least know someone who has.

I no longer worry or even wonder much about how I will help the young person in front of me. Every night and morning after mediation, I tell God, "Bring to me only those who I can best benefit and can best benefit me. Bring through me only what is for their highest and best good, whatever is Your will." And then I trust that no matter what, whatever comes through me is for his or her best good. I open my heart and trust that a higher power will guide me. This is what I teach my patients. Each youngster is different yet there are similarities, commonalities, no matter what background they come from. One of these is irresponsibility because of their lack of understanding the consequences of their behaviors. These kids are nice, usually smart, and they work at understanding, most of the time. However, they have either not been taught about consequences, or the lessons taught are not reinforced from a young age. So they get confused and angry or surprised when the consequences meet up with them face-to-face. That is sometimes at our office. They are to make their own appointments and keep track of them. If they miss an appointment without a forty-eight hour notice, they are billed. When responsibility is not taught and enforced at home, the child has to learn the hard way. They will not live with mom and dad forever. At some point they will be forced to learn, which is often very painful.

Tough love can be confusing at first for many of these kids. Teaching them responsibility does not win us popularity, at least not in the beginning. But then there is reward. The reward? Love and acceptance, even if they slip up, which most of them do. I have been asked, "Why are you so nice and caring and then make me pay money I don't have, because I had to miss an appointment?" This is where they begin to learn about responsibility. First I remind them that they had enough money to buy four bags of heroin a day, and if they have such a money problem, why miss an appointment? Then I tell them that sleeping in because they were playing video games all night is not "having" to miss an appointment. And third, "my caring about you has nothing to do with applying the rules that you agreed to." Many adults, as well as children, confuse love with rejection and anger. That is because many people were raised with rejection when they did something wrong or displeasing to a parent. Think of when little children are angry with mommy and tell her "I hate you!" That is because they have no understanding of how to express their anger so they confuse it with hate because that is a word they know. It would be better to tell children, "It's okay to be mad at me. I am mad too. I am mad that you hit your sister, but I will always love you. Loving and being mad are different." This teaches the child the difference between anger at the behavior, rather than at the child himself. When mommy and daddy are mad at their children rather than at the behavior, the children can grow up feeling unacceptable, not good enough, or a bad person.

The majority of the people I meet, whether in my office or private life, are interested in learning about metaphysics (the branch of philosophy that examines the nature of reality, including the relationship between mind and matter), but youngsters and young adults love it. They are able to grasp these higher and subjective concepts better than most of the adults I see. I have been amazed at how soulful and spiritual these kids are when someone is sincerely interested in listening to their deepest fears, desires, and confusion. It is as if they are bursting with questions relative to their realities, their environment, and their existence and purpose. There are many talented therapists I have met who are knowledgeable in subjective subjects, such as metaphysics; however, many do not use this valuable knowledge in their practices. Restrictions from institutions where they work often prevent them from using their knowledge in psychotherapy, but this is changing. I am not the first psychotherapist to discuss subjects such as past lives and future lives to get across cause and effect, among other life lessons. When I tell addicted patients that they need to overcome their addiction or they may take it with them "to the other side," some ask, "what if I don't believe that?" I ask them to wonder about whether I am right.

Arming patients with the knowledge and means to take back their inner power by understanding that there are consequences of their behavior, helps them begin to take responsibility for their own behaviors and empowers them and makes them strong and productive adults. Responsibility, responding to one's own ability, *is* power. In order to understand this concept and more, we have to open our minds in order to break through our limited understanding of the universe and ourselves in it, which is what I encourage others to think about, because in order to create change, we must be able to access our true potential. Ronald Wong Jue, PhD, President of the Association for Transpersonal Psychology, wrote in the forward for the book *Other Lives Other Selves*, by Roger Woolger, PhD, a well-known and respected Jungian psychotherapist, "Comfort and security levels often cloud our abilities to move deeper into knowledge of the images that impel and regulate our lives. Yet we yearn for ways to clear the clouds of unknowingness. In ourselves and our society, we are bound up with patterns that perhaps no longer serve us. If anything, these patterns which focus on materialistic values and self-centered orientations seem to create ecological havoc within ourselves and on our planet. On the other hand, these patterns have given rise to crises that are forcing individuals, groups, and nations to question old assumptions, models, and structures - and to develop a different perspective in order to deal with the perennial problems we face. As Ilya Prigogine, who won the 1977 Nobel Prize for a theory describing transformations, emphasizes, we are perhaps at a turning point where the stresses and conflicts of our time can thrust us into a new higher order. He is stating what Thomas Kuhn, a science historian and philosopher, calls a movement toward a paradigm shift - a paradigm being a scheme held by a community of individuals for understanding and explaining certain aspects of reality. We are presently emerging from a materialistic, control-oriented, self-centered scheme of reality into one which perceives life as an inseparable web of relationships. This new paradigm supports an awareness that there are intrinsically dynamic processes (forms of consciousness) that articulate the patterns and stresses of our lives. We are still hesitant to give up the belief that science deals with absolute truth rather than with a limited and approximate description of reality. It must be considered that personal truth is never an objective endeavor within the realm of science, but rather a personal path and inner revelation which all great spiritual teachers have revealed." [sic]

Because most kids and young adults have had less time being indoctrinated into "unknowingness," their minds are open, willing, and able to absorb other ideas. From there, they can gain new experiences and judge for themselves what is good for them.

This openness can save them. When teens start to develop self-esteem, they say things like, "I love doing better in school," or "at home, with family." One teen came in on a December day, excited because "it was the first time she was able to buy Christmas gifts for her family." That simple step forward made her feel better than she had in years…and without drugs.

Quitting drugs and taking responsibility for actions brings up what we repressed while on drugs. Gerald, a twenty-two-year-old, was two years into recovery when he told me he was getting married. He worried about future children being addicted, because several of his siblings and his father were addicts. For almost a year, he was anxious about the possibility of producing addicted children; it became an obsession. One day he came in and seemed at peace. When asked what happened, he said, "I talked it over with my fiancé and decided to have a vasectomy." Not something we would have suggested, but a resolution to his dilemma nonetheless. His sense of self-responsibility overwhelmed his need to be a biologic parent, and it resolved his psychological trauma. I commended his sense of responsibility, although I worried that he may be sorry later.

MEDITATION, SPIRITUAL GROWTH AND THE POWER OF THE MIND IN ADDICTION TREATMENT

"Of course, there are many mediocre therapists and many limited kinds of therapy. Just as in meditation, you should look for the best. Beyond the traditional psychotherapies of the '40s and '50s, many new therapists have been developed with a strong spiritual basis such as psychosynthesis. Reichian breath work, sand play, and a whole array of transpersonal psychologies. The best therapy, like the best meditation practice, uses awareness to heal the heart

and is concerned not so much with our stories, as with fear and attachment and their release, and with bringing mindfulness to areas of delusion, grasping and unnecessary suffering. One can, at times, find the deepest realizations of selflessness and non-attachment through some of the methods of transpersonal psychology."
—*Jack Kornfield,* "Even the Best Meditators Have Old Wounds to Heal" ©Buddha Dharma Education Association 1996-2012

Meditation is often confused with guided imagery, which is okay. However, true meditation is simply separating oneself from the outside world and going within. Meditation is relaxing into yourself, an important part of life, physically and emotionally. Meditation helps us become more aware of the deep and inner meaning to our lives, which is often scary in the beginning. Part of experiencing our inner strengths, abilities, and capabilities, is the willingness to reach into the deepest parts of our soul so we can transcend our fears. It is there that we find wisdom and strength to discover what needs healing and how to do that. To transcend inner fears, we must first discover that we are never alone. Emotions are behaviors; we can change behaviors. They are only in our minds. This thought is what gets me through fear. When I feel fear, I remind myself that, "This is only my thinking. I am doing fear." Once experienced, the inner sense of a loving and wise presence helps free us from the fear of looking closely at our deepest suffering. Daily meditation is the doorway to great wisdom. We cannot afford to not meditate daily.

There are many benefits to daily meditation, besides a higher awareness, such as increased concentration, relaxation, and the ability to regenerate cells. Studies confirmed greater gray matter concentration for meditators in the right anterior insula, which is involved in interceptive awareness, the ability to be aware of internal bodily states. According to *Merriam-Webster*, *interoceptive* is described as "relating to, or being stimuli arising within the body and especially in the viscera." This means that regular meditation causes changes in the functioning of organs and systems in the body, not just the brain. The necessary prelude to meditation is relaxation of the mind and body. Though addicted teens and young adults may seem calm on the outside, they are nervous, even hyper, inside. The benefits of daily meditation are many, psychologically, mentally, physically, and spiritually. Meditation releases endorphins and other calming neurochemicals. To quote Dr. Milton Erickson, "You have a conscious mind and you have an unconscious mind." Daily meditation helps teens reach into their unconscious minds to help them discover the "deeper reasons" for their addiction.

Sometimes as therapists we do not know what to do. I no longer think about that. I trust that when we ask to be a channel of healing, then we are. I also know that we can only do so much. No matter how hard we try or how much we care, the young patient has to be motivated to become sober and stay clean. That is our biggest challenge as therapists. We do our best to help people learn how to discover their abilities and capabilities, and since they do not see their worth at first, this can be hard to accomplish. Without drugs the very emotions, racing thoughts, anxiety, come to the surface with a vengeance. These intense feelings are symptoms of issues that need to be dealt with and have been ignored.

As a transpersonal psychotherapist, my therapy is somewhat different from most mainstream psychotherapy because it is spiritually based. Not religiously based, although I do incorporate patients' religious beliefs when it is important to them, especially as the basis for their belief in a higher power. However, whatever any of us has learned in any religion, it is what we have learned from what others have learned, and then given to us as fact. In reality, the "truth" depends on whom you ask, and that depends on what *they* were taught by others. I do not debate religion, either with my patients or in this book. That is personal. What I am saying is that to experience God, we have to open our minds to something much bigger than what we have been taught. Otherwise, our experiences of the omnipotent are limited. Actually, anything that has not been directly experienced for oneself, but has been taught by another's experience or learning is someone else's truth adopted by the listener, another example of a schema. I bring this up because it is important for us to understand that others, no matter how loving the intention, help form our beliefs. Certain connections, or anchors, are why people say they do not believe in God, or that God is punishing them or God does not love them or God loves them more than someone else. These beliefs are anchors infused by others' beliefs and told to us as fact. Whether we were raised very religiously, somewhat religiously, or not religiously at all, we all have anchors, to some degree, which are associated with religion that we have learned from others while growing up.

My main focus throughout therapy is teaching patients how to develop a deeper connection with what many of us call God, a higher power that resides within us. One of the truths that they need to know is the belief that deep inside, they already have all the abilities and capabilities they need to be anything and achieve anything they desire. This is a spiritual law. My job is to help them connect with that. It is one thing to *believe* and another to *know*.

A HIGHER POWER AS HELPER

"I could not say I believe. I know! I have had the experience of being gripped by something that is stronger than myself, something that people call God."
—When asked if he believes in God, C. G. Jung, *Time* Magazine, 1955

Most of us believe in a higher power that many of us call God. However, there are also people whose concept of God is negative and full of fear, which is counterproductive in therapy and in life. There are various reasons for this, but some people think of God as unapproachable and judgmental, simply because that is what they have been taught. Fears and misconceptions are why I use various names for God, so that my patients can tap into God's consciousness without firing up anchors that automatically connect them to learned and limited views of God. Nothing can compare to our own experience of that higher power, without the interference of indoctrination. Just one single incident in a child's life can anchor his or her perception of God, hopefully positive, but sometimes negative. How sad that some people are afraid of going within because of their fears. The fears are exactly where we need to go; we cannot heal what we do not see. Maybe it was something that people heard and it became associated with a belief that God would judge them harshly. If that perception were frightening, I would have a problem helping them to tap into that presence of love and serenity. Also, depending on how one is raised, God has many names. So I use terms like Higher Consciousness, Higher Self, Universal Life Force, The Source, and so forth, whichever helps the person in front of me feel comfortable with connecting to that higher power. This circumvents negative anchors to God. This higher power helps people to know that they are never alone and always loved. It is a space where we can go during our deepest needs. Simple meditation practiced daily becomes the doorway to the soul, which is connected to the source of our love, our light, to the God consciousness.

Of course it is good to hear that there is a higher power at work and that higher power resides in each and every one of us. That source becomes my biggest helper. However, just saying that is not enough; patients have to *feel* it, experience it. Connecting with that unseen force is what helps us get through anything. Innate in every person is the ability of connecting as one with the source of all there is. This knowledge through experience is not instant, and it certainly takes time and effort, but is the most powerful part of my therapy. This does not mean that it happens religiously, but it can be for some people, if that is what they rely on to help them get through hard times. Addiction is a tough road, with many ups and downs. But the path to healing addiction is possible, and daily meditation is an impetus for us to grow in wisdom, and later in the ability to help someone else. It is empowering to know that if we were not strong enough to face adversity, including addiction, then adversity would not present itself.

In the story of Maggie, you'll recall that Maggie was hurt, but she was also confused because she loved her little cousin and consciously knew her grandfather still loved her very much. But she still felt cheated somehow, a deep sense of loss and loneliness. It was a type of grieving process. The problem was that she did not know how to handle her emotions. Understanding the FTP and its RS opens the path to healing. So she took an opiate that helped her to feel a little better for a while. I helped Maggie learn coping mechanisms for difficult conditions and situations that she faced now and would probably face in the future. I showed her different ways of looking at things. We cannot change past events, but we have the power to change how we think about them. It takes patience, and it takes practice, and sometimes we need to fall down and get right back up again and learn from the fall.

One coping mechanism out of many is to look at the wisdom in our mistakes and slipups, rather than punishing ourselves, which hinders growth. We cannot change past events; only change how we think about past events. When we find at least one lesson from an event that hurt us or one for which we are sorry, then we can let it go. Dwelling on past events eats away at our life energy. Meditation helps reveal the wisdom needed.

Changing how we think about painful events can help us to see problems and painful events as opportunities to grow in wisdom and strength.

IMPORTANCE OF PARENTS

If you ever wonder why your children do not listen to you, do not do their chores, misbehave, do not work, do not do their homework, and why they take drugs, ask yourself this: "How would my child know to do or not do these things? How would my child know that some of the things he does are risky, rude, or unhealthy?" How would your child know that hard work and perseverance pay off if she has never been taught through example? How would she know that earning her own money through an honest day's work is rewarding? Has your child been taught the things that you want him or her to do? Has he been taught the consequences of bad behavior? Telling kids about responsibility has little or no effect. To understand, they would have to have something with which they can compare. Having kids experience cause and effect is powerful. If Sally has been in trouble before, have you let her pay the consequences that you threatened her with? Or did give in, showing her your weaknesses? Giving in also shows kids that what you say is not sincere. Are you consistent? Most parents would never tell their child that it is okay to skip school, but have you told her that it is okay to miss school because you are going on a vacation? Inconsistency is worse than being too strict or too lenient (except perhaps being so strict that it is dangerous or unhealthy). If you are too strict, you have no carrot to hold on the end of the proverbial stick. If children are shown that they need to earn privileges, then they will generally be hard workers as adults. If they have everything given to them without earning what they want, they will expect the same when they are adults. When parents are too strict, it is almost impossible to learn how to change for the better or to strive for a higher standard. Teens are rebellious at best.

For instance, if Sally works hard at school, babysits for spending money, and obeys her curfew, you might reward her in some small way. The small reward reinforces positive behaviors. You may be surprised how far your compliments go. Do you mention on a regular basis how happy you are about her hard work and good grades? Studying instead of going out on weekdays, having a part-time job rather than walking the mall with friends? These things need to be noticed by her parents. One of the best rewards you can give is some of your undivided attention, such as a lunch together, at home or out. If Sally is never rewarded for her positive behaviors, she may wonder what the point is of working hard. If, no matter what she does or how well behaved she is, she is not allowed extra privileges, such as going to a movie or a little extra toward what she has been saving for, eventually she may choose the easier path. If Sally has been saving for something that cost $75 and she has saved $65 by working hard, you might give her the remaining $10. If her brother of sister hangs out with friends and breaks curfew, smokes dope, and gets poor grades, and there is no differentiation by you between her positive behavior and their negative behaviors, then she may decide to stop working so hard. She may also wonder why you "like them better than her no matter how hard she tries to be a good girl." In this example, Sally likely does not learn the value of positive behavior and of focusing on positive goals. The message to Sally is "no one cares if you work hard and stay straight." Some parents think that by giving Sally a little extra reward for her good behavior they are comparing her to their other children. They think that the message may be that Sally is better than Joey and Brenda. She is not better, but her *behavior* is! Separate the child from the behavior and it will be easier to distinguish the differences in behavior between all of your kids. It will make it easier for them to know why Sally got a few extra dollars from you. Of course, teenagers will tell you how you love Sally more than them, how you're unfair, and so on. That is okay. Your job is not to be buddies; they have buddies. Kids want parents and time with their parents.

You can stay at home and still escape, which is often how people start addictions. Kids look for ways to escape unpleasantness. Children do not have much choice in these situations when you think of it. They live under your roof, you pay the bills, and they cannot make it on their own. When kids believe that they cannot talk to parents, their negative emotions exacerbate.

I believe there is a huge disconnect between parents and children today. Few families sit down at the dinner table together. It is important to commune with your children, and doing so over dinner is a great experience that they will likely remember into adulthood. Dinner together provides an opportunity to talk to and to understand one another. When problems do arise for kids, they usually wish they could talk to their parents. When they share a few dinners a week with mom and/or dad, they are likely to think they can talk to at least one of you. You will learn a lot about your kids, and they will learn a lot about you and what you think, too. Ideally we would sit and have dinner together with our children every night, but with our hectic way of life now that is not realistic. Everybody is very busy. But three nights a week, preferably more, will be very rewarding. Sometimes you have to demand it, especially if sitting down together is a new experience. I remember times when I told our kids they had to be home on a certain night in time for dinner, even if they complained sometimes because they had other ideas. But ask any one of them if they would change it if they could. The same holds true for our grandsons, who have lived with us. They are now grown men, and they will tell you that they value those times together over dinner. We are a close-knit family, and I believe a lot has to do with those dinners.

KIDS WHO DO TOO MUCH

A lot of kids today are stressed because they are doing too much, usually because parents think their child will do better if they are dancing, playing an instrument, playing football or hockey or even both, and other extracurricular activities. Try to remember, they have school, study time, and also need some down time. How many of these parents realize their child needs downtime? Oftentimes a child will want to do all of these things…for about five minutes. Children think they can do what comes out of their mouths. If they can think of doing five things, they think it's easy to actually do them. They do not realize the time involved, or how taxing all of the above can be. That is why they have parents. Be careful before allowing your child to do whatever he or she wants or you could be setting them up for failure. Does any parent want their child to become a "quitter"? With children just as with some adults, it's thinking out loud. Teach your kids how to truly think about something before they do it. Look at your kids' track record. Do they tend to start something and then quit it when the novelty wears off? You might want to check that track record, as well as go over the pros and cons of learning to play the piano before you go out and invest in one. Do your kids do their homework on time? Do they keep up their grades? Are your kids responsible? Do they stick to their word? Promises? If you cannot say yes to these questions, I would not advise getting a piano for Alice. Instead, remind her about the other things she said she "wanted" to do but did not stick to. Help Alice learn how to balance life so she learns how to do things for herself. There are some children who find school so easy, they don't mind being in two different sports and glee club. However, there are some children who struggle to keep up their grades, and having them overly busy just puts a tremendous stress on them, a way to set kids up for failure. If you wonder why some kids do not just tell parents that they are overwhelmed, it could be because they don't know how to tell them, or they have not been taught how to express their feelings and thoughts without the fear of their parents' anger. Another and more likely reason is that many kids have not been taught how to understand what they are feeling. Many kids may not know that they are overwhelmed, because their friends may be doing the same things. Your child may not realize his or her friends might be better equipped to do multiple things. That does not make one bad or good, just different. Just point out to your kids their qualities, rather than trying to convince them that they are as good as others, even if some of their friends can play six different sports with one hand behind their backs.

I am often asked, "What is the most important thing I can do as a parent to minimize my child's chance of becoming an addict?" The answer is, "Stop enabling your child when he repeats negative behaviors." Enabling is allowing. Think of enabling as "helping." Do you "help" your child repeat bad behavior by ignoring it? Continue to reward him? Enabling sends the message that you think the bad behavior is okay; worse, that you are afraid to stand your ground as a parent. You may say you do not approve, but your actions tell the truth. When you tell Jimmy that you do not want him to stay out past 11:00 p.m. and he strolls in at midnight, you enable him by pretending to yourself that you believe his lame excuse is valid. You also diminish his respect for you as a parent and role model.

It is natural for kids to experiment with life, stretching themselves and testing their boundaries. Babies test their boundaries by sticking anything in their mouths that they can get their little hands on. Mom or dad takes the item out of the baby's mouth. If there are no boundaries, kids feel unsafe and confused. They become especially confused as young adults. When parents allow kids to get away with whatever they want while growing up, those kids assume they can do that with everyone. Jimmy wants to go golfing and borrow his friend Tom's golf clubs. Tom isn't home, but Jimmy knows Tom keeps his clubs in the garage. Jimmy assumes Tom won't mind because he has loaned Jimmy his clubs before. Tom goes into the garage and takes them, fully planning on returning them the next day. The next day Tom notices his clubs are gone when he goes to use them. On a hunch, before calling the police, he calls Jimmy and asks him if he used the clubs. Jimmy tells him he did and that he forgot to bring them back. There is a heated argument between the two friends, and Tom never lets Jimmy borrow his clubs again. Tom is upset because Jimmy did not ask him to use his clubs, let alone to go into his parent's garage and take them. Jimmy's feelings are hurt, because he did not think it was a big deal and he thought Tom overreacted. Jimmy lost a friend over the incident and did not understand why. The confusion is the result of Jimmy growing up doing what he wanted, when he wanted. You can imagine how difficult it can be as a kid to learn about boundaries. It is much more difficult as an adult; however, it is often learned the hard way through pain and suffering, as in Jimmy's case.

GUILTY PARENTING

Enabling children also causes a lot of stress for you as a parent. We all have stress in our lives these days, so it might seem easiest to just ignore bad behaviors. In the long run, though, a little extra time now, setting and sticking to your rules, can save far more time and grief later. Another reason parents do not set rules and/or don't stick to their rules is what I call "guilty parenting." Guilty parenting is when parents feel guilty because they are gone all day at work and the kids are with a babysitter or at day care. They bring their children home or come home to their children, tired from a long day's work. It's late. The kids have to eat. Someone has to put the food on the table, maybe even cook. Kids are amazing miniature psychologists. They know how to play the parents because they know how to test boundaries. They get to eat what they demand rather than what is healthy for them. It is also easier to "prepare" food that is prepared, like mac & cheese, a high carbohydrate (sugar) dinner. They get to stay up late because they know if they complain or cry or throw a tantrum it will work, plus, mom and dad feel guilty for being gone all day. After all, how can you discipline your child after being gone all day? Giving in creates a pattern in the child, whereby "if I scream loud enough or complain, cry enough, I know I'll get my way. It's just a matter of time." This is a destructive pattern that continues into adulthood, but it just won't go over well with a teacher, boss, friends, or spouse. We do not always get our way in life. We all face disappointment from time to time. We learn to deal with it. As a parent, your job is to teach your children what is acceptable and not acceptable in the real world, rather than to try and be a friend. There are times when your kids do not like you. So what? At least they will respect you. Are you really concerned about your child, or are you more concerned about yourself? I know this will not buy me new friends, but parents who enable are parents who think more of themselves than of their kids. Think of your goal. Is it in the best interest of your kids or yourself? If it is your kids, then it is easier to do what is best for them. Keeping that goal in mind will help you make the right decisions for your children.

One way to test this is to notice how many times you speak in terms of "I" when thinking or talking about your child's behavior. For example, your daughter is on drugs. The therapist tells you to take away Jane's car, because she has not done anything to deserve that privilege. You say, "Gee, *I* feel really bad, because she paid for most of the car herself." We can feel bad for our kid, which is natural. Using the "I" word is a good indication that you are thinking more of what you want, rather than the best for your kids. Jane does not need a car, because after doing drugs and all the negative behavior that goes along with drug seeking, Jane should not have access to a car. At this point, the only things she needs is to go to school, come home, do her homework, and study until she earns back privileges, one at a time. I do not believe in making kids keep their room as clean as I would; however, there is no eating in the bedroom. Chores should be well defined, such as filling the dishwasher, emptying dishwasher, *being* the dishwasher. Teens are old enough to wash their own clothes and pick up after themselves "now," not when they feel like it. No cell phone, no curfew. She is consistently compliant in her addiction program. Furthermore, who needs a curfew when you are not allowed to go anywhere but home or church, synagogue, or mosque? A good therapist will help you define rules for your personal situation and stick to them. Sometimes your heart will break a little, but keeping your mind on the ultimate goal of helping your kid grow up to adulthood, free of drugs, will make it easier. How she earns back privileges is something that you need to discuss with your therapist and varies between families.

There are kids who were raised with both parents working full-time who have become successful adults. I have also seen kids with moms at home who turned to drugs. I have seen people drive without seat belts, too. That does not mean they will suffer serious injury or death in a car crash. Without seat belts, however, there is a much higher chance of serious injury or death. Young adults (18–24) have the highest crash-related injury rates of all adults, and seat belts reduce serious crash-related injuries by 50 percent. My experience, as a parent, grandparent, and psychotherapist, is that kids who don't have a relationship with both parents for more than just a couple of hours in the evening have a propensity for poor outcomes. By relationship, I mean most children are closer to their parents than they are with a computer, a social network, a cell phone, iPod, and so forth. In a restaurant recently we saw a baby about one year old, in a high chair. His father was trying to eat with one hand while holding an iPad in front of the baby's face with the other hand. What did parents do before all these electronics? I believe they actually talked, played, or colored with their child, helped him or her eat, while the baby learned how to behave in public. I hear people talk about why kids act rudely or do not know how to behave socially. What does one expect, when at home and in public, socialization happens through a tablet or smartphone, and by ignoring the people in one's company.

My advice to parents on this issue seems tough to some, but it is necessary for minimizing the risk of serious problems. Raising kids is not easy, and raising even the most normal of teens can be the epitome of challenge. If you are not having problems with a child then read no further; this book is geared toward people who are dedicated to helping children, those who already have a problem, or look as though they might, and for parents who want to save their kids or prevent them from disaster. Remember, once a child has a serious problem or has started drug use, your path to helping him or her will be possibly the toughest ride you have taken. I admit I have an issue with both parents of young children working all day, five days a week or more, without at least a family member watching them. The "formative years" has meaning. If you think that day-care workers care as much about your child as you do, you are kidding yourself.

When Dr. Ron and I presented a talk on teen addiction, a woman stood up and asked, irate, "And what the heck are the schools doing about these kids?" I could not believe my ears. I told her, "It is not the job of the school to monitor your child's behaviors or to teach kids right from wrong. It never has been. Teachers do not get a masters degree in babysitting. Sorry, ma'am, but that is a cop-out. The job of a teacher is to teach kids reading, writing, and arithmetic. It is *your* job as a parent to teach your children how to behave, including in school."

Today it seems as though parents have handed over the job of parenting to teachers or day-care workers, or that kids come home to an empty house. For some parents, there are few options. Some parents absolutely have to work. But six-week-old babies in day-care centers seems too harsh to me. Children need a parent, preferably a mom, in their younger years, and both parents in their lives is better, whether or not parents are divorced. Mom helps little ones early on how to become positive, confident, caring, and responsible for their behavior, and most of all, assures that babies are loved and loveable. Children need to know that when another child hurts their feelings, they will get over it, that they shouldn't let what other people say bother them. As you comfort them, you as a parent can teach them how to one day comfort themselves, because you have armed them with wisdom and the ability to do so. Teens definitely benefit from a parent being home after school; it is not necessary, but beneficial. *Addicted teens need to come home to adult supervision!* Most moms I have met feel torn between working full-time and being home with their children. They have worked hard for their careers. Those who kept their careers but cut back hours at work were less stressed than when working full-time, even when it meant less income. With guidance, they made it work. Parents tell me they both need to work because of finances. Most of the time parents who see me need to learn about budgeting. Determine if it is more to do with spending than with income. Your kids are only yours until they start kindergarten.

So what does this have to do with teen addiction? I am not suggesting that kids do not turn into great adults because both parents work. Many do. Think of the statistics on seat belts. Do you think anyone else is going to monitor, love, and nurture your child as you would? Who do you want your baby to bond to more, you or the person who is with her most? There are arguments on both sides. I am saying that there are people wondering what has happened to kids today, the same question asked for centuries and in many societies in the past. However, we have a real and serious problem in our society not seen in our history before. We have already lost much of a generation. We will feel the loss more acutely when baby boomers are no longer working. My answer to the question is, "What is different now, compared to when you, your parents, or grandparents, were raising children?" Think about it. Pretty much everything up to birthing is the same, so what *is* different? How many family dinners are there anymore? How many kids are afraid to disobey their parents? When we were kids, "respect" was spelled "f-e-a-r." There is a serious disconnect in the family unit, and it shows in our children as teens and adults. We see teenagers who act rudely, are self-centered and lazy, but expect more and more (and more expensive toys). How sad is it when television ads try to encourage kids to play for "sixty minutes or more." Most of these kids are nice kids. But if nobody teaches them how and when to be polite, how do they know they are being rude?

Teaching kids the notion that everybody's a winner, that nobody is a loser, does *not* prepare kids for the real world of adulthood that they will someday face. The truth of the matter is, there *are* winners and there *are* losers. The positive thing about losing is the opportunity it can give to learn that our strengths can come from that loss. Encouragement to try even harder the next time will reinforce the drive to achieve. It helps us to be positive, knowing that we have another chance to try harder, or differently. If losing is the same as winning, which it is clearly not (tell that to the Buffalo Bills), then where is the incentive to do better? Where is the incentive for the winner to continue striving for higher achievement? This is a serious "modern belief" for various reasons, one of which is creating a society of adults who give up and do not know how to pull themselves up by their bootstraps and motivate themselves to do better. In all walks of life, there is nothing like competition to make someone work harder. Think of the radio commercial where the guy calls in sick. His boss says, "Don't worry, we've got Bob." Suddenly the guy starts feeling better and tells the boss he can probably come in, and his boss says again, "No, no, don't worry. We've got Bob!" The point is, the ad demonstrates a human truth. The same is true with animals, domestic and wild. Two pets in the house will eat proportionately more than only one, because of perceived competition. I believe that people who teach kids that "everyone's a winner," even if the other team beats their team one hundred to one, do not want kid's feelings to be hurt. Nonsense. No one "hurts" us. "Hurt" is a behavior that we do. Many people believe that this concept will grow children into positive adults. Nothing could be further from reality. How might that happen? Failing at something is a message to do something different, or maybe to try harder. We inevitably learn more from our mistakes and failures than from our successes. I would rather see kids grow into adults who have been taught that to do better means to try harder. How is being a heroin addict a winner? However, a heroin addict who turns his or her life around and gains wisdom and healing from the experience and can help someone else is much more likely to be a better person than he or she ever would have been before that experience.

TEENS ALREADY ADDICTED; FINDING THEIR OWN ANSWERS

Treating Teens

It often takes a while and a lot of tough love for these kids to finally understand that there are consequences to their actions, but most of them do, with love, understanding, and strong support. To repeat: I reinforce to kids that I know that they have all the abilities and capabilities within them to achieve whatever they want in life. They just need support and guidance and that is my job. Their job is motivation. If they really, really, really want to have a good drug free life, they will. "I will support you as long as you do your part; I will explain to you what your part is. I will guide you in learning how to access and accentuate your abilities and capabilities. I will also show you how to access the Spirit within, the best counselor you will ever have. I will teach you how to find the answers to the most difficult questions and help you feel good about yourself. You will discover how to love yourself and love life, so that you will no longer need drugs to feel good. You will one day see the value in negative events, including this addiction, and learn how to grasp and utilize the positive from it. You will learn that you have a conscious mind and an unconscious mind and a spirit within, knowledge that is far more powerful than you can imagine right now. You just have to learn how to recognize each of these and how to utilize them for your highest and best good. Armed with all this, you can reach all your goals."

No matter how hard we try, how much we care, the young patient has to be motivated to become and stay cleansed of drugs. That is the biggest challenge for a therapist. We have to help young patients learn how to discover their abilities and capabilities, and since they do not see them nor believe they have them, that is tough. And it takes time; we are in a race together. Without drugs, the emotions, racing thoughts, and anxiety, come up to the surface with a vengeance. These intense feelings are symptoms of issues that need to be dealt with and have been ignored. As Carl Jung said, "what we repress will come out in a negative way." I tell my patients that we will work together to discover the message in those feelings. When asked why they started taking drugs, inevitably they say, "to fit in," or "everyone was doing it." These are superficial answers that they have heard from others, and because the deeper issue or trauma is lost in the unconscious mind, this is what they believe. However, experimenting with drugs, especially more than once, does not happen because everyone is doing it. Neither is it because you wanted to be a part of the crowd. It is because you wanted to feel different. If you take a drug to feel different, you did not like what you were feeling to begin with. That is psychological. After a time, you became dependent on or addicted to the drug, which then becomes biological. As some have verbalized, "Then there's hope for me?" Hope is a great start!

I give these young people a lot of new territory to think about, useful and interesting information to help them learn how to access help with changing their lives. They learn how to manage their stress and that which stresses them. If they can see that there is a higher power within them that they can reach for, they will be able to find answers to their problems. The answers they receive are specifically targeted for them and give them hope. Going within for answers to problems, as well as solutions to problems, also gives kids self-confidence. Just as weight-lifting builds strength in the body, meditation builds the inner strength needed for their journey ahead. By learning to go within through meditation, our patients find that on a deep level they know there is great wisdom inside themselves. They begin to strengthen critical thinking skills. Those who use these new skills later amaze me with their own solutions to problems and observations of their environment. They look for a higher purpose, not only in their lives, but also concerning the purpose of their addiction and the path they are meant to take. Adversity and despair forces them to into what I call a spiritual "redirect." Looking at addiction as the path to a spiritual redirect helps people look at a different path from the one that led to addiction, perhaps the path they were meant to take all along. The kids we treat are brave, though they do not see this themselves, at least not in the beginning. The skills they learn give them the strength to conquer fears that previously held them back. A therapist needs to keep them busy in the interim, which is not an easy task with teens. I give them processes that are exciting to them. Otherwise, we will lose them. That is why I use

Neuro-Linguistic Programming (NLP), hypnosis of various kinds, meditation with writing, Emotional Freedom Technique (EFT, a technique to collapse anchors and phobias, based on interrupting the energetic pathways in a behavior by tapping acupuncture points while verbalizing the unwanted behavior or thought), and the knowledge of the power of their own minds.

When our young patients first see me, they are anxious and do not know what to expect from me or what I expect from them. I want them to be comfortable in my office and with me. My main goal is to reframe negative beliefs and to show them that they can change behaviors by changing their beliefs. They need to know that they are never alone and there is help and guidance within themselves. Once they know that they have the power to change themselves by changing their thinking, with fortitude they will be able to beat this addiction. I want them to know that they have all the abilities and capabilities they need to achieve anything they want and that we are on their side. I like to combine neurochemistry profiles, simple ones, because this is also something that helps motivate people, especially when I can show them on paper that there is a reason for their anxiety; it's in the brain. A lot of people are afraid that there is something wrong with them, so I go over the four main reasons for addiction, the first of which is brain chemistry, which we address right away.

Goal setting is important in recovery. Reaching these goals starts with clearly defining the goals. One of the best ways to reach a goal is to be able to define it visually. If you cannot see it, you probably won't achieve it. Peter had great difficulty seeing a productive and happy future for himself, because he "felt" his goals but could not give me a picture. Because he could not give me a picture, I knew he had not defined them clearly for himself; feeling goals does not accomplish goals. Peter would soon learn how to reach goals by practicing visualization, using a different part of the brain. For example, I asked him what kind of house or apartment he would like if he won the lottery. He talked about how he would like to live in the country, in his own house, and would buy a new truck. Another problem that prevents people from reaching goals is that they don't believe they can. I told Peter to describe the house. How many bedrooms would it have? How far back from the road? What color would it be? Would there be trees around it? What color is the truck, the year, the make? Is it in the driveway or in a garage? What street is the house on? What town? What does it look like inside? Describe the colors in each room. In other words, I showed Peter how to visualize clearly, as if it were real. Waking visualization is not as clear as when dreaming, as it happens on a different brainwave. However, the longer you imagine what something will look like, the easier it becomes. That was less than two years ago. Peter has a new job doing what he loves. He makes more money than he previously thought he would and recently moved into a house in the country and has a new truck and is very happy. You have to see it to achieve it.

I ask patients what their belief is regarding God. It is important to utilize one's belief to help them actually *connect* with their God to help them on this journey. If someone says he or she does not believe in God, I say, "Interesting. What about God do you not believe?" Confusion sits on their faces. Many people think of God as a man who lives in the clouds, judgmental, who punishes some people and helps others, with no rhyme or reason. This God is an unfair and frightening God, certainly not one that will help everyone who asks, nor one who would be the inner source of a peace never before known. For several years, I shied away from calling the source of all there is as God. To actually experience God, one has to bypass fears and negativity taught to us. There are many names for God, so patients decide what to use. Whether we call God Consciousness "Universal Light," "The Source," "Great Spirit," or whatever suits people, makes no difference. It is personal for the purpose of experiencing that higher source without learned restrictions. Then they will be able to start fresh with their own experiences of a powerful and loving presence, rather than with the anchors or associations they have learned. Is it really God or a Higher Self? Maybe both.

We do not have to understand this Creative Source in order to use its power to heal us. The next step is to experience the feeling of oneness with our source, the source of our total being. This sense of oneness with a higher power that many call God makes it is easier to beat addiction. A connection with God can help us know how to get through the trials, pain, and fears that are inevitable in life. Whatever you decide to call this source, *it* does not care; it is our *intent* that matters, that draws us close. The source of our being, or God, resides within us all. Until you know it's there, though, you won't be able to use it. At some point many people have unconsciously given away their inner power as children. Most of our young patients feel out of control, totally anxious, and have lost hope of being able to beat their addiction. When they can "feel" that inner, spiritual ally, the loving wise one, they begin to sense that their struggle is not taking place by themselves and that there is powerful help and hope.

"The greatest personal limitation is to be found not in the things you want to do and can't, but in the things you've never considered doing"
— *Richard Bandler, PhD*

Chapter 9

PREVENTION

"People who experiment with drugs early in life are
more likely to be addicted later in life."
- National Institute on Drug Addiction, August 2010

Addiction is a disease that is prone to relapse. Preventing relapse is an essential part of the treatment. Relapse prevention is even more important in teenagers because they have a much longer time frame to remain sober than an older adult who has an addiction problem. It is also imperative that teens be treated early because their brain has a good amount of plasticity. This means that they are able to remold and rework connections that have been developed through the addiction. Scientific evidence shows that exposing a young brain to opiates may cause the brain to develop receptors to the particular opiate that is used. For instance, although heroin is not a natural substance, if the brain is exposed to it long enough, it will develop receptors to heroin, and it will not be satisfied until the heroin is given to it. The normal endorphin receptor may actually morph into a heroin receptor if that is all it is exposed to. This is due to the constant exposure, and the fact that the opiate may be more potent than the natural substance. The longer a teenager stays away from the substance, the more dormant the receptors become. In addition, teenagers may develop healthier more natural receptors as the opiate receptor to the illegal substance goes into dormancy. However, reintroducing the opiate may reactivate the receptor, and start the whole cascade of events, and behaviors, which lead to addiction.

WHY DO PEOPLE RELAPSE?

There are only three reasons people cannot change a behavior: (1) they do not know how to change the behavior, (2) it is physically impossible for them to change a behavior, and/or (3) they are not motivated to change. The buprenorphine treatment program teaches people how to change their behavior through counseling, lifestyle, supplementation, and substitution therapy, along with education. It is physically impossible for many addicts to change their addictive behaviors without substitution therapy, so they can continue in a treatment program. Without the substitution therapy, the statistics for trying to quit "cold turkey" are dismal. The main reason people relapse is that something disrupted or changed their motivation.

We have observed six reasons why motivation is lacking:

1. They deny they have a problem and therefore have no motivation to change.
2. They are ambivalent about change; they have some reasons to quit and some reasons to not quit.
3. They have no incentive to change, which can change if they are court ordered into treatment.   Also, their living situation may be threatened, or a relationship may be threatened, such as losing a boyfriend or girlfriend.
4. They may substitute other substances, or drugs, which modulates or controls their symptoms or behavior; therefore, they don't need treatment for the opiate addiction.

For example, they may substitute alcohol or another addictive substance as a way to get off of heroin.

5. They get into a pattern of recycling and relapse. They learned to live with episodic periods of staying clean through either treatment or rehab, and then when the going gets tough, they relapse. They relapse until it gets uncomfortable enough, and then they will get into treatment again. They have no motivation to change the cycle because the negative aspects of relapse do not outweigh the negative consequences of the recycling pattern they may have developed.

6. They view their problem as something other than addiction. They get picked up for a DWI and view it as a problem with the system, not with their addiction. If they do not drive anymore, they do not need to quit drugs, especially if they are not mandated into treatment or are not incarcerated because of their DWI. They can live without driving so they continue using drugs.

There are questions that should be asked to assess someone's motivation:

Question one: Are you making an attempt to quit, if so, what is that attempt? This is a test of whether they are able to behaviorally come to the conclusion that it is important to quit. If they are not making an attempt, then they are in the precontemplative phase and not ready or motivated enough to quit.

Question two: What is your attitude about quitting? If it is not important or valuable to them to quit, they are not likely to quit. The value of quitting has to be more important than the value of staying on drugs. This is where enabling parents make their biggest mistake. They do not make it uncomfortable enough for their child when they are on drugs, therefore their child has no incentive to quit.

What provokes a relapse?

One cause of relapse is drug re-exposure. If, for whatever reason, people take the addictive drug after they have been clean, they often will relapse. It is imperative that they not use opiates or any other addictive substance after they have been treated. The question inevitably arises: "When is it safe to use an opiate after treatment?" The answer is probably never. Everyone is different and it is impossible to predict where an addicted person may fall in the spectrum of relapse. A person may take a small amount of an opiate and relapse. It may take a larger amount in someone else, but both of these are unpredictable. This point should be constantly reinforced with teenagers. We know that the frontal lobes of human beings develop last. The frontal lobes are the areas that put the brakes on behaviors, so to speak. This is the area where the sense of right and wrong develops and will intervene if we are tempted with something that is dangerous. In humans, the frontal lobes may not be fully developed until well into the mid- to late-twenties. We all know of people who probably have not developed their frontal lobes even into their fifties. If the frontal lobes are immature or underdeveloped, as they are in teenagers, addiction does not have the same negative value that it would in an adult.

Stress can cause a relapse. When teens are stressed they may know of no other way to deal with it than to use drugs as a way to numb their thoughts and prevent other negative behaviors. Again, this is where counseling comes in as a way to deal with stress, and individuals can learn how to use more positive behaviors when stress occurs. We cannot prevent stress. All we can do is modulate its effect on us, and try to balance stressful exposure with more pleasant experiences. Exploring what stresses a person and what makes him or her feel positive is an important part of counseling. If we do not develop coping skills to deal with stress, relapse is much more likely.

Withdrawal symptoms can be a major cause of relapse. Before we used substitution therapy with buprenorphine, this was a major reason for people relapsing. As we have described, addiction is an intense hunger. The hunger overwhelms you, and you are powerless to resist. Imagine this magnified ten times. That is what addiction feels like. If you do not treat the withdrawal and craving with substitution therapy, relapse becomes the norm rather than the rule. Substitution therapy deals with this very well, and it is why it is now becoming state of the art in treating addiction.

Drug-related stimuli can be another cause for relapse. These are the classic associations with "people, places, and things." If addicts go to a place where they used or bought drugs, they may start craving and decide to relapse. If they associate with people who use drugs or have used drugs with them, or people who have dealt drugs to them, or that they have dealt drugs to, they will more likely relapse. If they get into situations where they used drugs as a way of coping and they have not learned ways to deal with these behaviors and situations without drugs, they are likely to relapse. The classic drug treatment, which involves avoiding people, places, and things, still has a tremendous amount of validity. All of the above are intensely ingrained anchors and almost impossible to fight against, especially until new and more desirable anchors are enforced. All we are adding is another dimension to this concept by introducing the new types of counseling as mentioned in the counseling chapter, lifestyle changes, and substitution therapies.

Inadequate family or social support can be a major reason for relapse. It is important to be supportive but not enabling. Some situations are harder than others. Without social support, it is difficult for a person to quit drugs. If others view the person as someone who is defective or someone who is not really ill, it is harder for this person to cope with their addiction. It is important for caregivers, family, and friends to be supportive and understand that this is a disease and should be treated in the same way any other disease would be treated. We would not shun someone who has diabetes and has to take daily insulin shots, but we often shun people who are addicted and/or on Suboxone. We would not tempt someone with doughnuts and sweets if they had diabetes; therefore, we should never ask addicted people if they would like an alcoholic drink or would like to use what we call soft drugs, such as marijuana. The brain does not make a distinction between legal, illegal, soft, or hard drugs. All it cares about is what effect it has on the brain. Soft drugs just need larger doses to have a similar effect as a hard drug. We also know that regardless of whether a drug is legal or illegal, it can have devastating effects on the brain.

Drug availability is a major factor in relapse. If a drug is highly available and relatively cheap, relapse is much more likely. When it is difficult to get prescription drugs because of legislation or providers unwilling to prescribe them, illegal drugs become more desirable. If heroin, for instance, becomes relatively cheap in a given geographical area, it is much more abused than illegally obtained prescription drugs.

Poverty can be a serious risk factor for relapse. One of the big issues with teenagers is that once they are addicted, they lose friends who do not use drugs, and they cannot be around friends who are drug users; they tend to end up with no friends. In addition, getting a job if you are an addict is hard, because many addicted teens drop out of school and do not have good job skills or experience. They may have been fired from multiple jobs due to poor attendance or performance. They may have been fired because they were impaired. Prospective employers can discover this, or they will call a previous employer who might make it difficult for the teen to get a new job. This results in the teenager having no money, no friends, and in many cases, no future. If they have been incarcerated, this compounds the problem when they get out. Poverty becomes a huge problem and one that is difficult to solve. They basically have to start with minimum-wage jobs, get involved in training programs, or rely on friends and relatives for money. The latter continues to chip away at an already poor sense of self-esteem, leading them back to the lifestyle of drug using, drug seeking, and drug dealing. It is what they are familiar with, and it becomes the "easy way out."

Good counseling is helpful, but as parents we may have to temporarily support addicted kids financially, tying their finances to tasks and performance. We have to teach them how to earn money even if it is with household tasks or chores for us. Giving anyone money without tying it to earning it is a big mistake. The best alternative is to get them retrained or back in school, or to earn an equivalency diploma so that they can restart their life. The sense of achievement and self-confidence once a kid gets that diploma exceeds their expectations. All of these examples contribute to their self-esteem, a huge problem with addicted teens.

Crime can also be a major problem with relapse or using drugs in the first place. Once they get into the downward spiral of abusing and dealing drugs, or stealing for drugs, it is difficult to break. They may get themselves into such a legal bind and see crime as the only way out. Unfortunately, incarceration for a short period of time may be the only answer for some teens. Experiencing time in jail helps them to develop the sense of right and wrong that is lacking in their frontal lobes and caused them to turn to drugs without realizing how dangerous they were. An understanding probation officer or judge could be the best thing that ever happened to them. The legal system takes it out of the hands of the parents but still creates enough of a negative aura around using drugs that they will avoid further use. On the other hand, if they go back to using drugs, stealing and dealing drugs may be the only way they can keep up their habit. These lead to the cycle of incarceration, recovery, and then relapse. I had a patient who at forty years old had been in jail fifteen times over twenty years. The only reason he came to me for treatment was because his last crime put him in federal prison. He hated federal prison so much, he told me, that he would seek treatment rather than go back to federal prison. He admitted, however, that quitting drugs was not something he wanted to do; it was the lesser of two evils. He had learned how to cope with county and local jails and could live in that environment. He could not deal with federal prison because it was stricter, and he could not obtain the drugs while there. This was not the case in the local or county jails. Needless to say, he did not stay clean for long. He relapsed and ended up back in federal prison. He did not have the incentive to stay clean. For him, staying clean was harder than staying in prison.

Teen and adolescent prevention has some distinct differences from relapse in the general adult population. First, genetics plays a role. When one or both parents have an addiction to alcohol or any other substance, their kids are more likely to become addicted and relapse. We cannot change this; we can only be more cautious and vigilant when one or both parents have an addiction problem.

Second, brain development is a major issue. Since the frontal lobes of kids are undeveloped, neither is their sense of right and wrong, so putting the brakes on their addictive behavior may be impossible. That is why parents need to install a sense of right and wrong by instilling responsibility in them. Think of a teenager's brain as a racecar engine and the frontal lobes are like bicycle brakes. The teenager does not have the ability to stop the racecar engine, because the brakes are not powerful enough. Some of this can only be prevented with time. We can accelerate the teen's sense of right and wrong by teaching them the lessons of cause and effect. Unfortunately, too many teens have to learn the hard way. We usually learn right from wrong through experience, or less frequently, we believe the advice of those wiser than us. Our culture has cultivated the school of hard knocks, and has shunned the role of authority and experience. As my wife would say, children do not come out of the womb any differently now than they did forty years ago. It is what they experience after they are born that has shaped the negative behaviors that we see today. We have to get back to the parents' and grandparents' sense of responsibility. Not so long ago, earning privileges was the norm. Today, teens think privileges are an entitlement. The sense of entitlement in our society has created a groundswell of irresponsible and nonproductive people. In response, we have created a culture of addicted teenagers.

Environment is a significant factor in teen addiction. There is more drug exposure in schools, workplaces, TV, movies, families, and even in medical providers' practices. As medical providers, we have ten to twenty times more opiate options than we did just thirty years ago. Drug exposure and drug using are ubiquitous. We see it all over movies and on TV. Drug use by movie stars, rock stars, and teenage icons is glamorized. Rather than exposing kids to the negative aspects of drug use, we show them how you can get away with it if you have enough money or the right lawyer.

Comorbidities, or other personality problems, are common in teenagers. Drug abuse rarely exists by itself. Many of the addicted teens have other mental issues or serious psychosocial issues that predispose them to addiction and relapse. Depression is much more common in teens than it was twenty years ago. ADD, ADHD, and learning disabilities are much more prevalent, and in my opinion, over diagnosed. To label someone as having ADD isolates him or her from the norm, and their peers. Labels can be damaging. We need to avoid labels whenever possible. We also need to stop relying on prescription medications to treat these maladies. It gets people into a belief system that there is a pill for every problem, and a pill is the answer. Depression is not a deficiency of Prozac or Effexor; it is a neurotransmitter problem that can be corrected and treated with lifestyle, diet, and natural methods. In the same way, ADD and ADHD are not deficiencies of Ritalin or Adderall. Both are deficiencies of essential nutrients, but even more so, deficiencies of parenting in many cases. When I was growing up, if

I could not sit in front of the TV for a prolonged period of time I was not diagnosed with ADD or ADHD. I did not get Ritalin to stop this behavior. It was more likely that I got reprimanded for not being able to sit still for a prolonged period. I occasionally even received a punishment that would not be allowed today, as it would be viewed as child abuse. I am not condoning corporal punishment, but we believe Ritalin is usually not the best treatment for a child who cannot focus or concentrate. We have to be careful not to make excuses for behaviors that perpetuate the use of Ritalin-type drugs. A more constructive approach would be to look at lifestyle changes and eliminate the negative labels attached to these active kids. Although our parents were generally stricter than parents today, and in many cases used punishments we would consider excessive today, our generation seems to have been quite successful compared to the present generation. Admittedly, there are more temptations and more dangerous things in our environment, like violence in TV and movies, but we have to move away from taking a pill for every mental problem or behavior.

WHY DON'T MORE DOCTORS PRESCRIBE SUBOXONE?

Lack of experience is a big issue for some doctors. Since a relatively small number of physicians are certified to use Suboxone, we do not have a large community experience. Physicians tend to be resistant to change. Until we get a critical mass of doctors who understand addiction and utilize Suboxone, it is impossible to serve the addicted population.

We do not have good support systems and networks of providers who understand the concept of substitution therapy or the concept of addiction as disease. Providers still view addicted people as undesirables who will steal from you and are difficult to manage. Although these patients require more time out of our busy practices, the protocols for treating them have good results and can be rewarding. In addition, since we are dealing with people who are a big cost to society, it is in our best interest to develop support systems and networks of providers to treat them.

Providers have a different set of responsibilities when treating opiate-addicted patients. We are mandated to make sure they get counseling, mandated to drug test them, and mandated to see them every thirty days. This causes stress in a busy provider's practice, because for one, we do not like mandates; we are bombarded by mandates from insurers, regulators, and state and federal laws. Another layer of mandates to treat what are perceived as relatively undesirable patients is not something most providers relish.

Many providers are suspicious of DEA regulations and oversight. By accepting patients who will be using buprenorphine, the DEA requires us to go through extra training and be subjected to excessive oversight. Excessive oversight is when DEA agents, with no complaints against the doctor, come unannounced to the doctor's office in the middle a full day of patient care. It is the only field in medicine where the DEA can walk in unannounced and scrutinize the provider at the same level as a criminal, even though there might have been no complaint. I have personally experienced this and it was unpleasant, embarrassing, and intimidating. All that patients see are agents barging in during work hours. Most doctors do not want to be any part of this. I do not see this changing much in the future. In fact, with the environment of increased regulation in medicine, I suspect it will get worse. I predict, as the addiction problem continues to increase, that the number of doctors willing to treat addictions will level off and then actually decrease. This will only compound the addiction problem.

Reimbursement by insurance companies in many cases is unfair for the amount of time we spend treating addicted patients. It is not the actual office time; it is the after-hours time our staff experiences when treating these patients. In my practice, almost

50 percent of calls after hours are related to Suboxone patients, or patients on opiate meds for pain. They want early prescriptions or have problems with their refills, such as "lost prescriptions," or they have other excuses for needing their prescription early. This is in spite of the fact that they sign a contract stating we will not fill prescriptions early, and there are no excuses for losing a prescription. Most doctors want no part of this, either.

Office staff is resistant to starting Suboxone treatment because of the stigma related to treating addicted patients. After they realize these patients have a disease much like diabetes, some of this goes away. However, many of these patients tend to be extremely demanding, irresponsible, and in many cases, abusive. This only reinforces the predetermined bias against treating them. It makes it very difficult for providers to justify treating large numbers of addicted patients under these circumstances. In our office, the fact that we focus on teen addiction attenuates this response to some degree, but it is still an issue.

Most physicians treat addicted patients with a reasonable amount of respect and dignity, which is not always true of pharmacies and mental health agencies. You might think a mental health provider or agency would be somewhat compassionate. However, it is my experience that some mental health providers associate a stigma to using substitution therapy and convey their prejudices to patients. I also see this with pharmacists who realize that a person on Suboxone is addicted. They may treat them with less respect than someone coming for blood pressure or diabetes medications. Although this issue is improving, it is still an ongoing problem.

To summarize, from a provider standpoint, opiate-addicted patients are more work, we are paid less to treat them, we are overly scrutinized by the DEA, we are mandated to do things that we are not mandated to do for other patients, it stresses our staff more, and the patients are in many cases difficult to deal with. As you can see, this is not something that physicians look forward to doing.

On the positive side, although these patients are all of the above, treatment with Suboxone can change lives, and in many cases, turn around an otherwise negative situation in young teens. It is one of the few things in my practice that is life changing. If we can intervene early enough and can be effective, we can turn around the lives of teenagers who were destined otherwise to end up in jail, with a horrible chronic disease, or dead. When evaluating the pros and cons of treating opiated addicted teens, the rewards outweigh the negative. Unfortunately, a physician has to experience the positive part of the treatment, because the perception is more focused on the negative aspects of opiate addiction.

WHAT CAN A PARENT DO TO PREVENT ADDICTION?

1. Be supportive. This is especially true before a child has an addiction problem. Try to support everything positive in your child's life, such as good grades, increasing grades, excelling at a sport or hobby, helping out a friend or relative, anything positive that he or she does. This reinforces the concept of positive behaviors resulting in positive reinforcement. Do not rely on teachers, friends, or others to support your child's good behavior. If your child becomes addicted, be supportive of treatment; he or she is working hard at it. Make sure he or she knows you will be there for him or her and reward sobriety. Do not enable. Do not reward your child with cell phones, cars, clothes, TVs, and so forth until he or she earns them.

2. Teach your child and demonstrate to him or her that negative behaviors have consequences. It is the parents that help instill a sense of right and wrong into a child's brains. The parents are the most important authority

figures and they are the ones who help a child's brain develop a sense of right and wrong. Parents will ask me what I would do if my child exhibited a negative behavior. My reply is, what would your parents do? They seem to understand that. They realize then that they are not as strict as their parents were. We point out that being strict is not the same as being "mean." Do not rely on teachers or other authority figures to teach your child right from wrong. Parents are the most important teachers in this respect.

3. Randomly drug test if you have any suspicion of drug use. It is not mean to drug test an addicted child! Do not assume that your child "could never" be involved with drugs. This is one of the biggest mistakes we see parents make. Drug tests can be bought at discount pharmacies for a relatively small cost. Some of our parents buy them from our office. Explain to your child that you are doing this for them and you will all feel better if it comes back negative. If they reply that drug testing them shows you don't trust them, your reply should be that trust is earned and not a God-given gift. Many teens initially protest but if they realize that drug testing is the way it is going to be, they will cooperate. This is a good way to catch addiction at an early stage; it can also prevent it.

4. Educate yourself about the signs of drug addiction. These are outlined in previous chapters. Make sure any unusual behavior in your child has an explanation. You are the best observers of unusual behavior, not the school, not your doctor, and not other authority figures. If you are not sure whether something is a sign of addiction, do a drug test. Have them on hand.

5. Be involved with constructive activities. Become involved in their sports, their hobbies, their interests, and school.

Reward the good behavior and teach the consequences of bad behavior. It is easier and more enjoyable to be involved in sports and hobbies than to be involved in lawyer visits, court dates, and counseling.

6. Do not assume it could not happen to your child. This is another huge error. The disease of addiction cuts across all social and economic levels, all races, all religions, and can happen in any family. There are things you can do to lower the risk. However, since the underlying problem is in most cases biochemical, you have to respect that it can happen to anyone. Believing it cannot possibly happen in your family could be your biggest disappointment.

7. Try to be a good parent as outlined in this book. Good parenting is *selfless*. It is a combination of rewarding good behavior, teaching the consequences of bad behavior, and being involved in your child's life. Being overprotective, overly punishing, too permissive, or absent will get you into trouble and increase the possibilities of a teen who is prone to addiction, because of the biochemical problem that may exist.

8. Look for signs of abuse by friends or relatives. If your child acts strange around a relative or friend, or seems to not want to be around them, this could be a danger sign. Do not believe that abuse could not happen in your family, as this is just as possible as addiction. Abuse is pervasive in our society at all levels. I do not believe it occurs more now than it did forty years ago; I believe that now it is more in the open than it was then. Young children will not come to you in many instances, because they are not sure what is going on when they are abused. The abuser usually threatens them, so they do not tell you. Pay close attention to how children react around certain people.

Abuse is the second most common denominator of addicted patients behind biochemical abnormalities.

9. Help build self-esteem in your child. Low self-esteem and a biochemical propensity for addiction is a lethal combination. Self-esteem issues are pervasive in addicted teenagers and are important to treat with counseling if they do become addicted. This relates to being involved in their lives and rewarding good behaviors. We are not all born good-looking, smart, or with perfect bodies. Some of us have emotional issues and lack social skills. It is up to us as parents to find the good in our children and build on that. Everyone has positive qualities and it is up to us to find them in our children.

10. Never take drugs with your child. Do not believe that your child should be your friend in the same way you are friends with people your age. It is true that sometimes a child can be like a friend, but a teenager may misinterpret this. They might believe they should be able to do whatever you do. If you use drugs with your child, it can only lead to negative consequences and loss of respect for you. If they become addicted, they will have issues of anger and guilt and will blame you for a part of their addiction. You, on the other hand, will have issues of guilt and will blame yourself for part of their addiction. I have yet to see a child who did drugs with a parent who in the long run thought it was a positive experience.

Chapter 10

FUTURE ISSUES

"We are all part of the addiction problem, and we must all be part of the solution, or we will lose the next generation of teens"
R. Santasiero M.D.

When we look at the future, we look at better ways to treat addiction, from a medical aspect, and as a society and culture. We also look at the ramifications of legalization of drugs, and how we got here in the first place. Ask yourself, what is the collateral damage that we have created with our addiction problem?

Look at the war on drugs. When we considered this war at the beginning of this book, we saw the tremendous amount of money spent, and that we really have not put a dent in the amount of drugs available to our fellow countrymen, our future, and our children. Many would conclude that the war on drugs is a waste of money. Right now the war on marijuana is essentially falling apart. A number of states have legalized it for medical use, and many states have decriminalized it. Most of this is due to the economic benefit of the government intervening with the growing of marijuana and taxing the distribution of marijuana. It is not because it is viewed as the right thing to do. I have not seen an argument for legalizing it as a way to control marijuana use. It is framed as a way for the government to control who grows, distributes, and sells marijuana. It is too hard to enforce the use of marijuana. We now know that decriminalizing it eliminates a large portion of the cost to society. Forty percent of all Americans over twelve years old have tried it, and at least thirty million people smoke it every day. An NIH survey in 2011 showed that 18.1 million Americans had used marijuana during the previous month. It is now medically dispensed in eighteen states and Washington DC. It is the largest cash crop in California, the nation's largest agricultural state. It is considered a legitimate pain reliever for cancer victims and is now available for an assortment of other symptoms, some of them conveniently vague and impossible to document. It was recently approved in Colorado for adult recreational use, and other states will soon follow, likely New York State. The government, however, still classifies pot as a schedule I controlled substance, the same as heroin and cocaine. This creates a dilemma for states because it is considered controlled at the highest level by the federal government, but decriminalized and legal in other states. The federal government has decidedly taken a hands-off approach to the decriminalization. The attitude is, relax the regulations, tax it, and make a ton of money from it. One of the benefits of decriminalization is eliminating the overworked police force and prosecutors who deal with mostly dead-end pot cases. Like it or not, marijuana use is deeply embedded in our culture and will not likely go away. The debate goes on as to whether legalization will increase consumption and abuse, or whether it will have no effect. A disproportionately large number of cases prosecuted tend to be Hispanic and African Americans, not the white college kids, who are using it at record levels. In most states legalization was an answer to huge debts and a way to raise a lot of money quickly. Mexican drug cartels will lose billions with the legalization and decriminalization. Up to 60 per cent of drug cartel money comes from the sale of marijuana.

Americans need to look at the facts. According to NIH statistics, 80 percent of alcohol is consumed by 20 percent of American drinkers. Eighty percent of illegal drugs are used by 20 percent of illicit drug users in the United States. Approximately three million people, less than 1 percent of the American population, consume 80 percent of illegal hard drugs. Alcohol and nicotine are the only addictive drugs that are currently legally available nationwide. When it comes to legalization, many argue that alcohol and nicotine are just as damaging, in some ways more damaging, than other legal and illegal drugs.

The argument for legalization comes from the following figures: More Americans are imprisoned for drug offenses or drug-related crimes than for all property crimes. We spend five times more putting drug dealers in prison than we did thirty years ago. This defies logic. If we were spending billions of dollars per year on the war on drugs, logically, the price of illegal drugs would be increased. Since the chance of imprisonment has dramatically increased, it should discourage dealers from selling drugs. However, the price of cocaine and heroin are almost 90 percent *lower* than they were thirty years ago. A $200 transaction on the street costs society approximately $100,000 for a three-year sentence for imprisonment and prosecution. In civilized and developed nations, cocaine sells for approximately $3000 per ounce. But in countries where cocaine and heroin are produced, it sells for 1 percent of its retail value in America. Ninety-two percent of the world heroin comes out of Afghanistan. Afghanistan is a country where we spend billions of dollars per year to defend the right of people there to have the freedom to grow whatever they want and to live the way they want. After we leave Afghanistan, they will likely go back to growing poppy, the plant from which opium is derived. How ironic that when Muslim extremists ruled the country, the crime for growing poppy was harsh. Ninety-two percent of the world's heroin is grown in a country that we support militarily, and we consume the majority of their heroin in the United States. In addition to opiates, Afghanistan is also the largest producer of cannabis (mostly as hashish) in the world. We are essentially supporting the destruction of our future with this practice.

If cocaine were legalized, a $2000 kilogram of cocaine could be sent via FedEx from Columbia for less than $50 and sold profitably in America for a small markup from its price in Columbia. Criminalization drives the cost of smuggling that same $2000 kilogram in America to $20,000, which retails for more than $100,000.

We used to believe that drug enforcement would raise prices but doubted that high prices would decrease consumption. We now know that consumption declines as price rises but wonder whether enforcement can substantially affect the prices. Drug cartels have almost unlimited money for corrupting law enforcement officials, because drugs are cheap to produce and so easy to renew. We also have created the greatest market for these illegal drugs in our own country. Fully legalizing marijuana would take up to $10 billion from violent and evil people, the dealers and producers, and shift much of that into tax revenue. Unfortunately because there is still a market, the drug cartels would switch their production and marketing to cocaine, heroin, and methamphetamines.

In 1990, 4 percent of Americans supported full legalization of marijuana. Today 50 percent support legalization. So what is the answer? Though I am not a proponent for legalization or for continued criminalization of drugs, I will describe what is happening in other countries and let the reader decide what is best.

In Portugal, opiates were legalized in 2000. Users were sent to counseling and mandated treatment. The programs were aimed at preventing users from going underground. Initially this resulted in a slight increase in illicit drug use, predominantly by people already addicted to drugs. The percent of heroin, cocaine, and marijuana users stayed about the same. However, drug-related court cases decreased by 66 percent, and drug-related HIV cases decreased by 75 percent. In 2002, 49 percent of AIDS patients were addicts. In 2008, only 27 percent of AIDS patients were addicts.

What happened? Essentially the number of people addicted stayed about the same. The number of people in jail went down dramatically. The number of people with AIDS, HIV, and drug-related hepatitis decreased dramatically. Most likely what would happen in the United States, is that the number of people addicted will stay the same. However, the cost to society will decrease because of decreased legal costs, incarceration costs, and the cost for treating drug-associated infections. In addition, the actual number of people with infection goes down dramatically, because people are now using clean needles versus shared needles. Although the facts may be surprising to some people, if you understand that addiction is a biochemical issue, you are not increasing the number of people in a society with a biochemical propensity. Legalization does not change this number. However, only legalizing soft drugs like marijuana could possibly cause the growers and marketers in the cartels to shift their attention and efforts to harder, more dangerous drugs. To date, we do not have much experience with legalization. It is clear that decreasing the criminal costs and decreasing the number of people infected with serious disease are benefits. If we take the next step and heavily tax the soft drugs, like marijuana, and control the disease and distribution of the harder drugs, like heroin and cocaine, we might have a better answer.

If we took the money generated through tax revenue from legalization and shifted it to education about the dangers of drugs, we might have a better answer to the problem. This is especially true with teens. I am not sure we could approach this without a wholesale change in our attitude about legalization. I also have serious doubts about the government using money generated from legalization and putting it toward the education of our young adults and children. Most likely it would go into the general fund and be shifted to pet projects unrelated to drug treatment and education. It is clear that we have lost the war on drugs, and it is clear that we cannot control the use of drugs or their distribution with our present criminal system. There is too much money being made by unsavory and corrupt people who have the ability to influence the system in their favor. We have to think outside the box for the answer. In addition, if parents took a more proactive attitude about drugs and we moved toward more self-responsibility, it could be to everyone's benefit.

One positive aspect of drug maintenance and treatment in the United States is the creation of drug courts. The first US drug court began in 1990. In a drug court, if you are charged of a minor offense and you have a drug problem, you are given the choice of drug rehab or jail. Drug rehab is relatively strict. You must remain clean and are drug tested on a regular basis. If you fail a drug test or you do not follow through with treatment, you are incarcerated. This has been a very successful program and has resulted in many more people completing treatment, with fewer people incarcerated. This program also has been positive for first-time offenders and teens that are caught selling or using drugs. It gives them a second chance, and for many it has been a positive experience. In 1990, there were 472 drug courts. In 2005, the number jumped to 1250, and in 2010, there were over 2400 drug courts associated with municipalities. A drug court can be in any size town or city, but the basic premise is the same: agree to treatment and you might save yourself incarceration, a more humane alternative than being caught with drugs and put in jail. Expanding the drug court to all 1.5 to 2 million drug offenders would cost approximately $13 billion. However, we would save approximately $40 billion per year, according to the Urban Institute's Justice Policy Center. This does not account for the collateral costs of saving a young person from a future of drugs, disease, incarceration, or death. The drug court story is a positive and effective aspect of our policy on drug addiction.

The objectives of maintenance treatment are to reduce the mortality from overdose and infection. Maintenance therapy helps to reduce opioid and other illicit drug use, and more importantly, helps reduce the transmission of HIV, hepatitis B, and hepatitis C. We have a hepatitis C epidemic in our country. One in every thirty-three baby boomers, those born between 1945 in 1965, are living with a hepatitis C infection, according to the Centers for Disease Control and Prevention. Sharing a needle while injecting an illegal drug is the biggest risk factor for becoming infected with this blood-borne virus. For many of those baby boomers, hepatitis C is related to something that happened twenty or thirty years ago when they experimented with drugs, sometimes as a one-time experience. About 3.2 million Americans are estimated to have chronic hepatitis C, and at least half of them do not know the source of the infection. The virus affects over 170 million people worldwide and can gradually lead to scarring of the liver and cirrhosis or liver cancer. It is widespread in Asia, mostly in China. In 2007, there were 15,000 deaths related to hepatitis C. The number surpassed the 13,000 deaths caused by the AIDS virus. The mortality will continue to grow in the next ten to fifteen years. It will become even worse than expected if we do not get a handle on teenage drug addiction. At the present time, we have a much bigger problem with hepatitis C than we do with AIDS. Both are potentially preventable diseases. As the numbers show, we can see that preventing disease is a huge part of the future of drug treatment policy in the United States. We have effective treatments for AIDS but to date we do not have good treatments for hepatitis C. It is likely that future effective treatment would be very costly to society for hepatitis C.

Also on the horizon are new threats to our teens. Designer drugs or "bath salts" are becoming more and more of a threat. These drugs can be manufactured in relatively unsophisticated labs. They have inherent dangers that we have not seen with other drugs. They can be made extremely potent; they may have side effects that we have not encountered, which are likely to be serious.

These drugs are mostly sold over-the-counter as legal products, because they were first marketed as bath salts and were supposedly not to be ingested. It is clear to the buyer that ingestion is a main purpose of these so-called legal products. As legislation catches up with the criminal chemists making these products, this problem will become less severe. However, criminals can be quite innovative and we have no idea what the future brings in this area.

Our teens also face the threat of addiction from designer drugs like ecstasy. Although these drugs do not have the addiction potential of opiates, the effects on neurotransmitters, brain chemistry, and hardwiring in the brain are probably worse than we see with opiates. In addition, we do not have good treatments for addiction to these drugs, as we do not have substitution therapies as part of the treatment. All of this speaks to us taking charge of raising our children and becoming more responsible. We need to show these concepts to our children. It does not matter what the drug is, the principles are still the same when treating and educating our children.

We must look to alternatives in treating our pain patients because opiates are not the answer. We must pressure our politicians to get insurance reimbursement for modalities such as acupuncture, massage, meditation, hypnosis, and other behavioral therapies to treat pain instead of always looking at painkillers and opiates. These natural modalities are also far less expensive. Reimbursement for these modalities would be a better alternative with no addiction potential.

As we increase regulation and oversight of prescription drugs, we will possibly shoot ourselves in the foot. By restricting physicians and regulating them more and more, physicians will opt out of prescribing opiate drugs altogether. Although there is a place for opiates in the management of acute and chronic pain, they are among the most overprescribed drugs in America. If your primary physician opts out of prescribing opiates, it will be left to pain management providers who may not know you as well. The other fallout that may occur is a patient who truly needs drugs and those that are dependent on drugs will look to illegal drugs, street drugs, or more dangerous alternatives for pain relief. A large number of people being treated for pain issues are actually dependent or addicted and essentially are using the opiate for their addiction problem and not their pain. We cannot ignore this population, as this will increase all the issues that we are trying to avoid such as crime and collateral diseases.

If you rely on the government to regulate controlled drugs, you may be disappointed. In February 2014, the FDA approved a new very potent opiate painkiller. This drug is dangerous for a number of reasons. The drug Zohydro ER is 50 mg of hydrocodone. The largest dose of hydrocodone prior to the approval was 10 mg per capsule. In addition, the 10 mg capsules had 325 mg of acetaminophen (commonly known as Tylenol, which is toxic to the liver in relatively low doses, 4000 mg per day). The addition of acetaminophen discouraged addicts from taking too many hydrocodone with acetaminophen capsules for fear of liver toxicity. In addition to that, the manufacturer did not include anything in the formulation to discourage addicts from grinding up and injecting the hydrocodone. This technology is well known and easily incorporated into the medication. The medication was tested in a study that involved subjects who had shown an ability to tolerate opiates. In other words, these people had used hydrocodone before and had some tolerance to opiates. This amount of hydrocodone can be toxic or lethal to opiate naïve patients (patients who had never used opiates). The FDA and manufacturer justified the drug approval for the severe pain seen in cancer patients. The problem with this stance is that we already have plenty of very potent drugs for cancer. Another problem is the drug, once approved, can and will be used by providers for patients that do not have cancer. We heard this same reasoning when Oxycontin was approved as a new drug for cancer patients. We know what happened with Oxycontin. It became the one of the most abused drug on the streets. The potency of a drug is not justification for approval. We already have plenty of potent opiate drugs. The scariest and most disturbing aspect of the approval was the FDA advisory committee voted eleven to two *against* approval of the drug, yet the FDA still approved its release. In addition, forty health care, consumer, and addiction treatment organizations urged the FDA to revoke the approval. This included the American Academy of Addiction Medicine, the premier addiction medicine body for physicians in the United States. If this decision and process is compared to the restrictions on prescribing buprenorphine, it appears the regulatory agencies operate with a double standard. Clearly we do not need another long acting pure opiate. This is a setup for abuse and diversion. If you believe the government and the FDA are looking out for our children and for us, remember this approval.

As medical providers, we have to understand that we are a significant part of the opiate addiction problem, but we can be a major part of the solution. The future will look at treating addicted patients more like we treat diabetics or patients with other medical problems. We will look for other substitution therapies for treating cocaine, alcohol, and other addictions in the same way we have used buprenorphine for opiate addiction. We will hopefully recognize that most addicted people have a neurotransmitter problem, and the behavioral symptoms are part of the disease, not the disease itself.

The future of understanding and treating addiction partially lies in our ability to understand brain function. As our technology improves, we will understand more about brain function and neurotransmitters. We can look at some of the work of pioneers in this field, such as Daniel Amen, MD. His work has some fascinating results. He found that the frontal lobes of the brain control our empathy, self-control, intuition, and appropriate responses to our environment. Interestingly, he finds that women seem to have more development and activity in these lobes than men. It is also interesting to note that these are the areas of the brain where self-control is not developed in teenagers. This prevents them from making good decisions, because they are unable to evaluate all aspects of the decision. Using drugs does not carry as much negative connotation to them, because they do not have the hardwiring developed at the age they first started using drugs. Since this part of the brain is underactive and underdeveloped, we need to look at ways to evaluate and use this information for better treatment. At the very least, we should be able to educate our teens using the technology of brain function. If you show them that part of their brain does not work at this point, and they need to be very cautious about decisions that they make, they may have second thoughts about using drugs.

We must also help pain patients to have realistic expectations about pain relief. We tend to give the impression that pain management is pain eradication, and that is not true. Use of narcotic and opiate pain relievers should be a last resort and should be done judiciously. We need to reassess treating someone who has acute pain with more than ten or fifteen opiate painkillers. A prescription for sixty or ninety pills is likely to end up on the streets or in the hands of a young teen. That is why a huge portion of our prescribed opiates ends up diverted or misused. When a prescription for Suboxone can be filled for eight dollars a pill at a pharmacy and sold for two to three times that much on the street, it does not take long for people to figure out that this is a good way to make money. When many of our prescriptions are written to patients with zero or very low copays, the profit margins increase dramatically. Providers should educate themselves better about pain management and addiction.

Although some drug companies are becoming more responsible with additives to opiate painkillers to make them less likely to be ground up, injected, or snorted, they can do better. It is relatively easy to add a full antagonist like naloxone to all opiate medications to prevent diversion or misuse. There are already medications on the market that address this issue and are not abused to the extent of drugs like OxyContin, Opana, and methadone. Some of these issues are legislative, some are medical, some are societal, and some are family. We must first start at the lowest common denominator, which is family. We need to take responsibility for getting our own houses in order to the best of our ability. That does not mean we will prevent all addiction, but we will certainly do a better job than we have in the past. The medical profession has to take responsibility for its part in this, and our politicians have to get serious about effective legislation to control this epidemic. We will not stop the addiction epidemic without the concerted efforts of everyone. We will never stop the supply of drugs into the United States; there is too much money to be made. We also have a *huge demand* for illicit and addictive drugs. We must *decrease demand* and the people supplying the drugs will look elsewhere for a market. We believe education is the great equalizer to decrease demand. It should be where many of our efforts are focused for our children.

It is not unusual for a teen to make one bad decision that turns out to be life changing, in a negative way. As parents, we have the responsibility for getting the education about drugs and addiction for our children. If you don't feel comfortable educating your children, find someone who will. If we do not do this in the near future, we increase the risk of having a lost generation, and the consequences will be catastrophic and permanent. We must help our children by giving them the tools to make the right decision when they face that crossroad. The time for change is now!

CROSSROAD

References

Introduction

1. National Institute On Drug Abuse, *"Drug Facts: High School and Youth Trends"* (2006).

2. National Institute On Drug Abuse, *"Drug Facts: High School and Youth Trends"* (2012, revised January 2014).

3. Bayard M. Shi C-W, "Abuse of Over-the Counter Medication Among Teenagers and Young Adults," *American Family Physician* 84, no. 7 (October 11, 2011).

4. National Institute On Drug Abuse, Info Facts: *"Prescription and Over-the Counter Medication"* (February 28, 2011).

5. *"Drug Abuse Recognition training,"* http://drugrecognition.com/

Chapter 1

2. "IMS Health Survey," ABC News (April 20, 2011)

Chapter 2

1. "The War on Drugs, a Trillion Dollar Failure," CNN (December 7, 2012)

2. "Decriminalizing Drugs: interview with Drug Czar, Gil Kerlikowski," Buffalo News (January 2, 2011)

3. Centers For Disease Control and Prevention, *2011 Causes of Death in United States.*

4. Substance Abuse and Mental Health Services Administration, "Emergency Department Visits By Adolescents involving Narcotic Pain Relievers," National Survey on Drug Use and Health (2009).

5. National Institute on Drug Abuse, Drug Facts: "Workplace Resources" (revised July 2008).

6. National Institute on Drug Abuse, Drug Facts: "Workplace Resources" (2009)

7. Drug Abuse Warning Network, "National Estimates of Drug Related Emergency Department Visits" (2009).

8. New York State Health Department Statistics "Controlled Drug Prescriptions" (2010).

9. S McCabe, "Medical Misuse of Controlled Substances Among Adolescents,"*Archives of Pediatric Medicine* 165 (2011), 729–735.

Chapter 3

1. American Psychiatric Association, *Diagnostic and Statistical Manual of Mental Disorders, 4ᵗʰ edition (DSM IV),* (Washington DC: American Psychiatric Press, 1994)

3. Graham, Shultz, Mayo-Smith, Ries, Wilford, et. al., *Principles of Addiction Medicine Third Addition,* (Chevy Chase, The American Society of Addiction Medicine 2003), 654–655, 1451–1454.

REFERENCES

Chapter 4

1. Gant, Charles, and Lewis, Greg,. *End Your Addiction Now,* (New York,:Warner Books, 2002), 8–9.

2. Prentiss, Chris, and Prentiss, Pax,.*The Alcoholism and Addiction Cure,* (Power Press, 2007).

3. N. Volkow, et. al., "Imaging Dopamine's Release In Drug Abuse and Addiction," *Neuropharmacology* (June 2009).

4. Sun, et. al "An Analysis of Relapse Factors of 615 Heroin Addicts," *Chinese Journal of Drug Dependence* 3 (2001).

5. SAMSHA, "Treatment Outcomes Among Clients From Residential Substance Abuse Treatment Centers: 2005."

6. N. Rodnay, "Causes of Painkiller Addiction Among Teenagers," http://EzineArticles.com/?expert=Nate_Rodnay

7. M. Sponagle, "Novel Methods To Cure Drug Addiction," *Life Extension* (October 2011), 69–76.

Chapter 5

1. L. Robinson, M. Smith, J. Saison, "Drug Abuse & Addiction," helpguide.org, (updated February 2014)

2. *"Prescription Drugs of Abuse in the Workplace,* " www.workplace. samhsa.gov (2009)

Chapter 6

1. *"Michigan* Youth Risk Survey," Michigan Department of Education, www.michigan.gov, (2011)

2. National Institute on Drug Abuse (NIDA), "Drug Facts: High School and Youth Trends." (revised January 2014)

Chapter 7

1. M. Larzeler, et al., "Promoting Smoking Cessation," *American Family Physician* 85, no. 6 (November 15, 2012).

2. Gant, Charles, and Lewis, Greg,.*End Your Addiction Now* (New York:Warner Books 2002).

3. *"Frequently Asked Questions,"* info@buprenorphine.samsha.gov/ Drug Addiction Treatment Act 2000

4. Braverman, Eric,.*The Edge Effect,* (New York:Sterling Publishing Co., 2005).

5. "Why are d*octors limited to only helping 30/100 people at a time?* National Alliance of Advocates for Buprenorphine Treatment,www.NAABT.org (updated April 2014)

Chapter 8

1. Jung, Carl,. *Memories, Dreams and Reflections,* (New York: Pantheon Books, 1962).

2. Prentiss, Chris and,Prentiss, Pax,.*The Alcoholism and Addiction Cure,* (Power Press, 2007).

3. Bandler, *The Ultimate Introduction to NLP* (New York:Harper Collins, 2012).

4. Woolger, Roger,. *Other Lives, Other Selves* (New York:Bantam Books, 1987).

5. "Medicine: The Wise Old Man," *Time* Magazine (February 14, 1955).

6. J.E. Young, J.S. Klosko, and M. Weishaar, *Schema Therapy: A Practitioner's Guide*, (New York: Guilford Publications, 2003).

7. R. Dilts, "*Anchoring*," www.nlpu.com/NewDesign/NLPU, (1999)

8. B. Holzel, et.al., "Mindfulness Practice Leads to Increases in Regional Gray Matter Density" *Psychiatry Research:Neuroimaging*, 191, (January 30, 2011)

9. CDC and Prevention can be found on the website: http://www.cdc.gov/motorvehiclesafety/seatbelts/facts.html

Chapter 9

1. M. Larzeler, et al., "Promoting Smoking Cessation," *American Family Physician* 85, no. 6 (November 15, 2012).

2. National Institute on Drug Addiction (NIDA), "Drugs, Brains, Behavior: The science of Addiction," www.drugabuse.gov, (updated August 2010).

Chapter 10

1. NIDA, "Marijuana," updated December 2012.

2. NIDA, "Alcohol," updated January 2014.

3. NIDA, "Illegal Drugs," updated January 2014.

4. G. Will, "Weighing Drug Legalization (editorial)," *Washington Post* (April 12, 2012).

5. C. Hiaason, "War On Pot Has Gone Up In Smoke," *Miami Herald* (January 7, 2013).

6. B. Hatton and M. Mendoza, "Decriminalizing Drugs," *Associated Press* (January 2, 2011).

7. "Opium Production in Afghanistan," *Wikipedia*, modified February 27, 2014.

8. NIDA, "Trends and Statistics," updated December 2012.

9. L. Neergaard, "Hepatitis C deaths up, Boomers most at risk," *Associated Press* (February 20, 2012).

10. C. Rosenbaum, S. Carriero, B. Kavita, "Here Today, Gone Tomorrow...and Back Again? A Review of Herbal Marijuana Alternatives (K2, Spice), Synthetic Cathinones (Bath Salts), Kratom, *Salvia divinorum*, Methoximine, and Piperazines," *Journal of Medical Toxicology* 8 (2012), 15–30.

REFERENCES

11. Amen, Daniel,. *Change Your Brain, Change Your Life,* (New York:Harmony Publishers, 1999)

12. "Groups Push FDA to Revoke Approval of Potent Pain Killer," CNN (February 26, 2014).

Resources

We recommend the following websites for statistics and background for drug related statistics, trends, treatments, and information:

- Coalition Against Drug Abuse: www.drugabuse.com

- National Institute on Drug Abuse: www.drugabuse.gov or www.nida.nih.gov

- Substance Abuse and Mental Health Services Administration: www.samhsa.gov

- Suboxone: www.suboxone.com

We recommend the following books for interesting and effective perspectives on understanding and treating addictions:

- Chris Prentiss and Pax Prentiss, *The Alcoholism and Addiction Cure,* (Power Press, 2007).

- Charles Gant and Greg Lewis, *End Your Addiction Now* (Warner Books, 2002).

- R. Bandler, *The Ultimate Introduction to NLP,* (Harper Collins Publishers, 2012).

- Eric Braverman, *The Edge Effect,* (Sterling Publishing Co., 2005).

About the Authors

Cherie Santasiero, Ph.D, M.NLP, is a Transpersonal Psychotherapist, with a doctorate in Jungian based psychotherapy from Delphi University. She is a master in neuro-linguistic-programming (NLP™) through Richard Bandler, PhD, co-creator of NLP, and is a clinical hypnotherapist and Reiki Master.

In her private practice, Dr. Santasiero enjoys her success working together with her husband, Dr. Ronald Santasiero, helping addicted teens and young people. With her counseling skills and understanding of the universe through meta-physics that she shares with her clients, 'Dr. Cherie' helps her clients empower themselves to reach the highest wisdom and potential within them and to become confident adults. A speaker and lecturer, Dr. Cherie Santasiero has several health related national and international articles to her credit and has demonstrated non-traditional psychotherapeutic counseling at Buffalo State College, D'Youville College, and SUNY Buffalo.

Ronald Santasiero, M.D., C.Ac is a Board Certified Family Physician with nearly 40 years of experience treating patients. He is a New York State Certified Physician Acupuncturist. Dr. Santasiero graduated from Medical School in 1975 at SUNY At Buffalo School of Medicine and Biomedical Sciences. He was one of the first 100 physicians in the nation to be American Board Certified in Acupuncture in 2001. He trained in Oriental Medicine and Acupuncture at the Acupuncture Foundation of Canada at the University of Toronto, and completed his second Acupuncture training at the UCLA Acupuncture for physicians training program, in 1994. A large part of Dr. Santasiero's training in Mind/Body Medicine was with authors Joan Borysenko, Ph.D., and Herbert Benson, M.D., at Harvard Medical School. He is a Clinical Assistant Instructor of Family Medicine at the SUNY School Of Medicine and Biomedical Sciences. Dr. Santasiero has been the Medical Director of the D'Youville College Physician Assistant program since it began in 1992. He is also an adjunct professor in the Physician Assistant program at D'Youville College, where he teaches Physical Diagnosis and Integrative Medicine. In 1995, Dr. Santasiero and his wife Cherie Santasiero, Ph.D., founded the Sedona Holistic Medical Centre in Hamburg, New York. Dr. Ronald Santasiero specializes in holistic primary care, pain management, integrative addiction care, and acupuncture. A speaker and lecturer, he has appeared on radio and television, where he mainly speaks on holistic medicine, acupuncture, and teen addiction. He holds a medical patent related to the HCG diet.

Since 2006, Dr. Ronald Santasiero has treated over 350 opiate addicted patients, the majority being teens and young adults. He was one of the first doctors in Western New York to be certified to use buprenorphine (Suboxone) for opiate addiction. He and Dr. Cherie Santasiero have lectured extensively on an integrative approach to teen addiction.

Since 1995, Sedona Holistic Medical Centre's founders, Ronald Santasiero, M.D., CAc, and Cherie Santasiero, PhD, MNLP, use their developed approach to health and Integrative care, using the latest studies and treatments for addictions and dependency, chronic pain, and other chronic conditions and illnesses. Their center relies first on nutrition, acupuncture, and emotional and spiritual wellness, before pulling out the prescription pad. They also have extensive experience treating anxiety disorders, stress, age-related and chronic diseases, and cancer.

Dr. Cherie and Dr. Ron live in the country and have four children and eight grandchildren. They have traveled the painful path of a loved one addicted to drugs. This book is based on personal and professional experience.

Made in the USA
Lexington, KY
04 August 2014